# Clinical Evaluation
# of Young Children
# with the McCarthy Scales

# Clinical Evaluation of Young Children with the McCarthy Scales

Alan S. Kaufman, Ph.D.
Department of Educational Psychology
University of Georgia
Athens, Georgia

Nadeen L. Kaufman, M.A., Ed.M.
Rutland Center
Athens, Georgia

No Longer Property of
Phillips Memorial Library

**Grune & Stratton**
*A Subsidiary of Harcourt Brace Jovanovich, Publishers*
New York    London    Toronto    Sydney    San Francisco

Phillips Memorial
Library
Providence College

**Library of Congress Cataloging in Publication Data**

Kaufman, Alan S

  Clinical evaluation of young children with the
McCarthy scales.

  Bibliography: p.
  Includes index.
  1. Learning disabilities.  2. Ability testing.
I. Kaufman, Nadeen L., joint author.  II. Title.
LC4704.K38    371.9′2    77-8969
ISBN 0-8089-1013-2

Grune & Stratton, Inc.
111 Fifth Avenue
New York, New York 10003

Distributed in the United Kingdom by
Academic Press, Inc. (London) Ltd.
24/28 Oval Road, London NW1

Library of Congress Catalog Number 77-8969
International Standard Book Number 0-8089-1013-2
Printed in the United States of America

*To our children*
*JENNIE, DAVID, and JAMIE*
*Our past, present, and future "subjects"*
*for demonstrating the McCarthy Scales,*
*with love*

# Contents

# Preface

We have been involved with the McCarthy Scales since 1969, which is before the test battery was standardized, subdivided into six scales, or even given its current name. One of us (A. S. K.) had the privilege of working with Dr. Dorothea McCarthy during the later phases of the development of the test and throughout the stages of standardization and manual preparation; N. L. K. served as a Field Supervisor during the standardization program, and conducted the first validity study with the McCarthy Scales, testing a group of minimally brain dysfunctioned children while the battery was being standardized.

Since moving to Georgia we have continued our research interest in the McCarthy and have broadened our experiences with the Scales to include teaching the administration and interpretation of the battery to graduate students (A. S. K.), and assessing youngsters referred for behavioral and learning disorders on neuropsychological batteries which feature the McCarthy (N. L. K.). The sum total of our experiences with the test has made us acutely aware of its potential value for the assessment of young children, especially preschoolers, learning disabled youngsters, and minority group members. Our long-term involvement with the McCarthy has also educated us to the limitations of the battery, as well as to problems concerning the administration and scoring of the separate tests and the interpretation of the scale and test profiles.

More than anything else, we have sensed a need for a book on the McCarthy to clarify and define the test's role in the clinical and psychoeducational assessment of young children. In writing this book we have tried to meet this need by orienting ourselves to practitioners in the field. Issues such as administration tips, quantitative and qualitative interpretation of the test scores, screening for learning problems, and communication of the test results in case reports are treated to make the McCarthy even more practical to use in clinical and school settings. The book is intended for graduate students who are learning the instrument, as well as for school psychologists, learning disabilities specialists, clinical psychologists, and others who routinely or occasionally evaluate young children's abilities.

Many persons merit our sincere acknowledgment for their direct or indirect contributions to this book. We are grateful to numerous psychologists and educators for their profound influences on our professional development, most notably the late Dr. Herbert G. Birch, Dr. Jeannette Fleischner, the late Dr. Dorothea McCarthy, Dr. Margaret Jo Shepherd, Dr. Marvin Sontag, Dr. Robert L. Thorndike, Dr. David Wechsler, the late Dr. Alexander G. Wesman, and Dr. Ralph Zalma.

We are thankful to Dr. William Swan and Dr. Mary M. (Peggy) Wood for their kind permission to let us adapt N. L. K.'s case reports written for Rutland Center in Athens, Georgia, and include these reports in the book as illustrative case studies. The encouragement and flexibility of Dr. E. Paul Torrance, and the supportive attitude of the College of Education at the University of Georgia, are also much appreciated since they facilitated a more rapid completion of the book. Mrs. Elizabeth Thigpen earns our gratitude for her tireless, cheerful, and competent typing of all drafts of the manuscript, and Mr. Cecil R. Reynolds merits our appreciation for his excellent job in preparing the Indexes. We also wish to acknowledge *Educational and Psychological Measurement* for permitting us to reproduce a figure, and The Psychological Corporation for permitting us to reproduce portions of the McCarthy record form and to use some of the standardization data in the preparation of tables.

Finally, we wish to express our deepest appreciation to our parents, Blanche & Max Kaufman and Hannah & Seymour Bengels, for their warmth, inspiration, and support during the writing of this book and throughout our lives.

ALAN S. KAUFMAN
NADEEN L. KAUFMAN

# List of Tables and Figures

## TABLES

## FIGURES

# Clinical Evaluation
of Young Children
with the McCarthy Scales

# PART I

# Practical Considerations

The main goal of this book is to enable examiners to use the McCarthy Scales as a clinical tool for evaluating preschool and primary-grade children. However, before an examiner becomes too concerned with issues relating to test interpretation, he should first understand thoroughly certain basic considerations. Practical issues pertaining to the McCarthy, such as its advantages and disadvantages and tips for administration, are therefore treated in Part I; interpretation of the profile and integration of the McCarthy with other tests are treated in Parts II and III, respectively.

Chapter 1 defines the role of the McCarthy in terms of the current assessment scene. The applicability of the battery for preschool and school age youngsters, learning disabled children, and black youngsters is discussed and a basic question is answered: Is the McCarthy an intelligence test? Chapter 2 is intended to serve as a supplement to the McCarthy Manual and presents a test-by-test discussion of how to handle ambiguities and other troublesome aspects of administration and scoring. Chapter 3 provides the examiner with an objective method for prorating Indexes when a test is spoiled or omitted. This chapter is of extreme practical importance because there is currently no way to obtain a complete Index profile when an examiner spoils a test, or to compute Indexes for some exceptional children (e.g., the blind) who cannot be given the entire battery.

# Chapter 1

## The McCarthy's Role in Assessing Young Children

The early 1960s witnessed a surge of interest in the preschool and kindergarten-age child, highlighted by the appropriation of federal money for Head Start and other assorted early intervention programs. The devastating effects of early sensory and cultural deprivation on the later abilities of animals and children had become widely known following the pioneering efforts of Hebb, Harlow, Hunt, and others. Piaget, after spending almost 40 years analyzing the development of children's cognitive abilities, finally became spotlighted in the United States. The result was widespread public acceptance of the importance of the preschool years for promoting the child's optimum intellectual development. Furthermore, optimism was rampant: Fill in the gaps in the young disadvantaged child's conceptual framework and watch him blossom as a school-age child.

With the passage of time, formal and informal evaluations of the special preschool enrichment programs were compiled and much of the optimism diminished (as did most of the federal money). Perspectives changed, but the vital importance attributed to the preschool years, and to the assessment of the child's abilities during this crucial period, remained steadfast. Unfortunately, the testing industry did not respond to the pressing preschool assessment needs of the 1960s and early 1970s; well-normed tests, designed with the interests and abilities of young children in mind, were just not developed. Though the situation is still far from ideal, there is at least one individually administered instrument that has enough merit to challenge the Wechsler/Binet monopoly on preschool intelligence testing: the McCarthy Scales of Children's Abilities (McCarthy, 1972).

The importance of the McCarthy Scales stems not only from its essential role in assessing the preschool child's abilities; the battery also meets many of the needs of clinicians engaged in a type of assessment that became prevalent during the 1960s—the psychoeducational diagnosis of learning disabilities. Today, the fields of preschool assessment and learning disabilities overlap dynamically. The current major focus in preschool measurement features the determination of a prekindergarten or kindergarten-age child's readiness for school and likelihood for success in conventional school programs. Similarly, a primary area of increasing interest within the field of learning disabilities is *early detection* of children with potential learning disorders. Hence, both areas have converged on one main goal: screening children for possible learning problems prior to their entrance into school.

Dorothea McCarthy was involved extensively both in preschool assessment and in the testing of exceptional children, and her test battery reflects this dual perspective. In view of current educational and psychological needs and emphases, and with consideration given to the relative paucity of well-designed instruments available for meeting these needs, it is necessary for the psychologist and learning disabilities specialist to comprehend fully the potential contributions of the McCarthy. That is our reason for writing this book.

## OVERVIEW OF THE McCARTHY SCALES

Although Chapter 4 presents a thorough analysis of the scales and tests constituting the McCarthy, a brief overview of the 1972 battery is in order before proceeding further. The McCarthy is intended for children aged 2½–8½ years, and was standardized on a representative sample of 1032 children (stratified on age, sex, race, father's occupation, geographic region, and urban versus rural residence) within this age range. The instrument comprises 18 short tests of mental and motor ability, and requires about 1 hour to administer, as does the

Stanford-Binet (Terman & Merrill, 1973) or a Wechsler battery (Wechsler, 1967, 1974).

The 18 separate tests have been grouped in various ways to form 6 reliable scales; the composition of each scale, and the interrelationships among the 18 tests, are depicted pictorially in Figure 1-1. Note that the Verbal, Perceptual–Performance, and Quantitative Scales are nonoverlapping (they do not share any tests), and altogether make up the global General Cognitive Scale. The Verbal, Perceptual–Performance, and Quantitative Scales are each unified by the *content* of their test items (words, concrete materials, and digits, respectively). In addition, the Verbal Scale requires vocal responses while the Perceptual–Performance Scale demands only nonverbal responses.

By contrast, the Memory and Motor Scales are *process* oriented, with the former assessing short-term memory and the latter measuring motor coordination. The Memory tests overlap with Verbal, Perceptual–Performance, or Quantitative, depending on their content (Fig. 1-1), and therefore are all included on the General Cognitive Scale. The Motor Scale, though overlapping somewhat with other scales, retains a good deal of uniqueness by including three noncognitive gross motor tests.

Based on an administration of the McCarthy, the examiner routinely obtains the following profile of scores for each child: the General Cognitive Index (GCI), a standard score with a mean of 100 and standard deviation of 16; Scale Indexes (standard scores with a mean of 50 and standard deviation of 10) on each of the five specific scales; and a rating of the child's hand dominance based on observations made during the administration of the Motor tests.

## CONTRIBUTIONS OF THE McCARTHY SCALES

Clinicians involved in early childhood measurement, psycho-educational diagnosis, and assessment of the minority child all stand to benefit greatly by the development of the McCarthy Scales. Even though these three broad areas often overlap in practical situations (e.g., when testing a 4½-year-old black child suspected of a learning disorder), the main contributions of the McCarthy to each area are discussed separately in the sections that follow.

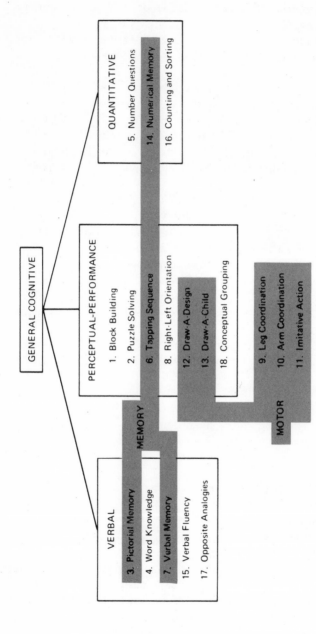

Fig. 1-1. The grouping of the 18 McCarthy tests into six scales. The tests in the Verbal (V), Perceptual–Performance (P), and Quantitative (Q) Scales are combined to form the General Cognitive Scale. Each of the Memory tests is also included on either the V, P, or Q Scale, and hence on the General Cognitive Scale. The Motor Scale contains three noncognitive tests which belong exclusively to it, and two tests which are shared with other scales. (Thanks are due Mrs. Fay B. Krawchick for designing the figure.) From "Factor structure of the McCarthy Scales at five age levels between 2½ and 8½" by A. S. Kaufman, *Educational and Psychological Measurement*, 1975, 35, 641–656. Reproduced by permission. Copyright © 1975 by Frederic Kuder.

### Early Childhood Assessment

Testing a young child is a difficult task even for the experienced examiner and requires special knowledge of children, perceptiveness, and a skillful testing technique. Goodenough (1949) provided valuable guidelines for testing preschool children in her book *Mental Testing*. Sattler (1974, pp. 67–68) summarized Goodenough's major points and presented a brief but valuable section on the testing of preschool children. The clinician who tests even an occasional young child should read Sattler's summary as well as McCarthy's (1972, pp. 44–45) section on establishing rapport. More desirable, however, is for the examiner to consult Goodenough's (1949) book directly, along with other pertinent references (e.g., Read, 1960), and to gain as much experience as possible with preschool youngsters.

McCarthy's test battery reflects the influence of her early training under Goodenough and the value of her many years of experience with young children. The test kit contains many attractive materials: familiar objects such as a ball and blocks, colorful pictures and puzzles, and gamelike equipment. As a whole, the kit was developed with the young child's needs and interests in mind. For example, the uninteresting cubes used for the Knox Cube Test (Arthur, 1947) have been replaced by an attractive, toylike xylophone for the analogous Tapping Sequence test.

Attractive materials facilitate the establishment and maintenance of rapport, which is perhaps the most essential ingredient in the valid assessment of a preschool or kindergarten-age child's abilities. However, an equally important aspect of rapport involves the *test sequence,* which ranks as an important feature of the McCarthy. Since rapport is most difficult to establish with a young child who is shy and nonverbal, the testing begins with two manipulative tasks. First comes Block Building, an easy test that requires mere imitation of the examiner's models. As the examiner begins stacking the blocks, while saying little, the young child is almost compelled to join into the activity. Next comes Puzzle Solving, a more conceptual nonverbal test. The bright, colorful picture puzzles maintain the child's interest, and the task itself often promotes the child's spontaneous verbalization.

The third test is Pictorial Memory, which requires the child to talk for the first time. Yet even for this first verbal test, an attractive set of pictures is used, both auditory and visual stimuli are provided to promote attention, and the child merely has to vocalize the names of pictured objects that were exposed (and named) briefly. Not until Word Knowledge, the fourth test, is the child asked to explain concepts in his own words. Even here, the child is gradually led from pointing to, and then naming, different familiar objects (Part I) to defining 10 words presented orally (Part II). Concrete materials are used for each of the first four tests; by the time the child is administered Part II of Word Knowledge and Number Questions, rapport has usually been well established. If not, the xylophone that is used for Test 6 may arouse the child's interest.

About midway through the test battery, the young child typically becomes restless and his interest starts to wane. The grouping of the gross motor tests in the middle of the battery provides a built-in break. The "intermission" tests include Leg Coordination and Arm Coordination, which permit the child and the examiner to stretch and move about actively in the testing room. Following noncognitive tasks such as walking backward, skipping, bouncing a ball, and aiming a beanbag at a target, the examiner must decelerate the child's "engine" and get him back to the testing table. This is facilitated by the nature of both Imitative Action and Draw-A-Design. Imitative Action is a simple gross motor test that must be administered sitting down. Draw-A-Design is a convergent design-copying test that virtually forces the child to attend to the task at hand; before it is over, the child is usually back in the proper frame of mind to complete the battery.

To reduce the effects of the child's fatigue during the end of the testing session, the child's vocalizing is limited to a maximum of one word per item during the last three tests: Counting & Sorting, Opposite Analogies, and Conceptual Grouping. In addition, two of these tasks involve the manipulation of blocks.

The 18 McCarthy tests are arranged with the Verbal, Perceptual–Performance, and Quantitative tasks alternating throughout the beginning and end of the battery, and the Motor tests occupying the middle portion. The systematic sequencing of the tests was intended to enhance rapport and to provide the child with an enjoyable testing experience. E. E. Davis (1974b, p. 58), in a review of the McCarthy Scales, commented that, "On the McCarthy young children seem to enjoy the experience of learning how to do each subtest and develop confidence before they are asked to engage in a new task." He found that better rapport was obtained with the McCarthy than the Stanford-Binet at the younger ages, and noted that the separate McCarthy tests were a more appropriate length than the short tasks in the Binet or the long subtests in the Wechsler Preschool and Primary Scale of Intelligence (WPPSI). In another review, E. E. Davis (1974a, p. 251) concluded that the McCarthy "is probably the best test that has been devised so far for testing the mental ability of individual young children."

Since preschool children tend to perform with great variability over time (even over a period of minutes) certain built-in precautions are included in the McCarthy to promote optimum measurement of the child's ability on each task. The use of toylike materials and a carefully conceived test sequence aid in this endeavor, but they are not enough. In addition, extra trials are permitted for many items (e.g., all Block Building and Leg Coordination items) to give the child a "second chance;" in all such cases, only the child's *best* performance is counted, not the averaging of his scores. On Draw-A-Design, if a child requests a second chance or spontaneously draws another design, only his best product is scored. Also, to ensure that the child understands the tasks at hand, he is frequently given feedback on the easier items; on Verbal Fluency, he is even given examples to start him off and help establish the proper mental set. Furthermore, the inclusion of many multipoint items rewards the child for virtually any response approximating correct performance. On Tapping Sequence, for example, the child is given one point for using the mallet purposefully, even if he cannot reproduce the simplest sequence.

Test–retest reliability coefficients (1-month interval) of about .90 for the GCI and .81, on the average, for the five Scale Indexes (McCarthy, 1972, p. 34) suggest that fairly stable measurement has indeed been obtained for children who typically exhibit marked variability in their test behaviors. The stability coefficient of .85 found for the GCI over a period of 1 year (Davis & Slettedahl, 1976) adds further credence to this contention.

Three additional topics relate to the benefits of the McCarthy Scales for young children and deserve mention. First, the *feelings* of the child are treated with respect: during Puzzle Solving, each picture puzzle is named "to minimize prolonged trial-and-error frustration," and the examiner completes unfinished puzzles so "the child sees that each task is possible before he attempts the next one;" for Verbal Fluency, a short 20-second time limit is used for each item to avoid "the prolonged strain of looking for more and more words in each category" (McCarthy, 1972, pp. 8, 11). Second, the progression of items in many tests—e.g., the transition from imitative drawing to copying a model in Draw-A-Design—reflects the application of numerous important findings from developmental research. Even the specific areas assessed by the battery correspond closely to the important primary abilities of young children identified by Thurstone and Thurstone (1941, 1953).

The third topic concerns developmental theory. Although the McCarthy Scales are not derived from theory, many aspects of contemporary developmental theories are incorporated in the battery. The influence of Piaget is clearly present in tasks such as Conceptual Grouping and Counting & Sorting, and in most of the other cognitive tests as well. The tasks assess the young child's abilities to organize and label his environment, interpret his perceptions, understand and apply basic concepts, demonstrate knowledge of objects in space, pit percept against concept, and recall stimuli that are seen or heard. These abilities are all consistent with Piaget's ideas of the way the preoperational child adapts to his environment and the general path he follows to enter the stage of concrete operations.

The Gesell tradition has made its mark on screening tests, infant scales, and readiness instruments, and is also prominent in the McCarthy. The inclusion of the gross motor tests in the McCarthy Scales is in accord with Gesell's treatment of cognitive and motor variables as two essential aspects of the total functioning organism (Gesell & Amatruda, 1947). Furthermore, the Draw-A-Design and Draw-A-Child combination parallels Gesell's Copy Forms and Incomplete Man tasks, which play a featured role in Ilg and Ames' (1972) Gesell School Readiness Tests.

### Psychoeducational Diagnosis

The movement that brought the concept of learning disabilities to the foreground in schools, child guidance clinics, pediatricians' offices, and the home has had its impact on assessment. The negative aspect of this impact is the weedlike sprouting of screening tests which purport to identify children with learning disabilities. These tests are then put into immediate use by groups of "believers" despite poor norms and inadequate validity information (or, in some cases, the complete absence of both). A brief administration time and testimonials by satisfied test users are often the keynotes for success.

By contrast, the positive aspect of the learning disabilities movement is the emergence of the dynamic process of psychoeducational
diagnosis, which features a thorough and comprehensive approach to
assessment. In psychoeducational diagnosis, many different types of
tests are used to learn about the child's strengths and weaknesses in a
variety of areas including mental ability, language skills, perceptual–
motor coordination, perceptual development, gross motor behavior,
achievement in school-related tasks, concept formation, memory, and
lateral dominance. Although a standard *core* of tests is typically used
by most clinicians, the diagnostic process is highlighted by flexibility.
Tests are chosen to coincide with each child's specific presenting problems, and many tasks are chosen (or even invented) on the spur of the
moment to test out hypotheses that are formulated *during* the testing
session. No test battery is considered sacred, and the examiner will
often administer only one or two subtests—sometimes only one or two
items—depending upon the specific type of information needed to help
complete the overall picture of the child's functioning. The ultimate
goal (besides accurate diagnosis) is to integrate the child's pattern of
relative strengths and weaknesses with his characteristic behaviors, and
then translate these findings into practical suggestions for remediation.

Psychoeducational diagnosis therefore shifts the focus from the
test to the child, which is a refreshing change. No single score, such as
an IQ, is overstressed; rather, each score forms a piece of the total
picture, where the whole exceeds the sum of its parts. (Often a multidisciplinary team including psychologists, educators, physicians, and
social workers is involved in the diagnosis, putting the test scores in
even better perspective.) Finally, the emphasis on finding out what the
child can do relatively well, so his own strengths can be utilized to
help him learn in school, puts testing in a positive light. The test
becomes the "helping agent" rather than the source of punishment,
and the test results are used in practical ways instead of being summarized by a single global score that then determines the child's
educational fate.

However, the psychoeducational diagnostic approach is limited
by the lack of carefully developed and well-normed tests. The clinician
is forced to choose the best available tests of each type even though
many of these instruments fall far short of meeting adequate standards. When the examiner tries to integrate results from numerous
tests, he has to make comparisons among scores derived from a

variety of normative samples; since some tests are normed on small or unrepresentative samples, the meaning of the scores they yield is suspect.

The McCarthy Scales are especially applicable to the psycho-educational diagnosis of the learning disabled youngster (Kaufman & Kaufman, 1977). The Motor Scale provides an immediate bonus over and above the information yielded by conventional intelligence tests. The child's gross and fine motor coordination on the McCarthy might suggest the need to administer selected additional motor tasks, but it would not usually be necessary to administer an entire supplementary battery of motor tests. The inclusion of Draw-A-Child in the McCarthy also makes it redundant to give a separate figure drawing test since the child's drawing of a boy or girl can easily be evaluated clinically or scored by supplementary systems (see pp. 189-191).

Whereas the Draw-A-Design test is not a substitute for the Bender-Gestalt (Bender, 1946), the child's design-copying perform-ance on the McCarthy and on the Bender can be integrated to yield a more thorough evaluation of his visual–motor functioning (see pp. 185-189). When testing time is at a premium, the McCarthy Draw-A-Design test may be used as a screening device to determine if the Bender should be given. Similarly, the child's hand dominance rating provides a means of evaluating whether a more thorough measure is needed, and the child's performance on Right–Left Orientation may be used in the same way.

In short, based on an administration of the McCarthy Scales, the examiner is provided broad exposure to the child's mental and motor functioning, thereby reducing the number of separate tests that are needed for effective psychoeducational diagnosis. The McCarthy's excellent standardization sample not only promotes confidence in the meaning of the obtained scores, but it also permits the use of a *com-mon norm* for comparing the child's relative abilities in diverse tasks. Furthermore, the specific areas assessed by the McCarthy—language, perception, conceptualization, and memory—correspond to the typi-cally problematic areas of functioning for learning disabled children; these children also commonly experience laterality confusions and/or motor problems.

The McCarthy has other advantages over conventional intelli-gence tests for the psychoeducational diagnostic process. Good short-term memory, for example, is essential for successful achievement in the primary grades as well as for the acquisition of concepts in the preschool years. This ability is not measured extensively by the Wechsler Scales or the early levels of the Stanford-Binet, but on the McCarthy it is assessed in two modalities, via verbal and nonverbal responding, and with a wide variety of stimuli. In addition, several of the McCarthy tasks tend to measure skills that are needed for school success, that lend themselves to educational interpretation, and that are remediable. McCarthy (1972, p. 10) notes that the skill required for Verbal Memory II (retelling a story read by the examiner) is a prerequisite for "such routine tasks as listening to a story read by a teacher, following oral directions, and remembering a homework assignment." Conceptual Grouping and Counting & Sorting provide two other illustrations of tasks measuring prerequisite school-related skills that may be remediated if necessary.

The results of two research studies with learning disabled children converge on one major point: on the average, the GCIs of these youngsters were about *15 points below* their IQs (DeBoer, Kaufman, & McCarthy, 1974; Kaufman & Kaufman, 1974). The mean WPPSI and Stanford-Binet (1972 norms) IQs of *normal* children have been found to be about equal to their GCIs (Davis, 1975; Davis & Rowland, 1974; McCarthy, 1972), so the tentative finding of a GCI–IQ discrepancy for learning disabled youngsters has implications for early screening as well as for psychoeducational diagnosis. If the discrepancy is consistently replicated in future studies, it will mean that the GCI is more in tune with the level of school achievement of learning disabled children than is the conventional IQ.

Another benefit of the McCarthy for psychoeducational diagnosis derives from the frequent presence in learning disabled children of behaviors such as hyperactivity, emotional lability, distractibility, and impulsivity. The same features of the McCarthy Scales that make it suitable for young children (e.g., the attractive materials and the test sequence) greatly facilitate the establishment and maintenance of rapport with a distractible or emotionally labile child. The "motor break" also provides the examiner with a chance to observe the child's behavior during tasks that are less structured than conventional sitdown tests (see Chapter 7).

One other aspect of the battery merits attention: its value to psychoeducational diagnosis even when a Wechsler test or the Stanford-Binet is used instead of the McCarthy. By comprising 18 separate well-normed mental and motor tests, the McCarthy serves as a source of tasks for *informal* assessment. As hypotheses arise during the psychoeducational diagnostic process about the child's functioning, it is reasonable to administer selected McCarthy tasks to test out these hypotheses. This topic is discussed at greater length on pages 211–214.

### Measurement of the Black Child's Abilities

The initial studies of the McCarthy for blacks and whites have produced promising results. Although additional research studies with new samples are essential, the early analyses with standardization data suggest the usefulness of the McCarthy for black youngsters. A comparison of the factor structure for separate groups of blacks and whites aged 3–7½ years revealed striking similarities and attested to the *construct validity* of the McCarthy for both racial groups (Kaufman & DiCuio, 1975). Equally important, samples of blacks and whites matched on many variables including social class did *not* differ significantly in their mean GCIs (or in their mean Indexes on the cognitive scales) at ages 2½–5½. Furthermore, the average GCI for the blacks at these ages was about 96, not substantially different from the designated mean (i.e., the so called "white mean") of 100. At ages 6½–8½, the picture was different, with the results paralleling the typical black versus white findings with the conventional IQ. White children scored significantly higher than black children on all cognitive scales, and the mean GCI for blacks was only 89. (See Kaufman & Kaufman, 1973a, for a more thorough presentation of the study of black–white differences, and see Kaufman & Kaufman, 1975, for an analysis of social class differences on the McCarthy for separate groups of blacks and whites.)

The McCarthy Scales seem, therefore, to yield significant racial discrepancies at the school-age level but not at the preschool and kindergarten-age levels, which are the main "targets" of the McCarthy Scales. Why might the McCarthy be "color blind" for younger children? The answer, though not obvious, is of extreme interest in view of the consistent findings of higher IQs by white than black children, even at the preschool and kindergarten ages (Kaufman, 1973b; Shuey, 1966). Probably two sets of variables are involved: those related to rapport, and those concerned with the nature of the items in the battery.

Rapport between a white examiner and black child often presents a problem during any individually administered test. The very young black child is likely to be especially nonverbal and inhibited when being asked questions by a white adult. Therefore, the facets of the McCarthy that are geared to the needs of any young child should pay extra dividends with the black youngster. The attractive and colorful materials, gamelike activities, clearly structured tasks, and the test sequence should help the black child overcome his anxiety in the potentially fearful testing situation and promote an adequate rapport. The focus on concrete materials permits the child to be task oriented, relieving the "social pressure" to interact with the examiner.

In terms of the tasks themselves, there are many aspects that are particularly pertinent to the black child's interests and aptitudes. None of the tests are as culture loaded as the Wechsler Information subtest or the Wechsler and Binet Comprehension items. Social understanding and the acquisition of specific facts, which are often a function of a child's subculture, are thus not reflected in the GCI. Conversely, short-term memory tasks—which usually do not produce significant differences between blacks and whites (Jensen, 1969)—are well represented in McCarthy's overall index of cognitive functioning. In addition, black children tend to perform poorly on tests heavily weighted in *verbal expression.* The McCarthy tests do not, in general, require the child to express his thoughts in phrases or sentences; in fact only Word Knowledge II, Verbal Memory II, and Verbal Fluency demand a substantial amount of verbiage in the child's responses. Finally, even the gross motor tests, which are not included on the General Cognitive Scale, may facilitate the black child's intellectual performance by sustaining interest and rapport throughout the entire session.

These speculations may not be related to the lack of significant differences between the Indexes of preschool and kindergarten age blacks and whites, but they do make sense. They should serve as reasonable hypotheses until cross-validation studies, and other investigations of the McCarthy's usefulness for black youngsters, are conducted. At that time the relationship between the GCI and IQ for black children should be more explicit, and the explanations for possible discrepancies in the two constructs may be better understood.

## LIMITATIONS OF THE McCARTHY

Any instrument that provides a broad range of information about a child's functioning based on about 1 hour of testing time must have certain limitations, and the McCarthy is no exception. Some of these limitations are of a practical nature. First, there is much clerical work that has to be performed by the examiner in order to transform scores on the 18 separate tests into Indexes on the 6 scales (Hufano & Hoepfner, 1974). Without extreme care, errors can easily creep in that may greatly distort the meaning of the child's profile. Also, the McCarthy may only be administered by a psychologist, learning disabilities specialist, or other professional who has been well trained in individual testing. Many school systems simply cannot afford to pay highly trained personnel to test children individually for screening purposes or for other large-scale assessment projects. Hence, the McCarthy will often lose out to a group instrument, or to an individual test that is short and can be administered by a teacher, even if the McCarthy is the more appropriate instrument. Furthermore, the McCarthy requires effort to learn to administer and score properly, which may discourage a number of potential test users. Mastery of the McCarthy tends to be more difficult than learning a Wechsler Scale, but not as problematic as becoming fluent with the Stanford-Binet or Illinois Test of Psycholinguistic Abilities (Kirk, McCarthy, & Kirk, 1968). As is true of most individual tests, however, the first several administrations of the McCarthy will require considerably more time than subsequent testings.

Other limitations of the McCarthy Scales go beyond mere practical considerations and should be thoroughly understood by test users. These shortcomings may be grouped in three distinct areas, which are discussed below: lack of social comprehension and judgment tasks; problems for testing school-age children; and difficulties pertaining to scale interpretation. Several of the McCarthy's limitations are "treatable," although some of the problems are built into the battery and may necessitate either using supplementary measures or choosing a different instrument altogether. The limitations that have solutions (e.g., the lack of a method for dealing with spoiled tests) are treated throughout the chapters of this book; Chapter 8 discusses the integration of the McCarthy with supplementary tests.

### Lack of Social Comprehension and
### Judgment Tasks

McCarthy's avoidance of highly culture-loaded items has obvious advantages, particularly for testing minority-group children. Nevertheless, many social intelligence or factual items measure a child's common sense judgment, his ability to evaluate familiar problem situations, and his acquisition of basic knowledge from the environ-ment. (What should you do when you are thirsty? How do we make water boil? Why do we need banks? Why is it important to go to the toilet before going to sleep at night? Why do we need doctors?) These represent important cognitive abilities since the items relate to the real world and often require application of knowledge; the child's perfor-mance on these tasks helps complete the overall picture of his func-tioning. Hence, supplementary sociocultural tasks are often desirable for thorough assessment (see pp. 181–185). The fact that the culture-loaded items in these supplementary tests will not affect the child's overall index of functioning (his GCI) is beneficial, however, espe-cially if he is disadvantaged.

### Problems for Testing School-Age Children

The McCarthy Scales were developed to meet the needs of the young child, and they do this well; but they do *not* provide adequate or complete measurement for many school-age children. The features that make the McCarthy so suitable for preschool, kindergarten-age, and first-grade children (e.g., the attractive materials, the test sequence, the many examples and second trials that are given) are unnecessary for most older children and do not contribute to the effec-tive measurement of their abilities. The Motor Scale, which assesses an important aspect of the young child's total functioning, measures a less crucial area of the older child's ability spectrum. In fact, at age 6½ and above the Motor Index is not particularly reliable or stable over time (McCarthy, 1972, pp. 30–34). With the possible exception of school-age children suspected of learning disabilities, other types of neurological impairment, or mental retardation—for whom the rapport-related aspects of the McCarthy and the Motor Index serve useful functions—the McCarthy should usually not be the featured ability test in a battery for older children. Even for the categories of exceptionality mentioned above, the examiner may prefer to give a WISC-R or Stanford-Binet to children above 6½ years of age, and use some McCarthy tasks for supplementary assessment.

The lack of social intelligence items in the McCarthy is a more severe limitation for older than younger children. The older the child, the more he interacts with his environment and the more independent he becomes from his home and parents. Social comprehension, maturity, and judgment cannot be omitted from an assessment of a school-age child's mental functioning without a considerable loss of pertinent information.

Social understanding tasks usually require the child to reason verbally by expressing his ideas in his own words. Other tasks, such as Verbal Absurdities in the Stanford-Binet, also demand verbal reasoning. Unfortunately, the important ability of reasoning via verbal expression is not tapped by any of the McCarthy tests. This represents no particular problem for preschool and kindergarten-age children; even on the highly verbal Stanford-Binet, verbal reasoning items (other than those categorized by Sattler, 1974, as social intelligence) are not introduced until age level IX. For school-aged youngsters, however, verbal reasoning is an essential aspect of intelligence both at school and at home. Its inadequate measurement by the McCarthy thus represents a serious shortcoming when testing children above $6\frac{1}{2}$ years of age.

A related limitation concerns the fact that few tasks in the McCarthy assess abstract problem solving. Puzzle Solving, Number Questions, and Conceptual Grouping do assess this high-level skill, but most McCarthy tests do not. Again, this is not of concern for young children. The Stanford-Binet has relatively few problem-solving tasks at the earlier age levels, and the abstract Picture Arrangement and Object Assembly subtests, which appear in the WISC-R, were replaced in the WPPSI by the convergent Geometric Design subtest. According to Piaget, the child progresses from preoperational thought to concrete operations at about 6 to 7 years of age. Problem-solving tasks are especially important for assessment of the concrete operational child, and the McCarthy does not adequately meet this need.

The lack of a sufficient *ceiling* on many of the 18 McCarthy tests for children aged 7 and above presents yet another problem. The average $8\frac{1}{2}$-year-old child earns at least *two-thirds* of the possible points on 16 of the 18 tests. At age $7\frac{1}{2}$, the average child earns two-thirds or more of the points on 14 tests. For ages $6\frac{1}{2}$ and below, however, most tests have a more optimum and age-appropriate difficulty level. Although the *scales* are quite reliable above age 7 (except for Motor), the measurement is based on tests that were designed for younger children and are more ideally suited for them both conceptually and statistically. Needless to say, the limited ceiling prevents effective assessment of the abilities of older *gifted* children, as McCarthy (1972, p. 28) points out.

The fact that the McCarthy does not extend above age 8½ years, coupled with the unavailability of a McCarthy-like battery for older children and adolescents, creates an additional consideration for the examiner. Exceptional children are often tested several times after they are diagnosed, either for reevaluation purposes or to determine eligibility for various school-related or institutional programs. The Stanford-Binet is normed on children aged 2–18 years, and the WPPSI—though spanning the narrow 4–6½-year-old age range—is succeeded by the similar WISC-R test battery. With these instruments, continuity of measurement over many years is quite feasible; with the McCarthy, the direct continuity ceases abruptly at age 8½.

The lack of continuity is not a pertinent issue for children aged 6½ and below. Accurate diagnosis is essential, and the best instrument for young children should be used for this purpose. Furthermore, for a young child, follow-up testing with the McCarthy is possible for several years, permitting continuity of measurement during the most rapid and crucial period of development. Interestingly, at the younger end of the McCarthy, the measurement is *more* continuous with infant scales than are the Binet or Wechsler tests. The McCarthy takes up where the Bayley Scales of Infant Development (Bayley, 1969) leaves off (age 2½ years), providing scores in the same two major areas— mental and motor. At the upper end, the less than adequate continuity with other available instruments should be considered by the clinician before choosing the McCarthy for an older child.

### Difficulties Pertaining to Scale Interpretation

A variety of other limitations are grouped under this heading because each, in its own way, affects the examiner's interpretation of the six scales. The first such limitation concerns the *internal consistency reliability* of several of the Indexes. If .80 is considered as an arbitrary criterion of satisfactory reliability, then the Perceptual– Performance and Quantitative Indexes each fall short of the criterion at 3 of the 10 standardization age levels; the Memory Index falls short at 5 levels; and the Motor Index falls short at 4 levels, including 2 values in the .60–.70 range for school-age children (McCarthy, 1972, p. 31). The band of error becomes uncomfortably large when coefficients dip below .80, necessitating cautious interpretation of some of the child's Indexes at certain ages. The reliability of the *difference* between pairs of Indexes also suffers when one of the Indexes has a large band of error.

Basically, though, no single Index or pair of Indexes should be overstressed for any particular child. All Indexes, including the GCI, should be interpreted as a whole, with the overall profile of abilities carrying far more weight than any single score. The approach that we propose for interpreting a child's Index profile (Chapter 5) is holistic and therefore consistent with this belief. Since the technique takes into account the reliability of each scale, clinicians who adhere to it will avoid overinterpretation of *any* Scale Index—whether it is one that merits cautious treatment, or one that is extremely reliable.

The *overlap* in content between some of the scales presents a second interpretive problem. In particular, the overlap of the Memory Scale with both the Verbal and Quantitative Scales is very substantial; not surprisingly, the average correlation of the Memory Index with the Verbal Index is .80, and the average Memory–Quantitative correlation is .75 (McCarthy, 1972, p. 39). The Motor and Perceptual–Performance Scales, which share the two drawing tests, also correlate a hefty .70, on the average. Just as the low reliability of an Index hinders interpretation of *differences* between Indexes, so do high correlation coefficients. McCarthy (1972, p. 35) recommended cautious interpretation of any observed differences in the three pair of Indexes noted above. However, judicious interpretation of Indexes does not solve the examiner's problems when trying to make sense of a child's profile. Fortunately, the method of profile interpretation described in Chapter 5 is not hindered by overlapping scales or highly correlated Indexes and partially alleviates this interpretive problem.

A third limitation pertaining to scale interpretation concerns the range of GCIs and Scale Indexes: each extends only about 3 standard deviations, in either direction, from the mean. McCarthy (1972, p. 24) did not extrapolate further because she was understandably concerned about the "inaccuracies that would result from too much 'educated' guessing." Certainly, a GCI range of 50–150 is sufficiently wide to classify the cognitive abilities of a great majority of children. The occasional child who scores outside the range presents no problem because the clinician has ample information to classify his ability level. Trouble arises, however, for the examiner who routinely tests extremely retarded or highly gifted children.

Consider, for example, the clinician who has to assess the abilities of numerous trainable mentally retarded (TMR) youngsters. Since the McCarthy goes down to age 2½, there is ample "bottom" to test TMR children aged 5 and above. The clinician may thus select the

McCarthy because it includes many items of appropriate difficulty and because its child-oriented nature is suitable for TMR youngsters. However, he is likely to become frustrated when many children obtain a GCI of "below 50" and the same Index on all five scales ("below 22"). He is unable to distinguish among the various children and cannot determine each child's relative strengths and weaknesses. The same type of frustration is likely to occur for the examiner who has to test a group of unusually gifted 3 and 4 year olds.

A technique utilizing Scale Ages (which are akin to mental ages) is offered to enable the clinician to assess the abilities of children who fall at the extremes of the normal curve (see pp. 122–124, and the case study of Elizabeth T. in Chapter 9). The technique permits the examiner to compare the ability levels of various individuals and to obtain a profile of strengths and weaknesses for each person. It also may be used for retarded children above age $8\frac{1}{2}$ and for gifted youngsters below age $2\frac{1}{2}$. However, age norms are not as versatile or psychometrically sound as standard score norms; the proposed technique treats the problem, but does not cure it. The ultimate solution would be to test substantial numbers of retarded and gifted children at each age level to extend the standard score norms without having to resort to guesswork.

A fourth problem concerns interpreting the scales for $2\frac{1}{2}$ year olds who are below average in ability. Just as there is an insufficient ceiling for bright school-age children, the McCarthy does not have enough bottom for $2\frac{1}{2}$ year olds. There really is no problem for children who have reached their third birthday, because a dramatic growth spurt typically occurs during the 6-month interim. Consider that the number of points earned by the average 3 year old on each of the six scales is double, or almost double, the composite raw scores obtained by $2\frac{1}{2}$ year olds (McCarthy, 1972, p. 36). In addition, the average $2\frac{1}{2}$ year old earns less than 1 raw score point on seven of the separate tests, indicating that most tasks are too difficult for him. As one might expect, it is not possible to obtain a meaningful profile of Indexes for the below-average $2\frac{1}{2}$ year old. By obtaining only 3 points on each of the five specific scales, the $2\frac{1}{2}$ year old will score close to average for his age (Indexes above 40) on the Quantitative, Memory, and Motor Scales. If he earns only 12 points on the entire General Cognitive Scale (less than 1 point per test), his GCI of 80 classifies him as dull normal. There is no solution to this particular limitation of the McCarthy. An infant scale such as the Bayley is preferable for the assessment of the mental and motor abilities of the below-average $2\frac{1}{2}$ year old and should be used whenever feasible.

A final limitation relates to interpreting a scale when one or more of its component tests is spoiled or cannot be administered. The WISC-R, WPPSI, and Stanford-Binet each have alternate tests in the event of spoilage, and each of these batteries has simple prorating procedures. The McCarthy has no alternates and the issue of prorating is not treated in the Manual. Since the child's weighted raw scores on *all* tests in a scale must be summed before conversion to an Index, spoilage or omission of a test prevents the examiner from obtaining a meaningful score. For example, if Verbal Memory is spoiled, the examiner cannot compute Indexes for the Verbal, Memory, or General Cognitive Scales unless a prorated score for the spoiled test can be determined. However, each McCarthy test has its own characteristic mean and standard deviation at different age levels, so conventional prorating approaches are not applicable.

In Chapter 3 a technique is presented that permits estimating a score for virtually any McCarthy test, should this be necessary. Though objective and psychometrically sound, the method for obtaining prorated Indexes is more complex than the procedures for the Binet or Wechsler batteries. Nevertheless, the examiner should be familiar with the technique because it is not uncommon for a young child to refuse a test, and even a highly skilled examiner will sometimes spoil a test. By prorating, no validly obtained test information is wasted. Furthermore, the technique permits the use of some of the McCarthy Scales for exceptional groups such as the blind, who cannot be administered the entire battery—which is a topic that is also treated in Chapter 3.

Overall, the limitations of the McCarthy apply primarily to older children. For youngsters aged $3-6\frac{1}{2}$ years the contributions and advantages of the battery far outweigh any shortcomings, and the McCarthy provides excellent measurement for children within this age range. The battery should also be extremely useful for special groups of school-age children, such as the mentally retarded and learning disabled, and for $2\frac{1}{2}$ year olds who are average or above average in ability. For a majority of school-age children (and for many $2\frac{1}{2}$ year olds), however, other instruments may be preferable for comprehensive intellectual assessment.

## IS THE McCARTHY AN INTELLIGENCE TEST?

Ultimately, test users seek a direct answer to a question that has practical implications: Is the McCarthy a type of intelligence test? A clinician who has to classify children as mentally retarded or normal to determine if they should be placed in an educable mentally retarded (EMR) class or stay in the mainstream, needs to know whether the GCI is essentially an IQ. The psychoeducational diagnostician who wants to compare the child's academic potential with his school achievement also must know if the McCarthy is an intelligence test.

In the Manual, McCarthy (1972, p. 5) stated that the term IQ was avoided "because of the many misinterpretations of that concept and the unfortunate connotations that have become associated with it." The choice of the term GCI instead of IQ was thus based on a semantic distinction rather than a conceptual one. However, the results of the black–white study (Kaufman & Kaufman, 1973a) and the investigations of learning disabled children (DeBoer et al, 1974; Kaufman & Kaufman, 1974) suggest that the GCI and IQ constructs are not identical.

Can one then conclude that the GCI is *not* a type of IQ? No such conclusion is possible based on the available research findings. Even different IQ tests are often found to yield divergent results for the same individual. For example, a 12 year old who is much better nonverbally than verbally will typically obtain a considerably higher overall IQ on the WISC-R than the Stanford-Binet. Furthermore, it is not uncommon for *gifted* children to score about 1 standard deviation higher on the Stanford-Binet than on a Wechsler scale (Zimmerman & Woo-Sam, 1970; 1972, p. 241). The existence of these well-known differences between the Binet and Wechsler tests for certain individuals or groups does not cause psychologists to claim that one IQ is "better" than the other; whichever battery is used simply becomes the criterion for intelligence, regardless of the different IQs that might be yielded by group intelligence tests or by other individual tests.

Therefore, the finding of differences between the GCIs and IQs of some individuals or groups does not mean that the McCarthy is not an intelligence test. The pertinent question is whether the McCarthy merits classification as a criterion of intelligence, and this should be answered on the basis of both rational and empirical considerations.

**Rational Evidence**

From the rational, or content validity, standpoint it should be demonstrated that McCarthy's cognitive tasks correspond closely to the type of items included in the Stanford-Binet, WPPSI, and WISC-R. The IQs yielded by these instruments are widely accepted as criteria of intelligence. In addition, the Binet and Wechsler scales are the tests that will generally be replaced by the McCarthy whenever it is used to measure a child's mental abilities.

Figure 1-2 shows the correspondence of each McCarthy test in the General Cognitive Scale with highly similar Binet tasks at Years II–X. Of the 15 McCarthy tests, 13 have direct analogs on the Stanford-Binet. Of the tests without analogs, Right–Left Orientation corresponds to the "Orientation: Direction" tasks at Levels XIV and AA of the Binet; and Tapping Sequence, though having no Binet counterpart at any level, is a clear analog of the Knox Cube Test (long accepted as a measure of nonverbal intelligence).

A close relationship (though not as close as the McCarthy–Binet correspondence) is also evidenced when a number of McCarthy tasks are matched with comparable WPPSI and WISC-R subtests, as shown below.

| McCarthy Test | Corresponding WISC-R and/or WPPSI Subtest |
|---|---|
| 2. Puzzle Solving | Object Assembly |
| 4. Word Knowledge | Vocabulary |
| 5. Number Questions | |
|     Items 1–3 | Information |
|     Items 4–12 | Arithmetic |
| 7. Verbal Memory | Sentences |
| 12. Draw-A-Design | Geometric Design |
| 14. Numerical Memory | Digit Span |
| 16. Counting & Sorting | Arithmetic |
| 17. Opposite Analogies | Similarities |

The congruence of the tests in the McCarthy Scales with tasks generally accepted as measures of general intelligence is extremely close. As mentioned above, however, certain types of intelligence test items are either not included in the McCarthy (social intelligence), or are underrepresented for older children (verbal expression, judgment and reasoning, abstract problem solving). Consequently, from a

| McCarthy General Cognitive Scale | Stanford-Binet Analogs at Years II–X |
|---|---|
| 1. Block Building | Block Building: Tower (II), Bridge (III) |
| 2. Puzzle Solving | Patience: Pictures (III-6), Rectangles (V) |
| 3. Pictorial Memory | Picture Memories (III); Naming Objects from Memory (IV) |
| 4. Word Knowledge | |
|    I. Picture Vocabulary | Identifying Objects by Name (II); Naming Objects (II-6); Picture Vocabulary (II, II-6, III, IV) |
|    II. Oral Vocabulary | Definitions (V); Vocabulary (VI, VIII, X); Abstract Words I (X) |
| 5. Number Questions | Making Change (IX) |
| 6. Tapping Sequence | ——————— |
| 7. Verbal Memory | |
|    I. Words and Sentences | Memory for Sentences I (IV) |
|    II. Story | Memory for Stories: The Wet Fall (VIII) |
| 8. Right–Left Orientation | ——————— |
| 12. Draw-A-Design | Drawing a Vertical Line (III); Copying a Circle (III), Square (V), Diamond (VII) |
| 13. Draw-A-Child | Picture Completion: Man (V) |
| 14. Numerical Memory | |
|    I. Forward Series | Repeating 2 Digits (II-6), 3 Digits (III), 5 Digits (VII), 6 Digits (X) |
|    II. Backward Series | Repeating 3 Digits Reversed (VII), 4 Digits Reversed (IX) |
| 15. Verbal Fluency | Word Naming (X) |
| 16. Counting & Sorting | Number Concepts (VI); Block Counting (X) |
| 17. Opposite Analogies | Opposite Analogies I, II, III (IV, IV-6, VI, VII) |
| 18. Conceptual Grouping | Comparison of Balls (III-6); Sorting Buttons (III-6) |

Fig. 1-2. Comparison of the tests in McCarthy's General Cognitive Scale with tasks in the Stanford-Binet at Years II–X. The age level(s) of each Binet task is indicated in parentheses following its name.

rational standpoint, the McCarthy is a better measure of the intelligence of preschool, than of school-age, youngsters.

### Empirical Evidence

Several studies have shown that the GCI correlates with WPPSI Full Scale IQ and with Stanford-Binet IQ to the same degree that these IQs correlate with each other. In the Manual, McCarthy (1972, p. 40) reported correlations of .71 and .81 with WPPSI and Binet IQs, respectively, for 35 normal first grade children. Davis and Rowland (1974) obtained a correlation of .77 between the GCI and Binet IQ for 33 normal 2½–8½ year olds, and Davis (1975) found a GCI–Binet IQ correlation of .91 for 53 normal younsters aged 5–6 years. Finally, De Boer et al. (1974) obtained a coefficient of .56 between GCI and IQ for 41 learning disabled children aged 4½–8½ years. (Of the 41 children, 33 were given the 1949 WISC, 7 the WPPSI, and 1 the Stanford-Binet.) The standard deviation of the IQs for the latter sample was a very restricted 9.7, since children were eligible for the sample only if their IQs were 90 or above; when corrected for restriction of range, the GCI–IQ coefficient jumped to .72 for the learning disabled sample.

Clearly, empirical data reported so far give evidence for a very close relationship between the GCI and the overall IQs yielded by the major intelligence tests. In addition, the GCI, Stanford-Binet IQ, and WPPSI Full Scale IQ displayed comparable predictive validities for a group of 31 first graders (Kaufman, 1973c); and the relationship of GCI to social class (Kaufman & Kaufman, 1975) paralleled closely the well-known relationship of IQ to social class (Anastasi, 1958, p. 517).

### Conclusions

More research is needed before the many facets of the GCI are well understood. Nevertheless, based on present information, *we feel confident that the GCI is an index of intellectual functioning and may be used interchangeably with the IQ.* The GCI does not provide a broad enough assessment of the requisite intellectual skills for school-age children; this limitation should be taken into account by test users, just as they carefully weigh the pros and cons of any intelligence test before selecting the most appropriate instrument for a particular child. However, the GCI should still be thought of as an IQ analog, even for a bright school-age child. Although the McCarthy is short on social comprehension and problem solving items, it still encompasses a diversity of mental tasks. It is important to remember that there is no one blueprint for an intelligence test. In fact, the Binet and Wechsler scales are as different from each other as they are from McCarthy's General Cognitive Scale. For example, only 30 percent of the Stanford-Binet tasks at Years II–XII measure Guilford's operation of "evaluation," as opposed to 70 percent of the WPPSI tasks (Kaufman, 1973a).

A few practical issues arise in view of the finding that two groups of learning disabled children obtained GCIs that were an average of about 15 points below their IQs (DeBoer et al., 1974; Kaufman & Kaufman, 1974). Assuming that the finding is replicated, should a child with a low GCI be categorized as mentally retarded? (He may be learning disabled.) What should be done when criteria for categorizing a child as learning disabled demand a *discrepancy* of a given magnitude between aptitude and achievement, or require the child to have an IQ of at least 90?

If the McCarthy really does provide indexes that reflect the *school-related aptitude* of learning disabeled children, then the GCI is a more relevant score than the IQ for *practical* purposes. How then should the questions mentioned above be handled? Surely a child should not be classified as mentally retarded (or multiply handicapped) simply because of a low GCI, when the overall picture suggests learning disabilities. The first part of the solution requires using the GCI or the IQ in conjunction with a measure of *adaptive behavior* (Lambert, Windmiller, Cole, & Figueroa, 1975; Mercer & Lewis, in press) when testing children suspected of mental retardation. Based on the American Association on Mental Deficiency guidelines, children must be retarded in *both* their intellectual functioning and their adaptive behavior to be classified as mentally retarded. Thus, when a low GCI is paired with low adaptive behavior, a diagnosis of retardation is reasonable; a low GCI, or IQ, coupled with normal adaptive behavior should *not* lead to a diagnosis of mental retardation.

The use of rigid criteria for classifying children as learning disabled is unfortunate in view of the research findings with the McCarthy. When rules are unbendable, additional testing will simply by necessary. Suppose a 7-year-old child obtains a GCI of only 74, but is suspected of having a learning disability in view of a neurological examination, his profile of cognitive and motor abilities on the McCarthy, his behavioral characteristics, and his pattern of scores on other tests of specific abilities and achievements. He should then be given the WISC-R Verbal or Performance Scale; his Verbal or Performance IQ may well be high enough to satisfy the rigid "average IQ" requirement and any other criteria regarding a discrepancy between ability and achievement. The Verbal Scale is a particularly good addition to the McCarthy since the Information, Comprehension, and Similarities subtests will provide valuable supplementary data regarding the child's social intelligence, problem solving ability, and verbal reasoning.

The best solution to the problem, however, is to alter rigid criteria to permit flexibility whenever possible. Bereiter (1973, p. 455) aptly stated that "IQ is important, not because it measures 'intelligence,' but because it predicts something important—school achievement." Binet was particularly intent on developing intellectual tasks that distinguished between good and poor students (Sattler, 1974, pp. 87–93). As better tests are built, they will account for more and more of the variance in school achievement. This improvement will reduce the discrepancy between aptitude and achievement for learning disabled children, and force criteria to become more flexible in the future.

# Chapter 2

## Administration and Scoring of the 18 Tests: Special Considerations and Helpful Hints

This chapter provides a description of the 18 separate tests in the McCarthy and a discussion of special tips and problems regarding the administration and scoring of each test. Before reading this chapter, the examiner should familiarize himself with Chapters 5 and 6 of the Manual (McCarthy, 1972). Administration of a few practice tests would also be helpful.

Chapter 5 of the Manual, "General Testing Guidelines," treats important issues such as establishing rapport and using the record form. Pages 48 and 49 of that chapter are particularly valuable since they list 10 general administrative rules that apply to most or all tests and need to be mastered (e.g., where to repeat an item, or how to score a response when the child changes his mind).

Chapter 6 of the Manual presents "Directions for Administration and Scoring," and is quite thorough in its coverage of the procedures to be followed. Many contingencies are anticipated, with rules provided to meet each special problem. However, every possible situation or scoring problem could not be anticipated, and questions arise about how to deal with unique circumstances.

An attempt has been made to clarify ambiguities in the administration and scoring rules for each separate test, to give suggestions for dealing with potential problems that may arise, and to offer aids that should facilitate smooth and accurate administration and scoring of the McCarthy. The particular points covered are based on our own clinical experiences of administering the McCarthy and teaching the battery to graduate students; comments and questions raised by other McCarthy examiners were also extremely helpful. Certainly as examiners throughout the country continue to adopt the McCarthy, additional problems will arise that are not covered in the Manual or in this chapter. Hopefully, the solutions to the various contingencies that are described in the pages that follow will provide useful guidelines for solving almost any subsequent administrative or scoring problem that an examiner may experience.

Each of the 18 separate tests is discussed below, in turn. The scale or scales on which each test is included (except for General Cognitive) is shown in parentheses following the test name.

### 1. BLOCK BUILDING
### (PERCEPTUAL-PERFORMANCE)

#### Description

The examiner builds structures out of blocks and leaves each model standing while the child builds one just like it. There are four items ranging from the simple stacking of blocks (Tower) to the careful placement of the walls and roof of a House.

Items are untimed. Two trials are allowed for each item, but only the *best* trial counts.

#### Administration and Scoring

The directions for administration are straightforward, although there are a few ambiguities that must be clarified. When a second trial is required for any item, it is not clear whether the examiner should provide a second demonstration. The answer is *no,* he should not; only one demonstration per item is allowed. The confusion arises because the correct procedure is stated only once, by item 1, and the rule does not explicitly mention the two trials: "For all items, the examiner's model is left standing during the child's attempts" (McCarthy, 1972, p. 55).

Along this line, children who accidentally knock down their structure should be encouraged to rebuild it. (Some do this spontaneously, others think they are not allowed.) However, the rebuilding is still considered part of the *same* trial. A second trial, when it is needed, is given only after the child has given his maximum effort the first time around. Children who start to build a structure *adjacent* to the examiner's model, matching the model block for block, should be stopped and told to start over in a place designated by the examiner. Again, the child's "error" does not count as a trial.

Another point that needs clarification concerns the number of blocks to give the child after the examiner builds the model and the child has to copy it. Some examiners give the child only the number of blocks required to build the structure (e.g., 3 blocks for the Chair), but this is not correct. Though not specifically stated, the examiner has to place before the child *all* blocks that are not used to build the model. This rule is important to remember because it is not uncommon for young children to make "bases" that are too long or to stack two blocks, instead of one, on top of a base.

A few other administrative precautions should be helpful. First, be sure to build each model about 8 inches from the child, as stated in the Manual. If it is built closer, the child does not have enough room to build his structure; if it is too far away, he may have difficulty seeing the model in its proper perspective. This point is particularly relevant to item 4 (House), which demands close attention to the precise alignment of the four-block base. The child must be able to see the examiner construct the base. (Short children should be encouraged to sit on their knees so they can look down at it; an alternative is to administer Block Building on the floor.) For all children, build the house in two clear steps, pausing about 5 seconds before placing the "roof" on the base.

Another point to remember is that the top block for the Chair and Building is placed from the *child's* perspective. Careful placement of the top block, and close observation of the child's placement of it, are essential since there is a penalty for "mirror images." Such reversals are also important for clinical reasons, since they provide clues about possible spatial or lateral confusions. Finally, it is not appropriate to start *all* children aged 5 and above at item 3. Older children who are suspected of mental retardation should begin with item 1. Insecure or extremely shy children might also be started at item 1 to virtually guarantee success and to help establish rapport.

When scoring Block Building, the examiner should remember that each trial is scored separately, and only the *best* score counts for each item. Difficulties may arise when evaluating some structures that are not covered by the scoring systems. For example, it is not clear how to score items 2 and 3 if the child rotates the figure. As indicated above, mirror images (180-degree rotations) are penalized; but what about 45- or 90-degree rotations? We suggest using 30 degrees as the criterion, since McCarthy used this criterion to determine rotations in several Draw-A-Design items. Thus, if the Chair or Building is constructed correctly, give full credit (2 points) so long as it is rotated by no more than 30 degrees. Rotations greater than 30 degrees receive the same score as mirror images—1 point.

For the same two Block Building items, a scoring problem arises if the child does not place the top block directly on the block beneath it. The Manual does give a rule for evaluating whether a *base* is correct (blocks must not be more than $\frac{1}{4}$ inch apart), but no rule is given for the *top* block. We suggest that the same $\frac{1}{4}$-inch criterion be used to determine whether the top block is correct; that is, give credit only if the top block is misaligned by $\frac{1}{4}$ inch or less.

Another scoring ambiguity arises in items 2, 3, and 4 when the child builds a structure correctly and then piles a second block on the "top" block. In such instances, the child should be penalized since the aim of the task is for the child to copy precisely the examiner's model. He should get credit for a correct base, but not for correct placement of the top block. (The logic is that he "spoiled" his response by placing two blocks on top instead of one.) When other responses are given that are not clearly covered by the scoring system, follow the general rule that full credit should be assigned only to a structure that closely matches the model.

## 2. PUZZLE SOLVING (PERCEPTUAL-PERFORMANCE)

### Description

The child assembles six cut-up picture puzzles which depict either a common animal or food. Each of the first two puzzles comprises only two pieces, while the last couple of items are fairly complex six-piece puzzles.

All items are timed, with 30–120 seconds allotted depending upon the complexity of the item. Bonus points for rapid *perfect* performance may be earned on the last three puzzles.

### Administration and Scoring

As with Block Building, the examiner may begin at item 1 (instead of item 3) for children aged 5 and above who are suspected of retardation or who are very insecure or shy. In fact, any child who had to return to items 1 and 2 on Block Building (because he got less than a perfect score on item 3) should begin with item 1 of Puzzle Solving.

The biggest problem in administering Puzzle Solving is for the examiner to avoid negative transfer from Wechsler's Object Assembly test. The following rules apply only to the McCarthy and must be learned well by the examiner: (1) *all* puzzles are named before they are attempted; (2) each puzzle is *completed* by the examiner, if the child does not get a perfect score, before going on to the next item; (3) the examiner lays out the puzzle pieces in full view of the child, *without* a screen.

Also remember to lay out the pieces for each item, give the instructions, and *then* begin timing. In addition, for item 1 *only*, allow a *second trial* after demonstrating the correct response. (Do not, however, give the child credit for success on the second trial; it is for practice only.) Finally, it is worth noting that some young or behaviorally disordered children become frightened when they realize that item 5 is a Bear, and give a verbal or nonverbal indication of their fear. It is permissible to calm the child by statements such as "Don't worry, this is a friendly bear!"

Scoring the six items is quite objective, although there are important differences in the scoring of the first three items versus the last three. For items 1–3, less coordination is demanded of the child. Puzzle pieces may be separated by as much as ¼ inch, or be out of alignment by the same amount, and the child will still earn full credit. For items 4–6, a greater premium is placed on the child's fine motor coordination. Although misalignments of ¼ inch or less are tolerated, the puzzle pieces *cannot* be separated ("pieces must be touching or virtually touching"). Furthermore, quick perfect performance is rewarded with 1 or 2 bonus points.

Thus, the last three items (Pear, Bear, Bird) are not only more complex; they are also scored more stringently, with good coordination required for success. This distinction in scoring the two halves of the Puzzle Solving test has to be learned at an automatic level since each puzzle must be rapidly evaluated as soon as the child completes it.

One other point about scoring Puzzle Solving: there is no penalty, on any item, for rotating the puzzle. Nevertheless, note any rotations on the record form since they provide valuable qualitative information if similar behaviors are observed on other tests; however, there is no basis for drawing inferences solely from rotated puzzles. (Some children may build a puzzle upside down so the examiner can see it!)

### 3. PICTORIAL MEMORY (VERBAL, MEMORY)

#### Description

The examiner shows the child a card containing six pictures and names each pictured object during a total exposure time of 10 seconds. The child names from memory as many of the objects as he can in 90 seconds.

#### Administration and Scoring

This one-item test requires careful practice to achieve mastery of the administration procedure. The problem is synchronizing every-thing—securing and maintaining the child's attention, naming the objects, and allowing a few seconds for inspection—without exceeding the total exposure time of 10 seconds. Inexperienced examiners will often allow 12–15 seconds of exposure, which is a serious error for a short-term memory task. The only answer is practice.

When giving Pictorial Memory, say the introductory statement slowly and clearly so the child understands what is expected of him. Then expose the card, placing it *flat* on the table, and begin timing immediately. (The card must be flat. This helps the child focus his attention and ensures that the examiner's fingers will not block any pictures.) Name each object in turn, while pointing to it, taking care to pronounce each word clearly. The "naming time" should take 6 or 7 seconds, leaving a few seconds for inspection. *However, do not allow more than 10 seconds exposure to the card even if it takes longer than planned to name the objects.*

If the child does not respond at all when the card is removed, encourage him ("You can do it," "Try your best") and repeat the instruction "Now tell me what you saw" a few times, if necessary. Once the child has given his first response, only *two* prompts are to be given if he hesitates or stops responding (see p. 66 of the Manual); no other probes are permissible.

One change in the directions for administration is acceptable. The word "padlock" is obsolete, so "lock" may be substituted for it when naming the objects. Other substitutions are not allowed, however.

The scoring of Pictorial Memory is easy. Nevertheless, one important rule is implied in the Manual, but not spelled out: there is *no penalty* if the child names objects that do not appear on the card.


### 4. WORD KNOWLEDGE (VERBAL)

#### Description

On Part I, Picture Vocabulary, the child identifies (by pointing) five objects pictured on a card and then he names four other pictured objects. For Part II, Oral Vocabulary, the child defines a steeply graded list of 10 words ranging from concrete objects ("towel") to abstract concepts ("loyal").

#### Administration and Scoring

Children above 5 years of age who are suspected of mental retardation should be given Part I first, as should older children who have been extremely nonverbal through the early part of the testing session. When Part II is given first (as it will be for most children aged 5 and above), it is essential to evaluate carefully the child's responses to the first two items ("towel" and "coat"). Although examiners sometimes forget, Part I must be given in its entirety if the child scores 0 on *either* item 1 *or* item 2.

The rules for administering Word Knowledge (pp. 67–69 of the Manual) should be internalized completely. Many prompts are permitted (indeed required) to encourage the child to respond appropriately to the various pictures and words. The examiner must be ready to supply all of the relevant probes to ensure that the child is given every opportunity to respond correctly. Along this line, note that unlike the rules for Wechsler's Vocabulary test, *all* 1-point responses are questioned by the examiner. (Ambiguous 0-point responses are also questioned.)

Extra effort is needed on the part of the examiner to learn and use local pronunciations of the words and to articulate each word carefully. Whereas this rule holds true for all words spoken by the examiner during the test, it is especially crucial for the items in Word Knowledge II. Here each and every word is a multipoint item, and there are no context clues to facilitate understanding. The examiner should also be very alert to the possibility that the child is responding to a word that he thought he heard (cow instead of towel; colt instead of coat; threat instead of thread; etc.). When this ambiguity occurs, the examiner is instructed to repeat the question with an extra stress on the key word. However, if the examiner is not "set" for an auditory misperception, he will often score as a failure a response that should have been followed up.

When administering Part I, the examiner should place each card flat on the table (for the same reasons mentioned above for Pictorial Memory). Card I includes six pictures, although only five are asked, to ensure that the child does not get the last picture correct ("Show me the cow") by a process of elimination. However, some children will spontaneously point to or name the extra picture (a horse), perhaps thinking that the examiner made a mistake. Young children often seek extra praise for knowing the horse, whereas school-age youngsters may worry that they will not get credit for their response. When this occurs, reassure the child appropriately before presenting Card 2. (With a preschool child, either praise or a playful remark such as "Poor horsie, he always gets left out!" is usually sufficient.)

Scoring Part I of Word Knowledge is simple and objective. Note, however, that items 2–5 are scored quite leniently; for example, "ship," "canoe," and "ocean liner" are all acceptable names for a picture of a sailboat. Part II presents some of the problems that invariably arise when scoring any individually administered vocabulary test. Still, the distinction between 0-, 1-, and 2-point responses for most of the items is fairly clear, minimizing the amount of subjective judgment that is required for scoring the test. To further reduce subjectivity in scoring, the examiner should learn thoroughly the four paragraphs on page 70 of the Manual (under the heading "Scoring Standards"), and study carefully the sample responses that are provided for each item.

The scoring system for Part II of Word Knowledge does not adequately treat *nonverbal* responses. Is a child credited, for example, if he defines the word "towel" by giving a clear demonstration of a person using a towel? McCarthy does give partial credit (i.e., 1 point) to the following definition of "coat:" "like that (points to a coat)." Hence, it seems reasonable to give 1 point to a nonverbal response that communicates at least some understanding of the word. Like all 1-point responses, these answers should be queried by the examiner to see if the child can upgrade his response to a 2-point level. (A completely nonverbal response should be probed by saying "Tell me in *words* what a _____ is.") It is permissible to give the child 2 points for a response that is partly verbal and partly gestural, so long as the child clearly evidences his knowledge of the concept. A common illustration of this occurs with the word "shrink:" e.g., the child who says "like when pants shrink," while using his hands to show something getting smaller, earns 2 points. However, a purely nonverbal response (e.g., defining "tool" by making the motions of hammering a nail) should not be given more than 1 point.

### 5. NUMBER QUESTIONS (QUANTITATIVE)

#### Description

The child responds to oral questions that involve numbers in some context. The first three items assess knowledge of number facts (e.g., "How many heads do you have?"). Two other items measure quantitative concepts (half, dozen), while the majority of items demand use of simple computational skills to solve oral arithmetic problems.

There are a total of 12 items, all untimed. The skills assessed by this test are generally of a higher level than the ones measured by Counting & Sorting (Test 16). Children who do well on Number Questions (9 or more items correct) are therefore exempted from taking Counting & Sorting, and are given full credit for it.

#### Administration and Scoring

Read each item with some animation and at a deliberate pace. Give a slight emphasis when reading numbers or other key words such as "half" or "dozen." Questions should be repeated whenever a child does not respond within about 10–15 seconds. (Adjust the time interval to suit the child's pattern of responding.) Repetition of a question, either because of the child's request or the examiner's judgment, is an essential aspect of valid test administration. Some of the items are rather long; the goal of Number Questions is *not* to assess the child's short-term memory.

For item 1, be alert to the possibility of the child responding to "How many ears do you have?" by giving his age. (He may hear "years" instead of ears.) When this occurs, repeat the question with an extra stress on the key word.

Item 4 is the first computational problem and represents an abrupt departure from the first three "number fact" questions. Some children develop a set and are not prepared for a different type of item. To help break the possible set, the examiner should pause for a few seconds after item 3 and then say, "O.K., now let's try this one," before reading item 4.

The record form shows the correct answers to the items in words rather than numerals to protect against "peeking." Nevertheless, be sure to keep the answer column in the record form shielded, and be especially careful not to expose the Manual (which includes an easy-to-read answer column).

### 6. TAPPING SEQUENCE (PERCEPTUAL-PERFORMANCE, MEMORY)

#### Description

The examiner taps sequences of notes on a xylophone, and the child copies each sequence from memory. The first item requires tapping each of the four notes in succession (three trials are allowed, if needed); the remaining eight items involve more complex sequences, ranging from three to six notes.

#### Administration and Scoring

Correct administration of Tapping Sequence, especially the last few items, requires practice. Striking notes at a rate of 1 per second is far more difficult than reading digits at a steady rate. Good motor coordination is required by the examiner to strike each note flush. Furthermore, the examiner has to memorize each sequence before administering it because it is not feasible to glance back at the record form or Manual once the sequence is begun. This requirement creates the tendency to speed through the sequence or to tap the notes in distinct "chunks"; both practices invalidate the test items.

For best results, take a long moment to study the sequence and begin tapping only when it is surely committed to memory. Hold the mallet not more than 3 inches above the xylophone to avoid grazing a key or hitting the plastic. Then, strike each note while maintaining a relaxed grip on the mallet, and pause long enough between taps to produce the appropriate rate of administration. When handing the child the mallet, take care to present it at his midline, so he can choose the hand he wants to use. (Some examiners inadvertantly hand it over to the right of center, virtually placing it in the child's left hand.)

Do not begin tapping unless the child is clearly attending to the test materials. If he starts to look away once the sequence is started, the examiner may need to stroke the child's chin with his free hand to redirect his gaze. Also, it is not uncommon for a child to give a strong verbal or nonverbal response (e.g., screwing up his face) when he first hears the nonmelodious "tunes" that emanate from the xylophone. It is a good idea for the examiner to show agreement with the child's feelings while, at the same time, encouraging him to try his best.

What should be done if the examiner makes an error while administering an item (e.g., tapping a wrong note or hitting the plastic)? If it happens once, the examiner should stop the item immediately, perhaps by using a nonverbal gesture that suggests "erasing" the notes, while saying something like: "Oops! Let me start this one all over." A pause of several seconds is desirable before trying again. If the examiner makes a second error during the test, however, then Tapping Sequence should be considered *spoiled*. (See Chapter 3 for rules on prorating.)

One final word of caution: do not let the child handle the xylophone after the test is over. Although it is good practice to let the young child help put away test materials after a task is completed, be sure to put the xylophone in its box without his help. Otherwise, the fragile xylophone and mallet will live a short and uneventful life.

Scoring Tapping Sequence with accuracy requires the same concentration that is needed to administer it properly. The examiner must recall the exact sequence after administering it so he can evaluate the correctness of the child's response. Again, it is the longer sequences that cause the most trouble.

Although the scoring system is objective, the examiner sometimes has to exercise his subjective clinical judgment. For example, a child will occasionally tap the same note twice in a row—not because he thinks he is supposed to, but because be barely grazed the note the first time or he was dissatisfied with the tone. If the item is otherwise correct, the examiner should give the child credit as long as he is reasonably certain of the child's intentions. (Thus, the rule about penalizing a child for tapping a key more than once, on page 78 of the Manual, should not be applied rigidly). Another potential scoring problem arises when the child taps an incorrect sequence, but realizes it (usually by attending to auditory cues) and spontaneously taps the right sequence. Based on McCarthy's rule about spontaneous changes in a response (point 10 on page 49 of the Manual), the child should be given credit for the item.

## 7.  VERBAL MEMORY (VERBAL, MEMORY)

### Description

The child repeats a series of three or four unrelated words spoken by the examiner for each of the first four items of Part I. For the last two items of Part I he repeats sentences from memory, and for Part II he tells the essential ideas in a story read to him by the examiner.

### Administration and Scoring

Just as in Part II of Word Knowledge, Verbal Memory demands careful articulation and thorough knowledge of local pronunciation and dialect. On the first four items of Part I, in particular, the lack of context clues in the series of unrelated words makes the child very dependent on the examiner's accuracy in communicating the stimuli. In addition, practice is required to master reading the words in items 1–4 at a rate of 1 per second (a different cadence is necessary for 1- versus 2-syllable words), and to read the sentences slowly, clearly, and with good intonation.

For Part II, the examiner should read the story with expression, rather than in a monotone, but he should avoid overanimation. In particular, visual cues such as gestures to suggest the wind blowing the letters must *not* be provided. The task assesses *auditory* skills; visual stimuli distort the meaning of the test to an unknown degree. (Non-verbal gestures have to be avoided on Part I for the same reason.) Finally, the story should take approximately 30 seconds, or slightly more, to read. Practicing several times with a stopwatch will facilitate its proper administration.

Young children sometimes have difficulty on the first four items of Part I waiting for all of the words to be spoken before beginning their response. Apparently not grasping the nature of the task, they repeat each word as it is spoken. To try to prevent this from happening, read the statement "Wait until I have finished saying all the words before you start to answer" slowly and with proper emphasis. If the child begins to respond before the examiner has completed the entire item, a quick nonverbal gesture indicating "wait" or "shhh" is permissible to try to squelch the response, and the examiner may point to the child when it is his turn. Then, the statement "Wait until I have finished . . ." should be repeated before administering the next item. These extra cues may be given until the child understands the task, although if he fails to grasp the idea by the third item, then Part I is discontinued. However, the apparent reason for the child's poor performance should be noted as an important clinical observation.

The instructions for items 1–4 of Part I are ambiguous because they do not convey the importance of repeating the words in *sequence*. ("Now I am going to say some words and I want to see how many of them you can say after me.") This is an unfortunate oversight, but the examiner may not alter the directions in any way and he *must* deduct 1 point from the child's item score if the words are repeated out of sequence. These procedures were followed during standardization and cannot be changed now without distorting the meaning of the norms.

Some examiners have trouble deciding what constitutes a sequencing error even though the Manual is quite clear on this point. The basic rule is that an error in sequencing occurs *only* if 2 or more words are reversed. There is no sequencing error if a word or two is omitted, or if extra words are added that were not in the stimulus—so long as there are no reversals. Consider the item "doll–dark–coat." One point is deducted for each of the following illustrative responses: "coat–dark–doll," "doll–coat–dark," "dark–doll." However, there is no sequencing error for "doll–coat," "dark–coat," or "big–doll–dark–black–coat." Interestingly, the latter response is given full credit because the child is not penalized on Part I or Part II for adding words or ideas that were not included in the original stimulus.

Despite the lack of a penalty for extra words (or for sequencing errors in the sentences and the story), such occurrences are of clinical importance and should be noted. The added words or events may reflect *perseveration* (e.g., including a word from item 2 in the answers to items 3 and 4), or they may reveal topics that are preoccupying the child's mind (see Chapter 7). Sequencing errors may suggest disorders in the child's logical thought processes or in his auditory sequential ability.

To score the story efficiently and accurately during the test administration, the examiner should master the general scoring rules on the bottom of page 80 of the Manual and learn the essence of passing and failing responses to the 11 items. This familiarity will permit the checking off of correct responses as they are spoken. The only words that should be jotted down are the terms used for "Bob," "woman," and "letters" (items 1–3) and any phrases that are of borderline quality and require further thought. The alternative of recording the story verbatim and scoring it at a later time should be avoided. Some children speak too quickly to make copying the story practical; others slow down to accommodate the examiner, and may forget part of the story in the process.

It is important to remember *not* to give Part II to children who score below 8 (of 30) points on Part I. If it is given inadvertently, the examiner has to discount any points the child may earn on Part II (although the great likelihood is that he will score 0). The danger in giving it by mistake is the child's possible emotional response to the frustration or boredom he is bound to face; it will probably be necessary to reestablish rapport before continuing with the battery.

## 8.  RIGHT–LEFT ORIENTATION
## (PERCEPTUAL–PERFORMANCE,
## FOR AGES 5 AND ABOVE)

### Description

The child demonstrates knowledge of right versus left with regard to his own body on items 1–5 (e.g., "which is your left ear?"). For the last four items, the child shows the maturity of his right–left concept by answering questions pertaining to a picture of a boy—e.g., "Show me Roger's right elbow."

## Administration and Scoring

Extra prompts to elicit a response are allowed only on the first item. However, it is permissible to repeat the question verbatim for any item, and the examiner should feel free to do this throughout the test whenever the child is hesitant to respond. Since chance guessing plays a role in the score earned by almost any child who has not yet mastered right versus left, it is important for a child to be given every opportunity to answer each item that is administered. (However, do *not* urge a child to guess if he still does not respond after the item is repeated.) Furthermore, a child with a poor memory will have trouble remembering the instructions to the two-part items. By repeating questions, when necessary, the child's knowledge of right and left will be tapped rather than his short-term memory.

Questions should be read slowly, with an extra stress placed on the words "right" and "left." The picture of "Roger" should be placed *flat* on the table in front of the child for items 6–9. If the child picks the card up and holds it so it faces the examiner (i.e., so it is oriented in the same position as the child), return it to the table and explain that it is not fair to move the card. The child's answer to each successive Right–Left Orientation item is sometimes a function of the feedback he receives from the examiner. It is therefore essential that no verbal or gestural reinforcement, either positive or negative, be given until the entire test is completed. At that time, a positive word about the child's effort (regardless of his success) is in order.

## 9. LEG COORDINATION (MOTOR)

### Description

The examiner demonstrates or describes several motor tasks involving the lower extremities. The child is given two trials, if necessary, to try to perform these activities. The items include walking backward, walking on tiptoe, walking a straight line, standing on one foot (first the preferred foot, then the other one), and skipping.

### Administration and Scoring

Some time can be saved by prearranging the testing room for the gross motor tests: the 9-foot tape can be fastened to the floor, and the target set up against the wall before the child arrives. However, the tape and target may distract young children during the first part of the testing session, or be moved out of position by an active child who is unable to stay in his seat for more than 15 minutes at a time. In addition, a prearranged room deprives the child of the chance to help the examiner set up the equipment. When testing a preschool child or an active older youngster, it is therefore more advantageous *not* to set up the room ahead of time.

The most difficult aspect of administering Leg Coordination (and Arm Coordination) is controlling the child during these less structured "games," while still adhering to the standardized procedures. Another problem is what to do with the Manual and record form while administering the Leg Coordination items. The examiner needs two free hands to control the child, to protect him (e.g., if he loses his balance and starts to fall, or if he is about to bang into a wall while walking backward), and to participate in the games in a natural manner. If the examiner tries to manipulate the Manual, a record form, and a pencil while in the center of the room, then the gamelike aspect of the task is lost and it becomes just another test.

The record form and pencil should be left on the table during the test. The examiner should go to the center of the room, away from any furniture, to demonstrate the items and to start the child on his attempts. The child should be aimed in the direction of the table whenever feasible; then, when he is through walking, tiptoeing, or skipping, the examiner will be in a position to easily record his performance. If things do not go as planned, however, then the examiner should return to the table as often as necessary to record the pertinent information. This may be after every item for a child who requires two trials and gives variable performance, or after the entire task for a well-coordinated child who passes every item easily; the examiner's memory will also be a factor. The inexperienced examiner will need to keep the Manual in his hand during the entire test. With practice, however, the directions for administration and scoring are easy to master and the Manual can join the record form on the table (available for quick reference, if needed).

Demonstrations are required for the first trial of walking backward, walking on tiptoe, and standing on one foot. Although not specified in the Manual, it is good practice to demonstrate before the second trial as well if the child's first response suggests that he does not understand what is expected of him (e.g., if he walks on his heels instead of on tiptoes). This rule is consistent with McCarthy's instructions for walking a straight line (item 3) and skipping (item 6), which require a demonstration only if the child apparently does not under-stand the verbal directions. Incidentally, for the latter two items the examiner should routinely demonstrate the tasks whenever a second trial is needed to ensure that the child comprehends the task. For item 6, children seem to answer the question "Can you skip?" with an auto-matic "yes," regardless of their ability or their understanding of the word "skip;" therefore, do not put too much stock in their verbal response. In general, when administering Leg Coordination keep in mind that it is intended to measure motor coordination, not memory or verbal comprehension.

The importance of being a good model cannot be overstated. Demonstrations must be given conscientiously: take six or seven large strides backward, not just a perfunctory two or three; stand on one foot for at least 5 seconds, keeping the elevated foot perpendicular to the foot on the the floor; etc. Be sure that the child is attending closely before beginning any demonstration.

Item 4, which requires standing on one foot, often causes prob-lems for the young child. When a second trial is needed he is told to "use the same foot as before." The concepts "same" and "before" are fairly difficult, and he may not understand the command; or, he may simply forget which foot he was standing on. The examiner therefore has to pay close attention to the foot the child chooses to stand on for the first trial, and use nonverbal means (pointing to, or even touching, the child's leg) to help communicate the instructions, whenever necessary. A similar problem arises with item 5 when the examiner says "Now let's see how long you can stand on your other foot." Again, the examiner's attentiveness and deft use of nonverbal cues will facilitate communication and minimize the child's frustration.

Walking on tiptoe (item 2) also presents some potential pitfalls. The examiner should avoid wearing loose-fitting or high-heeled shoes since they make it difficult to give a clear demonstration of this motor task. Similarly, if the child wears sandals or shoes that are too large it is hard for the examiner to evaluate his tiptoeing performance. In some cases, the child may have to remove his shoes for this item in order to assess his ability. In general, though, the examiner will be able to evaluate children accurately by facing the child's *profile* and kneeling down whenever necessary. (This type of positioning is also helpful for scoring the items requiring the child to stand on one foot by providing a better angle for determining if his elevated foot is still in the air or barely grazing the floor.)

Clearly, the scoring of Leg Coordination occasionally demands subjective judgment. As indicated, it is difficult to tell if some children are really performing the desired task. In addition, a *discontinuous* 2–1–0 scoring system is often hard to apply to behaviors that tend to be *continuous;* distinctions between terms such as "good balance" and "some imbalance" are ambiguous at best, and require clinical judgment. As a rule, a perfect score should be earned only when the child's response is well-coordinated (i.e., almost effortless) and unambiguous.

It should be noted that a child who runs, gallops, or takes huge steps on item 3 (walking a straight line) does not earn any credit even if he stays completely on the tape. His response does not count as a trial unless he persists even after one or two demonstrations. A child who cannot perform a task during the Leg Coordination test does not earn any credit for responding appropriately later in the session (e.g., a child who fails the skipping item, and then skips around the room after the entire session is over). The reason is that only two trials are permitted, and the later success would constitute a third trial.

## 10. ARM COORDINATION (MOTOR)

### Description

The child performs three motor tasks involving the upper extremities. For Part I he has to bounce a rubber ball, with 15 consecutive bounces required for perfect credit. In Part II, the child and examiner engage in a beanbag catch game. The child attempts to catch nine tosses—three with both hands, and three with each hand separately. (Children who miss all three attempts with both hands do not try one-handed catches, however.) Part III requires the child to aim the beanbag at a target. The goal is to throw the beanbag through the hole in the target on each of six attempts (three with each hand), although partial credit is earned for just hitting the target.

### Administering and Scoring

Several of the administrative problems mentioned above for Leg Coordination also arise for Arm Coordination: whether or not to set up equipment in advance; what to do with the Manual and record form during the tasks, especially while participating in the beanbag catch game; how to deal with the child's inability to understand the verbal directions or to remember which hand he just used for throwing or catching. The same suggestions given for the Leg Coordination items hold as well for the three Arm Coordination tasks. For example, set up the tape and the target so the examiner's position offers him easy access to the table.

The ball and beanbag are potential weapons for a hostile, aggressive, or behaviorally disordered child (see Chapter 7). Either test material may be aimed at a lamp, a window, or the examiner with little or no provocation. Even a child who is merely showing off can injure the examiner during the beanbag catch game with a fast overhand throw. During Leg Coordination, it is essential for the examiner to be alert for the *child's* safety; with Arm Coordination, he must be equally alert for his *own* safety.

The "Test Limits" on page 89 of the Manual are a bit unclear. The rules are simply: (1) administer all three parts to all children, and (2) for Part II, do not give items 2 and 3 if the child fails item 1.

For Part I, Ball Bouncing, be sure to use a ball that is "live." Check the ball periodically and buy a new one (at a local store or through the publisher) as soon as it loses too much of its "bounce." Never administer this task on a carpet even if it is inconvenient to locate a hard surface. It is better to administer it outside (weather permitting), or on a bathroom floor, than to hinder the child's performance with a carpeted floor. Be certain that the child begins to bounce the ball as far away as possible from furniture and walls; children sometimes cover quite a bit of ground during ball bouncing, and should not be required to navigate an obstacle course. The directions for administration are such that the examiner has to give the instructions ("Can you bounce a ball like this? Try it and see . . .") *while* demonstrating the task. This feat requires practice, and points again to the importance of reducing dependency on the Manual while administering the gross motor tasks. (As with the Leg Coordination items, a clear and well-executed demonstration is essential.)

Part II of Arm Coordination, the Beanbag Catch Game, demands good motor control by the examiner in order to throw "strikes." Any toss that is poorly thrown does not count as a trial, but if misthrows occur too frequently the child may become frustrated, lose his concentration, or imitate poor throws out of silliness. The examiner has to watch his own feet to be sure that he is standing exactly at the edge of the 9-foot tape, and he must attend closely to the child's feet. Some children accidentally move closer or take a long stride forward when catching the beanbag; others may do these things on purpose, hoping that they will not be caught. Regardless of motivation, children are not credited for any catch covering a distance less than 9 feet. Each time an infraction occurs, warn the child that it is not fair to move closer and tell him that his catch does not count (if he was successful). Do not count the *first* violation as a trial, but fail all subsequent infractions.

In Part II, children sometimes have difficulty keeping one hand behind their back for items 2 and 3 (see p. 164). If their hidden hand "escapes," remind them of the rule but do not penalize them as long as they only use the intended hand for the catch. If, however, the hidden hand becomes a "helping hand," then the child does not receive credit for a catch. The first time it occurs, give a warning and disregard the trial; subsequently, continue to warn the child, but count each trial as an unsuccessful attempt.

The one-hand catch items also demand the examiner's close attention to the hand the child uses for each trial. Though he may choose to use his right hand for the first trial of item 2, he may switch to his left hand for the second or third trial (with no trickery intended); an examiner who is not set for this possibility may be too engrossed in the administration and scoring of the items to notice the switch. Each trial of the items in Part III requires the same degree of observational skills. In the latter task, the examiner not only must be alert to the hand used to throw the beanbag, but he must attend closely to the target, which is occasionally knocked out of position by a hard throw and has to be reoriented before the child's next attempt.

With the Beanbag Target Game, remember that the target *must* be set up against a wall (*not* in the middle of the floor). Sometimes a child will throw the beanbag against the wall and the beanbag will land *behind* the target, or bounce off the wall and then go through the hole in the target. The scoring rules clearly state that responses such as these are scored 0. However, the child may clap his hands or shout, thinking he has scored a bull's-eye. Should this occur, give the child tactful feedback so he will not deliberately aim at the wall on subsequent attempts.

Some children experiment with novel positions for throwing the beanbag (kneeling, lying on their stomach, etc.), but these are not permitted. The child has to stand up while aiming at the target, and he should be told so if he tries to experiment. (Disregard any throw from a novel position; demonstrate the correct position if necessary.) The child may lean over the line with his arm or body, as long as his feet remain behind the line when he releases the beanbag *and* during his "follow through." Crossing the line just after the toss indicates that he was leaning too far and counts as a foul. The same procedure used to deal with children who step over the line in the Beanbag Catch Game are applicable to the Beanbag Target Game.

One final thought about administering Arm Coordination merits careful attention. Although these "games" are fun to many children, they may thoroughly frustrate a very young or an uncoordinated child. The examiner should be sensitive to the child's feelings and comfort him if necessary. Missing an occasional throw from a child who is having trouble catching the beanbag is a good idea since it will show him that even an adult can miss. Similarly, a child who fails to hit the target with any toss may be placated if he sees the examiner aim at the target and miss. (Actually, many examiners miss the target even when trying hard to hit it!)

Scoring Arm Coordination is fairly straightforward, although a few points deserve mention. With ball bouncing it is sometimes hard to discern if the child who bounces the ball, but fails to hit it again, should be credited with 0 or 1 bounce. As a rule of thumb, a child who throws the ball down to begin the task gets credit for 1 bounce if it bounces up somewhere near him (i.e., not more than 2 or 3 feet away); he earns a score of 0 if he throws it down at an angle and it bounces away from him, if he throws it against the wall, if he merely drops it, etc. Judgment is also needed to detect whether a child who starts to lose control of the ball actually makes contact with it, or if the ball is bouncing on its own momentum. Follow the child if he needs to cover a lot of territory, so these decisions can be as objective as possible; give him the benefit if there is a reasonable doubt.

In the Beanbag Catch Game, a child earns credit on item 1 (two-hand catches) whether he uses one hand or both hands to make the catches. If he makes a one-handed catch during item 1, he is encouraged to use both hands, but this is only to remind him that he should use both hands on subsequent trials. It is not specified in the Manual, but give credit to a child who catches the beanbag (with one or both hands) against his chest, stomach, side, etc., so long as he has control of it. If the child fumbles the beanbag but manages to catch it before it hits the ground, he also receives credit.

## 11.  IMITATIVE ACTION (MOTOR)

### Description

The child imitates the following simple gross motor tasks: crossing one foot over the other at the ankles, clasping hands, twiddling thumbs, and sighting through a tube.

### Administration and Scoring

The main administrative consideration involves item 1—crossing feet at the ankles. The examiner has to pull his chair away from the table with his entire body in full view of the child. He should have the child's complete attention before demonstrating the action, and he should make sure that he does not fold his arms since competing movements may distract the child. For items 1, 2, and 3 the examiner should continue to demonstrate the appropriate action until the child responds. This repetition obviously cannot be done for item 4 because the tube is handed to the child.

Scoring item 3, Twiddling Thumbs, is sometimes difficult. A child who folds his hands incorrectly (e.g., interlocking two fingers at a time instead of alternating the fingers of each hand) *fails* the item, even if he twiddles his thumbs adequately, because he did not succeed in imitating the entire action. Some children fold their hands so loosely that their thumbs rotate independently. As a general rule, give the child with a loose grip credit *only* if his thumbs overlap—even slightly—so they can be considered to rotate about each other.

## 12.  DRAW-A-DESIGN
## (PERCEPTUAL-PERFORMANCE,
## MOTOR)

### Description

The child copies three simple figures drawn by the examiner (a circle and two lines), and a series of six designs printed in a booklet that range in complexity from a right angle to a hexagon with an "X" inside it. None of the items are timed.

### Administration and Scoring

Items 1–3 require the examiner to construct the models. Do this with the Drawing Booklet directly in front of the child, and do not begin until he is clearly attending to the task at hand. There is a tendency for the examiner to draw the figures too large. Even though the scoring system takes this possibility into account so the child is not penalized, it is best to administer the items exactly as stated. Practicing the circle and lines with a ruler available for immediate feedback greatly facilitates the examiner's learning process.

The general rules of administration on pages 95–96 of the Manual should be read carefully because they include some pertinent points that must be followed: using a short pencil *without* an eraser for the child, folding the booklet back so only one design is exposed at a time, dealing with a child who rotates the booklet, etc.

For items 4–9, the child may experience a figure–ground problem and start to copy the barely visible image of the design on the *back* of the page. This is, of course, a noteworthy clinical observation, suggestive of a visual perceptual problem. The first time this behavior occurs, point to the appropriate design and say "Draw one just like this." Ignore his first response and score only the second one. Should he repeat the figure–ground error on subsequent items, make no further comment.

Scoring any design-copying task requires subjective judgment as well as a disproportionate amount of scoring time, and Draw-A-Design follows this tradition. Fortunately, however, the rules for scoring each item are explained in detail and numerous sample responses are provided. With practice, most designs can be scored by simply comparing them to the sample designs, although the verbal rules *must* be consulted whenever there is even mild doubt how to score an item. (Doubts often arise for items 6–9, especially when distinguishing between 2- and 3-point responses.)

The examiner should study the general scoring rules found on page 97 of the Manual because they are applicable to all Draw-A-Design items. For example, it is essential to note that only the *best* drawing is scored if the child produces two or more responses to the same stimulus. (The child may draw more than one design spontaneously, or he may ask permission to try again.) Note also that items 4–9 include minimum and additional criteria; the *additional* criteria are only referred to if the child's response passes the minimum (i.e., pass–fail) criteria.

A clarification is needed in the scoring rules for item 6 ($\circledcirc$) since no mention is made of gaps or overlaps in each circle. The rule used for items 7, 8, and 9 should be applied to item 6 as well: a gap of no more than ⅛ inch is permitted; an overrun of no more than ¼ inch is also permitted. Thus, gaps such as the ones in samples G and I on page 105 of the Manual, and the overlap in sample N, are tolerated. However, if either one of the circles has a gap that is too large or an overrun that is too long, the design *fails* the first minimum criterion (which deals with the quality of the circles).

## 13. DRAW-A-CHILD
## (PERCEPTUAL-PERFORMANCE,
## MOTOR)

### Description

Boys draw a picture of a boy, and girls draw a picture of a girl. There is no set time limit, but if the child has not finished after 5 minutes, he is encouraged to complete his picture. The same scoring system is used, regardless of the sex of the child.

### Administration and Scoring

It is permissible to encourage the child to begin drawing if he is hesitant, but no prompts are allowed once he has begun. For example, if important body parts are omitted, the examiner may *not* urge the child to complete the picture. When the child stops drawing, the examiner has to say "Is it all done?" This question may impel the child to add more parts spontaneously which, of course, is fine; but it is the only probe permitted. After the child has worked for 5 minutes, the examiner is instructed to encourage the child to finish. However, the examiner may *not* take the booklet away until the child is satisfied with his picture.

The scoring system is fairly easy to use after a little practice. Furthermore, the many illustrations throughout the scoring rules and the seven sample drawings (pages 121–126 of the Manual) help make the system quite objective. Of the 10 items used to score the drawing of a child (each scored 2–1–0), the first seven follow the same pattern. Each deals exclusively with a different part of the face or trunk: 2

points are given if the part is drawn in proper proportion or with appropriate detail; 1 point is given for any representation of the body part, however crude; and 0 points are given if the part is absent from the drawing. The last three items, which concern the limbs, have equally clearcut distinctions between the response categories.

## 14. NUMERICAL MEMORY (QUANTITATIVE, MEMORY)

### Description

In Part I, the child repeats series of digits in the same order they are presented by the examiner, while Part II requires the child to repeat series of digits in the reverse order. Part I comprises six items with the spans ranging from two to seven digits. The five items in Part II include spans of two to six digits.

### Administration and Scoring

McCarthy has avoided the number 7 in the Numerical Memory items since it is the only two-syllable digit. This omission facilitates the administration of the items at a rate of 1 digit per second, although practice is still needed to master the appropriate pace and to avoid the unconscious grouping of digits. The problem of a child starting his response prematurely occurs for Numerical Memory, just as it does for Verbal Memory I. In fact, the sample items ("Say 2." "Now say 6.") sometimes instill the wrong response set for the actual items, leading children to begin responding as soon as the first digit is spoken. When this happens, the *nonverbal* gestures suggested above for Verbal Memory (see p. 41) should be used. If the child does not grasp the aim of the task, even with the extra cues, this fact should be noted to aid interpretation of his test profile. We do not advise using Glasser and Zimmerman's (1967, p. 18) suggested technique of grasping the child's hand while saying the numbers, and letting go when the series is completed. This method seems to overstep the bounds of the normative procedures, although it may be used to "test the limits" (see pp. 196–199).

On Part II, the child may not know the meaning of the concept "backward" and he may fail to grasp its connotation from the sample items. Should this occur, the child receives a score of 0 for Part II. The examiner may *not* teach the concept, and must adhere strictly to the administrative procedures described on page 128 of the Manual.

## 15. VERBAL FLUENCY (VERBAL)

### Description

The child names as many "things" as he can in a given category within 20 seconds. There are four such items, with the child asked to name Things to Eat, Animals, Things to Wear, and Things to Ride.

### Administration and Scoring

The time limit of 20 seconds must be strictly obeyed; responses given 1 or 2 seconds overtime do not count. In addition, once the timing starts do *not* stop the stopwatch when making a comment to the child, or for any other reason, until the time limit elapses.

Only *one* verbal prompt per item is given if a child is having difficulty responding. The examiner says "Try to tell me some things to ride" (or things to wear, etc.) to a child who has given no responses, or only 1 *correct* response, after 5 seconds. But no other comments are permitted to encourage a child who stops suddenly after, say, 10 or 15 seconds. Nonverbal encouragement by the examiner is permissible, however; that is, he may sit with his pencil poised and ready to write, and show a look of "hopeful expectancy."

The only other comment that may be made during each item serves to *redirect* a perseverating child who uses the same *word* in three consecutive responses. Thus, if a child responds with "baked ham, country ham, Virginia ham," to item 1, the examiner says, "What other things to eat can you think of?" The examiner may *not*, however, redirect a child who "loses" the category—e.g., no feedback may be given to a child who, while naming animals, says "dog, horse, cow, barn, grass."

The directions to the child should be read slowly and clearly with an extra stress on the words that define the category for each item. Enunciation is especially important for item 4 since the word "ride" may be heard as "write." Sometimes a child with immature or defective speech will give responses that are not immediately understood by the examiner. Such responses should be recorded phonetically. After the *entire* Verbal Fluency test is over, the child should be questioned about the unclear responses, and given credit for appropriate answers if the child can convey his meaning. Example: "For things to eat, you said 'top-door.' What is that?" If the child communicates the idea that "top-door" is "popcorn," give credit for the response.

The five general scoring rules on page 130 of the Manual provide consistent ways of handling potentially ambiguous responses such as synonyms or modifications of the samples. The "borderline" acceptable and unacceptable responses provided for each item should be read carefully since some distinctions are not intuitive (e.g., "milk" is not an acceptable Thing to Eat).

To avoid scoring errors, it is helpful to follow these steps for all four items: (1) cross out any responses that are obviously wrong such as irrelevant things, repetitions of the examiner's examples, and duplicates of acceptable responses; (2) check questionable responses by consulting the five general scoring rules and the samples of borderline responses, and cross out all answers that are not credited; (3) sum the acceptable responses for each item, keeping in mind that the maximum score for each item is *9 points* (even if an exceptionally fluent child names 14 things in one category).

### 16.  COUNTING & SORTING (QUANTITATIVE)

#### Description

The child has to count blocks, sort them into equal groups, and demonstrate knowledge of ordinal terms (second, fourth). Nine items assess these basic but essential quantitative concepts.

#### Administration and Scoring

For school-age youngsters, routinely check the child's perform-ance on Number Questions before administering this test. Any child who passes 9 or more of the 12 items on the earlier test is exempted from taking Counting & Sorting, and is given full credit (9 points) for it. For these children, be sure to enter a 9 in the total box on the record form before proceeding to Test 17.

When setting out the blocks for the two sorting tasks (items 4 and

6) be careful not to put the blocks into two equal groups. Even if the blocks are evenly spaced, be certain that half of them are not accidentally placed in front of one card with the other half of the blocks in front of the second card. For each sorting item, remember that a child who makes an error is given a second chance ("Are you sure you have the same number of blocks on each card?") If he corrects his mistake, he earns full credit for the item. If the child still sorts the blocks incorrectly, the examiner has to correct the error before going on; the child's response to the item following each sorting task is dependent on having an equal number of blocks on each card. (The examiner has to correct any errors made by the child on items 1 and 2 for a similar reason.)

Most of the items in Counting & Sorting require nonverbal responses, with vocalization expected only for items 3, 5, and 7. Since this test is not on the Verbal Scale, the child should be given credit for any of the three items if he indicates the correct answer nonverbally (e.g., by raising the appropriate number of fingers.)

### 17.  OPPOSITE ANALOGIES (VERBAL)

#### Description

The child completes nine analogies by providing the appropriate "opposite." For example: "An elephant is *big,* and a mouse is _____."

#### Administration and Scoring

Read each item slowly, placing a slight emphasis on the italicized word and pausing briefly before reading the second part of each phrase. As indicated in the Manual, be certain to avoid any gestures while reading each statement since these visual stimuli may provide unwitting clues to the correct response.

If the child does not understand the word "opposite," it is not permissible to teach him its meaning, except by following the procedures in the Manual exactly as stated. He is given feedback for each of the first two items to try to teach him the "ground rules" of the task. Note, however, that the child who fails the first two items is discontinued. Thus, the child who finally catches on after the second bit of feedback is not given the opportunity to demonstrate his understanding. It is usually a good idea to administer item 3 just to find out if he has grasped the concept. Success on that item, or on subsequent items, does *not* count toward the child's score on Opposite Analogies, but it provides valuable clinical information.

## 18. CONCEPTUAL GROUPING
## (PERCEPTUAL-PERFORMANCE)

### Description

The child shows his understanding of basic shape, color, and size concepts (items 1–3); demonstrates classification skills (items 4–6); and shows his ability to figure out logical rules for grouping (items 7–9). The items, which are untimed, utilize a set of 12 colorful blocks.

### Administration and Scoring

For items 1–3, the examiner has to remember to correct errors made by the child, but only after each item is *completed*. Since subsequent items depend on the child's knowledge of basic concepts such as "square" and "little," it is important for the child to be given feedback.

Whereas a "lesson" on shape, color, or size is clearly inappropriate, pointing to each block on the card and supplying its label may be done two or three times before going on to the next item. Since chance guessing may be responsible for some children's correct answers to items 1–3, it is essential for the examiner to remember to give appropriate feedback on these items even when the child is right (e.g., "Yes, this is the little one (point) . . .").

Read each item slowly, placing a stress on the key word or words in each statement. Items 5 and 6 require the child to manipulate two or three variables at a time to answer correctly. When administering these items it is especially important to enunciate clearly and to give an equal stress to each adjective. (e.g., "Now see how many *big round red* ones you can find. Remember, you're looking for *big round red* ones.")

The examiner may repeat the instructions to an item *before* the child begins his response, if necessary, but not *after* the child has already begun selecting blocks. For example, a child who starts putting *circles* on the card for item 4 cannot be "reminded" to find all the *square* ones. Similarly, a child who selects *most* of the square blocks, and then stops, cannot be coaxed to find *all* the squares; and a youngster who loses the set and adds some circles to the pile of squares cannot be told to find *only* the square ones.

For items 7 and 8, it is important to scatter the blocks on the card in a *random* fashion; for item 9 it is just as important to arrange the blocks neatly, and slightly off center, as pictured on page 138 of the Manual. If the child selects more than two blocks for item 9, he is told to find only two. This extra help is given to facilitate the child's performance on this very complex item. Such help may *not* be given to children who select too many blocks in items 4-8.

When scoring item 4 ("Find all the square ones . . ."), remember to convert the difference between right and wrong choices to the 2–1–0 system shown in the manual. Entering the value of "rights minus wrongs" in the Score column by error may inflate the child's score substantially and lead to incorrect interpretation.

Children sometimes exhibit perseveration or lack of impulse control on several of the Conceptual Grouping items. For example, on item 5 a child may put the two big yellow blocks on the card and then start to add the *little* yellow blocks. When this occurs, the child *fails* the item even if he seems to be violating the rule deliberately or "for fun." If the child *pauses* for a few seconds after adding the last correct block, however, the examiner should gather up the blocks and prepare for the next item, rather than giving the child the opportunity to spoil his response. (This latter rule applies to all Conceptual Grouping items. Some children interpret the examiner's failure to react to their correct response as an indication that something is wrong with it.)

Some young children fail to grasp the notion that the blocks go on the cards. Instead, they may put them in a separate pile, give them to the examiner, or keep them in their hands. Encourage them to put the blocks on the card, but there is *no penalty* so long as the blocks they choose are clearly intended as their response, and are separate from the rest of the blocks.

The scoring of item 9 has been of concern to some examiners who claim that several 0-point responses are as good as the responses that earn 1 or 2 points. We would dispute that any failing responses are as good as the 2-point response, which requires manipulation of all three variables simultaneously; but there is at least one response (i.e., two yellow blocks) that is probably better than the designated 1-point responses. Nevertheless, credit may *not* be given to any response except the ones specifically listed in the Manual because that system was used to score all standardization cases. If a child does give a logical response that earns no credit, however, this fact is of clinical value and should be noted.

# Chapter 3

## Computing Prorated Indexes When a Test is Spoiled or Not Given

The practical issues pertaining to the administration and scoring of the McCarthy are not limited to the clarification of ambiguities or the listing of helpful hints and aids. A very real problem that is not treated in the McCarthy Manual is how to deal with tests that are spoiled or not administered.

Spoiled or omitted tests are often a function of a clinician's lack of experience. The inexperienced examiner may expose the Pictorial Memory card for 15 (rather than 10) seconds, fail to query several 1-point responses in Part II of Word Knowledge, or forget to return to a test that was refused earlier in the testing session. However, even the experienced clinician will sometimes be faced with this problem. For example, an older acting-out child may grab the record form and read some of the items in Verbal Memory I, thereby spoiling that part of the test, or the examiner may decide to terminate the testing of a young child before completing the battery, sensing that he is no longer able to cooperate fully.

In addition, it is sometimes necessary to omit tests because of a child's handicap. A blind child, for example, can be administered most, but not all, of the Verbal and Quantitative tests. The examiner would learn much about the blind child's abilities if Verbal and Quantitative Indexes could be estimated.

Clearly, a technique for prorating Indexes is needed to deal with spoiled or omitted tests. (Of course, administering an omitted test at a subsequent testing session is always preferable to prorating, should this be feasible.) Unfortunately, prorating on the McCarthy is not as simple as prorating on the WPPSI, WISC-R, or Stanford-Binet. All Wechsler subtest scores are standard scores having the same mean and standard deviation, and all Binet tasks are weighted equally within each age level. Consequently, a score for a spoiled or omitted Wechsler or Binet task may be prorated by using simple averaging techniques; the equal units also permit the substitution of an alternate or optional task for one that is spoiled.

The McCarthy test scores, however, are not in equal units. The weighted raw scores for each test have their own characteristic range, mean, and standard deviation at each age level. One test cannot be substituted for another, and mere averages of the child's weighted raw scores on the validly administered McCarthy tests will *not* give a reasonable prorated score for a spoiled or omitted test.

Nevertheless, the importance of having a technique for prorating McCarthy Indexes is apparent. Without such a technique, a spoiled or omitted test prevents the computation of Indexes for all scales that include that test. If Tapping Sequence is spoiled or omitted, for example, the examiner has no way of computing the child's Perceptual-Performance Index, Memory Index, or GCI. We have therefore developed the straightforward procedure for prorating described in this chapter.

## THE COMPUTATIONAL PROCEDURE

The aim of prorating is to estimate the weighted raw score that the child would have obtained on a valid administration of the task. This estimated score can then be entered in the appropriate box(es) on the back of the record form, and his prorated Index(es) can be computed.

A good estimate of the child's weighted raw score on a spoiled or omitted test may be obtained by averaging his *level of functioning* on similar tests. For example, if Opposite Analogies is spoiled, then the child's performance on other Verbal tasks should be used to determine his likely score on the spoiled Verbal test. If he performed as well as the average 6½ year old on the other tests in the Verbal Scale, then a reasonable estimate of his Opposite Analogies score is the mean score obtained by 6½ year old children (even if his chronological age is only 4).

Since weighted raw scores are not comparable from test to test, the scores have to be converted to a common metric before they can be averaged. Table 3-1, which presents *test age* equivalents of weighted raw scores for all cognitive tests, offers an easy method of making these conversions. The table was developed from McCarthy's Table 17 (1972, pp. 204–205), which shows means and standard deviations of test raw scores across the age range. (The test ages for Right–Left Orientation at ages 2½–4½ were obtained from standardization data provided by The Psychological Corporation.)

In Table 3-1, the Verbal, Perceptual–Performance, and Quantitative tests are each grouped separately. This grouping facilitates prorating since only the Verbal test ages are averaged to estimate a score for a spoiled or omitted Verbal task; only the Perceptual–Performance test ages are averaged for a spoiled or omitted Perceptual–Performance task; and only the Quantitative test ages are averaged for a spoiled or omitted Quantitative task. The gross motor tests are not included in Table 3-1 because prorating the Motor Index presents some additional problems and is treated later in the chapter.

The steps to follow for prorating when a *cognitive* test is omitted or spoiled are listed below.

**Step 1. Obtain test ages for all validly administered tasks in the pertinent scale.** For example, if a Perceptual–Performance test is spoiled or omitted, determine test ages for all other Perceptual–Performance tests. Enter Table 3-1 with the child's *weighted* raw score on each relevant test, and convert it to a test age. For example, a weighted raw score of 7 on Block Building equals a test age of 3½ years; a weighted raw score of 7 on Puzzle Solving equals a test age of 6 years. Weighted raw scores that do not appear in Table 3-1 correspond to test ages "below 2½" or "above 8½."

**Step 2. Compute the mean of the test ages obtained in Step 1.** When computing the mean of the several test ages, values of "below 2½" and "above 8½" should be treated as 2½ and 8½, respectively. (Exception: if the child obtains two or more test ages of "below 2½" in the same scale, then a prorated Index should *not* be computed for that scale.) Round all mean test ages to the nearest *half year*. Mean test ages ending in the fraction ¼ or ¾ should be rounded *up*. (For example, round 4¼ to 4½ and 7¾ to 8.)

**Table 3-1**

Test Age Equivalents of *Weighted* Raw Scores on the Verbal, Perceptual–Performance, and Quantitative Tests

| Tests | 2½ | 3 | 3½ | 4 | 4½ | 5 | 5½ | 6 | 6½ | 7 | 7½ | 8 | 8½ |
|---|---|---|---|---|---|---|---|---|---|---|---|---|---|
| **Verbal** | | | | | | | | | | | | | |
| 3. Pictorial Memory | 1 | — | 2 | — | 3 | — | — | 4 | — | — | — | 5 | — |
| 4. Word Knowledge | 7-8 | 9-10 | 11 | 12-13 | 14-15 | 16 | 17 | 18 | 19 | 20 | 21 | 22 | 23 |
| 7. Verbal Memory | | | | | | | | | | | | | |
|    Part I | 2-3 | 4-5 | 6-7 | 8-9 | 10 | 11 | 12 | — | — | 13 | — | — | 14 |
|    Part II | 0 | 1 | 2 | 3 | 4 | 5 | 6 | — | 7 | — | 8 | — | 9 |
| 15. Verbal Fluency | 2-3 | 4-5 | 6-7 | 8-9 | 10-11 | 12-13 | 14-15 | 16-17 | 18-19 | 20 | 21-22 | 23 | 24 |
| 17. Opposite Analogies | 0 | 2 | 4 | 6 | 8 | — | 10 | — | 12 | — | 14 | — | 16 |
| **Perceptual–Performance** | | | | | | | | | | | | | |
| 1. Block Building | 4-5 | 6 | 7 | 8 | — | 9 | — | 10 | — | — | — | — | 11 |
| 2. Puzzle Solving | 0 | 1 | 2 | 3 | 4 | 5 | 6 | 7 | 8 | — | 9 | 10 | — |
| 6. Tapping Sequence | 1 | — | 2 | — | 3 | — | 4 | — | — | 5 | — | — | 6 |
| 8. Right–Left Orient. | 2 | 3 | 4 | 5 | — | 6 | — | 7 | — | 8 | — | 9 | 10 |
| 12. Draw-A-Design | 1 | 2 | 3 | 4 | 5-6 | 7 | 8 | 9-10 | 11 | 12 | 13 | 14 | 15 |
| 13. Draw-A-Child | 0 | 1 | 2-3 | 4-6 | 7-8 | 9 | 10 | 11 | — | 12 | 13 | 14 | 15 |
| 18. Conceptual Group. | 1-2 | 3 | 4 | 5 | 6 | 7 | 8 | — | 9 | — | 10 | — | 11 |
| **Quantitative** | | | | | | | | | | | | | |
| 5. Number Questions | 2 | 4 | — | 6 | — | 8 | — | 10 | 12 | 14 | 16 | 18 | 20 |
| 14. Numerical Memory | | | | | | | | | | | | | |
|    Part I | 2 | 3 | 4 | — | 5 | — | 6 | — | 7 | — | 8 | — | 9 |
|    Part II | — | — | 0 | — | — | 2 | — | 4 | — | 6 | — | 8 | — |
| 16. Counting & Sorting | 1 | 2 | 3 | 4 | 5 | 6 | 7 | — | 8 | — | 9 | — | — |

**Step 3. Determine the child's estimated weighted raw score for the spoiled or omitted test.** Table 3-2 was constructed to enable the examiner to estimate the child's weighted raw score on the spoiled or omitted test. Locate the column in Table 3-2 that corresponds to the *mean test age* computed in Step 2, and locate the row with the name of the spoiled or omitted test. The estimated weighted raw score appears at the intersection of the row and column. For example, suppose an examiner spoils Pictorial Memory. If the child's mean test age on the other Verbal tests is found to be $4\frac{1}{2}$ years, then an estimated weighted raw score of 3 may be determined for him from Table 3-2.

**Step 4. Enter the estimated weighted raw score on the back of the record form in all appropriate boxes.** If a drawing test is spoiled or omitted, then the same score that is estimated from the child's Perceptual–Performance test ages should also be entered in the Motor column. Similarly, an estimated score for a short-term memory task is entered in the Verbal, Perceptual–Performance, or Quantitative column, and also in the Memory column. Whenever an estimated weighted raw score is entered on the back of the record form, add the abbreviation PRO (or the word "prorated") to the right of each pertinent box.

**Step 5. Compute composite raw scores and Indexes in the usual manner.** Once weighted raw scores have been estimated for all spoiled or omitted tests, the regular procedures for computing composite raw scores and Indexes (described on pages 143–148 of the Manual) may be followed. Be sure to add the designation PRO to the right of each prorated composite raw score on the *back* of the record form, and to the right of each prorated Index (including GCI) on the *front* of the record form.

**ILLUSTRATION**

The following case is used to demonstrate the procedures for prorating. It also serves to illustrate an instance where prorating is essential for salvaging meaningful results from potentially chaotic test information.

Martin G. is a $4\frac{1}{2}$-year-old boy suspected of a behavior disorder. Previously labeled untestable, Martin expressed interest in the McCarthy materials and was cooperative for Tests 1–6 and for Part I of Test 7 (Verbal Memory). During Verbal Memory II, Martin decided he did not want to hear the story. When the examiner was half-way through the story, Martin put his fingers in his ears and began to hum loudly, thereby spoiling the task.

Rapport was regained during the gross motor tests and was maintained through Test 17. As soon as the blocks were brought out for Test 18 (Conceptual Grouping), however, Martin lost interest in the test and refused to cooperate. He insisted on playing with the blocks, and began to throw them when the examiner tried to redirect him to the task at hand. All efforts by the examiner proved fruitless, and the session was terminated. It was not feasible to set up a second appointment.

Prorating was therefore necessary, or it would not be possible to compute four of the six Indexes: Verbal, Perceptual–Performance, Memory, and General Cognitive. The steps to follow to estimate weighted raw scores for Verbal Memory II and Conceptual Grouping, and to prorate Indexes for the four scales, are described below.

**Step 1.** **Obtain the pertinent test ages.** For Verbal Memory II, the relevant ages correspond to the remaining tests in the Verbal Scale; for Conceptual Grouping, the ages correspond to the other Perceptual–Performance tests.

Martin's weighted raw scores on the validly administered Verbal and Perceptual–Performance tests are listed below. Test ages, obtained from Table 3-1, are shown next to the weighted raw scores.

| Test | Weighted Raw Score | Test Age |
|------|--------------------|----------|
| Verbal | | |
| 3. Pictorial Memory | 3 | $4\frac{1}{2}$ |
| 4. Word Knowledge | 6 | Below $2\frac{1}{2}$ |
| 7. Verbal Memory I | 10 | $4\frac{1}{2}$ |
| 15. Verbal Fluency | 6 | $3\frac{1}{2}$ |
| 17. Opposite Analogies | 4 | $3\frac{1}{2}$ |
| Perceptual–Performance | | |
| 1. Block Building | 9 | 5 |
| 2. Puzzle Solving | 6 | $5\frac{1}{2}$ |
| 6. Tapping Sequence | 3 | $4\frac{1}{2}$ |
| 12. Draw-A-Design | 11 | $6\frac{1}{2}$ |
| 13. Draw-A-Child | 10 | $5\frac{1}{2}$ |

**Step 2.  Compute mean test ages.**  The mean of the Verbal test ages is 3.7, which rounds to 3½. (The test age of "below 2½" on Word Knowledge was treated as 2½ in the computation.)

The mean of the Perceptual–Performance test ages is 5.4, which rounds to 5½.

**Step 3.  Estimate weighted raw scores for Verbal Memory II and Conceptual Grouping.**  By entering Table 3-2 with Martin's mean Verbal Age of 3½, an estimated score of 2 is obtained for Part II of Verbal Memory. Similarly, an estimated weighted raw score of 8 is obtained for Conceptual Grouping by entering Table 3-2 with the mean Perceptual–Performance age of 5½.

**Step 4.  Enter the estimated weighted raw scores on the record form.**  Figure 3-1 shows the back of Martin's record form, revealing the weighted raw scores he actually obtained along with the two that

**Table 3-2**
Prorated Weighted Raw Scores for General Cognitive
Tests, by Test Age

| Test | | 2½ | 3 | 3½ | 4 | 4½ | 5 | 5½ | 6 | 6½ | 7 | 7½ | 8 | 8½ |
|---|---|---|---|---|---|---|---|---|---|---|---|---|---|---|
| 1. | Block Building | 4 | 6 | 7 | 8 | 9 | 9 | 10 | 10 | 10 | 10 | 10 | 10 | 10 |
| 2. | Puzzle Solving | 0 | 1 | 2 | 3 | 4 | 5 | 6 | 7 | 8 | 8 | 9 | 10 | 11 |
| 3. | Pictorial Memory | 1 | 2 | 2 | 3 | 3 | 4 | 4 | 4 | 4 | 4 | 4 | 5 | 5 |
| 4. | Word Knowledge | | | | | | | | | | | | | |
| | Part I | 7 | 8 | 8 | 9 | 9 | 9 | 9 | 9 | 9 | 9 | 9 | 9 | 9 |
| | Part II | 1 | 2 | 3 | 4 | 6 | 7 | 8 | 9 | 10 | 11 | 12 | 13 | 14 |
| 5. | Number Questions | 2 | 4 | 4 | 6 | 6 | 8 | 8 | 10 | 12 | 14 | 16 | 18 | 20 |
| 6. | Tapping Sequence | 1 | 1 | 2 | 2 | 3 | 3 | 4 | 4 | 5 | 5 | 5 | 6 | 6 |
| 7. | Verbal Memory | | | | | | | | | | | | | |
| | Part I | 2 | 4 | 6 | 8 | 10 | 11 | 12 | 12 | 13 | 13 | 13 | 14 | 14 |
| | Part II | 0 | 1 | 2 | 3 | 4 | 5 | 6 | 7 | 7 | 8 | 8 | 8 | 9 |
| 8. | Right–Left Orient. | 2 | 3 | 4 | 5 | 5 | 6 | 6 | 7 | 7 | 8 | 8 | 9 | 10 |
| 12. | Draw-A-Design | 1 | 2 | 3 | 4 | 6 | 7 | 8 | 9 | 11 | 12 | 13 | 14 | 15 |
| 13. | Draw-A-Child | 0 | 1 | 2 | 5 | 7 | 9 | 10 | 11 | 11 | 12 | 13 | 14 | 15 |
| 14. | Numerical Memory | | | | | | | | | | | | | |
| | Part I | 2 | 3 | 4 | 4 | 5 | 6 | 6 | 6 | 7 | 7 | 8 | 8 | 9 |
| | Part II | 0 | 0 | 0 | 0 | 0 | 2 | 2 | 4 | 6 | 6 | 8 | 8 | 8 |
| 15. | Verbal Fluency | 2 | 4 | 6 | 9 | 11 | 13 | 15 | 17 | 18 | 20 | 21 | 23 | 24 |
| 16. | Counting & Sorting | 1 | 2 | 3 | 4 | 5 | 6 | 7 | 8 | 8 | 9 | 9 | 9 | 9 |
| 17. | Opposite Analogies | - 0 | 2 | 4 | 6 | 8 | 10 | 10 | 12 | 12 | 14 | 14 | 14 | 16 |
| 18. | Conceptual Group. | 1 | 3 | 4 | 5 | 6 | 7 | 8 | 9 | 9 | 9 | 10 | 10 | 11 |

COMPUTATION OF COMPOSITE RAW SCORES

1. Enter the *weighted raw scores* which are in the shaded boxes on pages 2-7 of the record form. For each test, enter the score in the box(es) bearing that test's number. (For example, the score for Test 3 is entered in 2 boxes.)
2. Sum the scores in each of the 5 columns. Enter the totals in the *composite raw score* boxes at the foot of the page.
3. Transfer the *composite raw scores* to the front cover. (Open the booklet and turn it over so that the front and back covers are side by side.) Enter the scores in the Composite Raw Score column in the box labeled "Composite Raw Scores and Scale Indexes."

(For more detailed directions on the completion of the record form, see Chapter 7 of manual.)

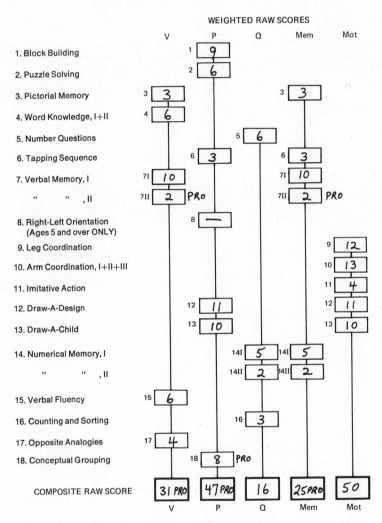

Fig. 3-1. The back page of Martin G.'s record form, showing his actual weighted raw scores along with the scores estimated for him via the prorating technique. Note that all estimated weighted raw scores and composite raw scores are followed by the abbreviation "PRO" to indicate that prorating was performed.

# McCARTHY SCALES OF CHILDREN'S ABILITIES

## Record Form

NAME *MARTIN G.*      AGE *4½*   SEX *M*

HOME ADDRESS *1721 JAMES DRIVE, RURALTOWN, GA.*

NAMES OF PARENTS OR GUARDIAN *MIKE AND KATHY G.*

SCHOOL *NONE*      GRADE ___

PLACE OF TESTING *MARTIN'S HOME*      TESTED BY *LYNN SCOTT*

REFERRED BY *PARENTS*

---

### MSCA PROFILE

Enter the 6 Scale Indexes on the appropriate lines below. Then circle the mark representing the Index for each Scale. Draw a line connecting the circles. Note that the values for GC are different from those for the other Scales.

|  | Year | Month | Day |
|---|---|---|---|
| Date Tested | *1976* | *3* | *28* |
| Date of Birth | *1971* | *9* | *21* |
| Age | *4* | *6* | *7* |

| SCALE INDEX | Verbal | Perceptual-Performance | Quanti-tative | General Cognitive | Memory | Motor |
|---|---|---|---|---|---|---|
|  | *35 PRO* | *60 PRO* | *46* | *93 PRO* | *47 PRO* | *71* |

(profile chart with scale values 22–78 and SD markings +3SD, +2SD, +1SD, Mean, –1SD, –2SD, –3SD)

### COMPOSITE RAW SCORES AND SCALE INDEXES

Enter the composite raw scores from the back cover. *Obtain the composite raw score for GC by adding V+P+Q.* Determine the corresponding Scale Indexes from Table 16. (See page 151 of manual for detailed directions.)

| Scale | Composite Raw Score | Scale Index | |
|---|---|---|---|
| Verbal (V) | *31* | *35* | PRO |
| Perceptual-Performance (P) | *47* | *60* | PRO |
| Quantitative (Q) | *16* | *46* | |
| General Cognitive: Add composite raw scores V+P+Q | *94* | *93* GCI | PRO |
| Memory (Mem) | *25* | *47* | PRO |
| Motor (Mot) | *50* | *71* | |

### LATERALITY

(Enter information from Laterality Summary on page 5.)

Hand *R*

Eye *L*

---

Fig. 3-2. The front page of Martin G.'s record form. Note that all prorated Indexes are clearly labeled with the abbreviation "PRO."

were estimated. Note that "PRO" is indicated to the right of all appropriate boxes.

**Step 5. Perform computations in the usual manner.** Figure 3-1 shows that composite raw scores were obtained by summing all weighted raw scores in each column, whether they were earned or estimated. The composite raw scores were then converted to Indexes, using the appropriate pages in the normative table (McCarthy, 1972, pp. 168–169). The front of Martin's record form, shown in Figure 3-2, reveals an interesting profile of Indexes—thanks to the prorating technique.

### THE MOTOR SCALE

It is reasonable to estimate a score for a spoiled or omitted cognitive test from a child's performance on similar tests because the intercorrelations among the tests in the Verbal, Perceptual–Performance, and Quantitative Scales are substantial in magnitude. Unfortunately, the intercorrelations among the five Motor tests are substantial only at ages $2\frac{1}{2}$–$3\frac{1}{2}$. For children aged 4 and above, the two drawing tests correlate about .50, but the other intercorrelations among the gross and fine motor tasks tend to fall between .00 and .20 (data from the correlation matrices used for factor analysis by Kaufman, 1975b). Thus, a child's score on a spoiled or omitted Motor test cannot be estimated too efficiently from his level of performance on the remaining tests.

We would suggest computing a prorated Motor Index only under the three circumstances indicated below.

1. If a drawing test is spoiled or omitted. The weighted raw score for Draw-A-Design or Draw-A-Child can be estimated from the child's test ages on the remaining Perceptual–Performance tests. This estimated score should be used to compute prorated Perceptual–Performance *and* Motor Indexes.

2. If one of the parts of Arm Coordination is spoiled or omitted. Even though total score on Arm Coordination does not correlate very highly with scores on the other Motor tests, the separate parts of Arm Coordination correlate respectably (.30 to .40) with each other. Consequently, if one part of Arm Coordination is spoiled or omitted, it is reasonable to estimate a child's total weighted raw score on Arm Coordination from his performance on the two validly administered

parts. A table developed on the same principle used to estimate scores on cognitive tests is shown below to facilitate this estimation.

| Sum of Scores on Two Parts | | | Estimated Score on |
| I + II | I + III | II + III | All Three Parts |
| --- | --- | --- | --- |
| 0 | 0 | 0 | 0 |
| — | 1 | 1 | 1 |
| 1 | 2 | 2 | 2 |
| 2 | — | — | 3 |
| — | 3 | 3 | 4 |
| 3 | — | 4 | 5 |
| 4 | 4 | — | 6 |
| — | — | 5 | 7 |
| 5 | 5 | 6 | 8 |
| 6 | 6 | 7 | 9 |
| 7 | — | — | 10 |
| — | 7 | 8 | 11 |
| 8 | — | — | 12 |
| — | 8 | 9 | 13 |
| 9 | — | — | 14 |
| 10 | 9 | 10 | 15 |
| 11 | — | 11 | 16 |
| 12 | 10 | 12 | 17 |
| 13 | 11 | 13 | 18 |
| 14 | 12 | 14 | 19 |
| 15+ | 13+ | 15+ | 20 |

Suppose that a child who earns 4 points on Part I and 5 points on Part II adamantly refuses to participate in the Beanbag Target Game (Part III). Locate the sum of his scores on Parts I + II (9 points) in the appropriate column in the above table. Then read horizontally across to determine his estimated weighted raw score on all three parts of Arm Coordination (in this case, 14 points). Enter this value on the back of the child's record form, appending the designation "PRO."

3. If Imitative Action is spoiled or omitted. Imitative Action is a short test that is quite easy, even for most young children. It contributes relatively little to the Motor Index, although it serves the useful function of providing a "bottom" for children who do poorly in the other two gross motor tests.

When Imitative Action is the only spoiled or omitted Motor test, it is unreasonable not to be able to compute a Motor Index. To estimate a weighted raw score for Imitative Action, sum the child's scores on the other gross motor tests (Leg Coordination and Arm Coordination), and use the conversions shown below:

| Sum of Leg and Arm Coordination Scores | Estimated Score on Imitative Action |
|:---:|:---:|
| 18+ | 4 |
| 9–17 | 3 |
| 4–8 | 2 |
| 0–3 | Do not prorate |

Estimating a score on Imitative Action for children below age 4 is defensible because the intercorrelations among the Motor tests (especially the gross motor tests) are substantial for young children. At ages 4 and above the estimation is also sensible since virtually all children obtain perfect or near perfect scores on Imitative Action. Hence, there is little risk of making an error of any consequence when estimating a weighted raw score for Imitative Action.

If Leg Coordination or more than one part of Arm Coordination is spoiled or omitted it is not advisable to compute a prorated Motor Index. The examiner may, however, interpret the child's scores on the validly administered Motor tests using the procedures described in Chapter 6.

## PRECAUTIONS ABOUT PRORATING

The availability of a straightforward procedure for prorating should *never* be an excuse for omitting any McCarthy task. A prorated Index is *less reliable* than an Index based on all tasks in a scale. The consequences are an increased band of error around the prorated Index and a decreased reliability of the *difference* between the child's prorated Index and his Indexes on other scales. Thus, the prorating technique fulfills an important practical need as long as it is not abused.

The reliability of the GCI will suffer the least from a few prorated tasks. As the most global and comprehensive of the McCarthy Indexes, the GCI enjoys an impressive degree of accuracy. However, the abilities assessed by even the briefest of tasks on the

General Cognitive Scale contribute *functionally* (not just statistically) to the unique construct labeled GCI. Eliminating one or more tasks alters the nature of the construct, and hence the meaning of what is measured. In addition, whenever a General Cognitive task is not given, at least one of the specific Indexes must also be prorated; this diminishes the effectiveness of the differential measurement that plays so important a role in the administration of the McCarthy. Sometimes, differential measurement must be sacrificed for the sake of a brief administration time. In these instances, it is essential to select the tasks to be administered in a careful and systematic fashion. (See the discussion of a six-test McCarthy short form on pp. 205–210.) Random or whimsical decisions about which tests to omit do not constitute sound testing procedures under any circumstances.

Ordinarily, no more than *one* weighted raw score for a test or part-test should be estimated for any of the five specific scales. It is acceptable (though not desirable) to estimate scores for *two* tests or part-tests on the Verbal and Perceptual–Performance Scales, since these are the most reliable scales among the five (McCarthy, 1972, p. 31). However, if more than one Quantitative, Memory, or Motor task is spoiled or omitted, it is not advisable to compute a prorated Index.

If the number of spoiled or omitted tests is large enough to prevent the examiner from computing a Verbal, Perceptual–Performance, or Quantitative Index, then he should *not* prorate a GCI. The examiner may, however, interpret all valid Indexes and test scores in accordance with the procedures discussed in Chapters 5 and 6.

### APPLICATIONS OF PRORATING FOR TESTING HANDICAPPED CHILDREN

Youngsters with impaired sensory functioning or other physical handicaps typically cannot be given the entire McCarthy Scales. However, selected tasks can usually be administered validly to these children with the precise tasks dependent on the nature and severity of their handicaps. A technique such as prorating thus permits the examiner to obtain one or more estimated McCarthy Indexes for some physically handicapped children, thereby unifying what would otherwise be isolated test scores. These practical issues will be addressed more specifically for three groups of handicapped children: blind, deaf, and cerebral palsied.

### Blind Children

The prorating technique is especially valuable when testing blind youngsters. All of the Verbal tasks except Pictorial Memory and Word Knowledge I, and all Quantitative tasks except Counting & Sorting may be administered to blind children. The procedures described above permit the examiner to obtain prorated Verbal and Quantitative Indexes, imposing a sense of order on the test data gathered for a blind child.

Sometimes a Quantitative Index can be computed for a blind youngster without having to prorate. McCarthy (1972, p. 76) states: "If the child passes 9 or more items on Number Questions, he should be given full credit (9 points) for Counting & Sorting (Test 16)." Consequently, when a blind child does very well on Number Questions, his Quantitative Index can be obtained in the conventional manner.

Similarly, McCarthy (1972, p. 67) instructs the examiner to give full credit (9 points) on Word Knowledge I (Picture Vocabulary) to children aged 5 and above who pass *both* item 1 and item 2 of Word Knowledge II. For blind youngsters, the examiner should follow this rule for everyone, including preschoolers. When a child is "exempted" from Picture Vocabulary, only a score on Pictorial Memory has to be estimated in order to compute a prorated Verbal Index.

Even though a GCI cannot be computed for a blind child, and Indexes cannot be obtained on the Perceptual–Performance, Memory, and Motor Scales, a considerable amount of information may still be derived from the child's level of functioning on the Verbal and Quantitative Scales and the difference between his two Indexes. McCarthy (1972, pp. 33–35) reports that a difference of about 11 points is needed for significance ($p < .05$) when comparing a child's Verbal and Quantitative Indexes. Because prorating reduces the reliability of an Index to some extent, differences of *15 points* should be required for significance when comparing a blind youngster's prorated Verbal and Quantitative Indexes.

In addition to evaluating the Indexes, the examiner may wish to determine the blind child's relative strengths and weaknesses on the separate tasks. The same procedures described in Chapter 6 should be applied. To use these techniques, the examiner needs an overall level of mental functioning for the blind youngster; such an estimate may be obtained from the table shown below. Sum the child's prorated *composite raw scores* on the Verbal and Quantitative Scales, and consult the table to determine his estimated General Cognitive Age.

| Verbal + Quantitative Composite Raw Scores | Estimated General Cognitive Age |
|---|---|
| 11-26 | 2½ |
| 27-38 | 3 |
| 39-51 | 3½ |
| 52-64 | 4 |
| 65-75 | 4½ |
| 76-85 | 5 |
| 86-93 | 5½ |
| 94-103 | 6 |
| 104-111 | 6½ |
| 112-119 | 7 |
| 120-125 | 7½ |
| 126-131 | 8 |
| 132-137 | 8½ |

**Deaf Children**

The number of McCarthy tasks that can be administered to a deaf child depends upon the examiner's skill and experience and the child's communication abilities. Most young deaf children require pantomime instructions to understand what is expected of them. Several Perceptual–Performance and Motor tests can easily be communicated nonverbally and may be administered without violating the norms: Block Building, Puzzle Solving, Draw-A-Design, Leg Coordination, Arm Coordination, and Imitative Action. Tapping Sequence can also be communicated in pantomime, but it would be wise *not* to administer this task because (1) the lack of auditory stimuli changes the task to an unknown degree, and (2) the deaf child who knows that a xylophone plays music may become upset by the task.

Draw-A-Child is not as easy to give with pantomime instructions as an imitative task like Draw-A-Design or a self-explanatory test such as Puzzle Solving. A skilled examiner can undoubtedly communicate the nature of the task to most deaf children, especially those of school age. Indeed, a number of research studies have been conducted to evaluate the human figure drawings of deaf children (Harris, 1963, pp. 28–29). However, it is likely that the visual aids needed to convey the instructions nonverbally will distort the McCarthy Draw-A-Child norms to some extent.

Although Indexes cannot be obtained, and should not be prorated, for deaf children who are limited in their communication skills, the tables shown below will provide some summary information about their skill areas. Visual–motor ability may be determined by converting the *sum* of the deaf child's *weighted* raw scores on Block Building, Puzzle Solving, and Draw-A-Design to an age equivalent. Similarly, the sum of weighted raw scores on Leg Coordination, Arm Coordination, and Imitative Action may be converted to a gross motor age equivalent. The child's age level on the visual–motor tasks may be considered as a rough estimate of his nonverbal intelligence. However, both the visual–motor and gross motor age scores should be interpreted cautiously since neither "half-scale" score is as reliable as the complete Perceptual–Performance or Motor Indexes.

| Visual Motor | | Gross Motor | |
|---|---|---|---|
| Sum of Block Building, Puzzle Solving, and Draw-A-Design | Age Equivalent | Sum of Leg Coordination, Arm Coordination, and Imitative Action | Age Equivalent |
| 5–7 | 2½ | 5–9 | 2½ |
| 8–10 | 3 | 10–13 | 3 |
| 11–13 | 3½ | 14–16 | 3½ |
| 14–16 | 4 | 17–19 | 4 |
| 17–19 | 4½ | 20–22 | 4½ |
| 20–22 | 5 | 23–24 | 5 |
| 23–25 | 5½ | 25–26 | 5½ |
| 26–27 | 6 | 27–28 | 6 |
| 28–29 | 6½ | 29–30 | 6½ |
| 30–31 | 7 | 31–32 | 7 |
| 32–33 | 7½ | 33–34 | 7½ |
| 34 | 8 | 35 | 8 |
| 35 | 8½ | 36 | 8½ |

The three visual–motor and three gross motor tests represent the minimum battery for a deaf child. As the deaf youngster's facility with language improves (e.g., he learns how to read, use sign language, express himself verbally, read lips), additional McCarthy tests can be administered. The number and nature of the tests that can be administered validly are a function of the child's integrities and the examiner's skill at utilizing these integrities to communicate the various tasks. Whenever virtually all tests are administered to a deaf child, the procedures for estimating test scores and prorating Indexes should be applied.

### Cerebral-Palsied Children

Children with cerebral palsy have a neuromuscular impairment stemming from a brain injury which may affect their visual, auditory, motor, and speech functions (Cruickshank, 1966). Administration of a cognitive and motor battery such as the McCarthy obviously presents problems and must be adapted to the specific capabilities of each child. The visual or auditory difficulties of some cerebral-palsied children lead to test-related problems similar to the ones discussed for blind and deaf children and need not be reiterated.

A valid Motor Index cannot usually be obtained or prorated for a cerebral-palsied child, but some of the cognitive scales can often be given in their entirety. If the cerebral-palsied child has adequate speech and the use of one hand, it is possible to obtain Indexes on all five cognitive scales. Only Puzzle Solving, with its time limits and bonus points for quick performance, may be unfair for a child who does not have the use of both hands. If a child's score on Puzzle Solving seems depressed because of his handicap (based on observations of any coordination difficulties), the examiner may consider the test invalid and estimate a score for Puzzle Solving using the prorating techniques. In general, children with cerebral palsy frequently solve manipulative problems in a laborious fashion and may be unduly penalized by timed tasks such as Puzzle Solving (Sattler, 1974, pp. 82–83).

A child who has limited use of his hands but can talk and hear adequately may be given the Verbal tests and all Quantitative tests except Counting & Sorting. A prorated Quantitative Index can be computed, just as it is for a blind youngster. Conversely, a child with good hands but poor speech can be administered the entire Perceptual–Performance Scale. In fact, the Perceptual–Performance Index provides adequate measurement of the nonverbal intelligence of any child with an expressive speech problem since none of the items require talking.

It is difficult to obtain valid test data for a child with multiple handicaps. The examiner has to determine the child's sensory and motor capabilities, particularly as they relate to taking standardized tests. An instrument such as Katz' (1954) Survey of Degree of Physical Handicap (see Sattler, 1974, pp. 80–81) may prove valuable for this purpose. The examiner should strive to administer as many McCarthy tasks as possible without deviating from the standardized procedures. If most tests in a scale can be given under valid conditions, then a prorated Index can usually be computed. Even if no Indexes can be obtained for a child, the examiner can determine an overall level of functioning from the average of his test ages on all cognitive tests that are given. The procedures in Chapter 6 may then be used to formulate hypotheses about specific areas of strength and weakness.

The examiner of cerebral-palsied children should remember that even when a task is administered under apparently valid conditions, the child's failure may be due more to physical than mental factors (Garrett, 1952). Considerable experience with handicapped children is necessary to assess their intellectual capacity, and even experienced clinicians need to exercise caution when interpreting cognitive and motor test data for young children with cerebral palsy. Nonetheless, it is usually worth the effort to assess the mental abilities of these children. As Sattler (1974, p. 83) states: "In spite of the difficulties in using standard tests, it is still important to compare the cerebral-palsied child's performance with that of the normal child, because the latter sets the standards in the world at large."

# PART II

# Interpretation of the McCarthy

The aims of Part II are to describe the abilities that are measured by the scales (Chapter 4), provide empirical approaches for interpreting the scores yielded by the McCarthy (Chapters 5 and 6), and offer suggestions for analyzing the tests clinically (Chapter 7). Taken together, the chapters constituting Part II serve to enhance the examiner's ability to interpret the McCarthy profile both quantitatively and qualitatively.

Chapter 4, which discusses what each scale measures from empirical, developmental, and theoretical perspectives, is largely *descriptive*. In contrast, Chapters 5 and 6 are *prescriptive,* offering suggested quantitative techniques for interpreting the McCarthy profile of scores. The latter two chapters proceed from the general to the specific (from global findings to the more precise areas of the child's integrities and deficits) to parallel the organization that ought to characterize the test results sections of case reports. Thus, Chapter 5 begins with an interpretation of the GCI, and then treats the Scale Index profile; Chapter 6 continues with an approach for interpreting fluctuations in the child's scores on the 18 tests.

The quantitative methods described in Chapters 5 and 6 are not merely descriptions of the obtained scores in terms of means, standard deviations, reliability coefficients, and the like; these topics are covered quite well in the Manual (McCarthy, 1972, pp. 24–43). Rather, our approach to interpretation is to build upon these basic topics, add common sense to psychometrics, and offer techniques that permit dynamic understanding of the child's profile of abilities. The qualitative test interpretation in Chapter 7 complements the empirical procedures and is a necessary ingredient for enabling the examiner to achieve the above goal.

# Chapter 4
## The Six Scales and What They Measure

Before interpreting a child's profile of scores in a test battery, the conscientious examiner should assume a challenging and inquisitive attitude regarding the meaning of each score. What specific skills are required for successful performance in each area? Do the obtained scores correspond to "real" abilities in the child? Is the meaning of the scores the same across the age range, or do important developmental changes occur?

To answer these questions about the McCarthy Scales, a few different approaches were taken. The specific skills assessed by the tests in each scale were enumerated in a logical fashion. The abilities assessed by similar tasks in the Stanford-Binet, WPPSI, and WISC-R (e.g., see Sattler, 1974) were used as guidelines for describing the major skills measured by McCarthy's tests, as were our clinical experiences with a variety of individually administered instruments. Guilford's (1967) structure of intellect model was also used to define each cognitive task in the battery, thereby providing an alternative means of analyzing the abilities required for success on each test.

The empirical results of factor analysis at several age levels offered a useful method for determining whether McCarthy's scales correspond to unitary abilities in the child, and for shedding light on the meaning of the Indexes at different age levels. The developmental issue was also approached by studying qualitative changes in the child's test performance across the age range. In analyzing developmental trends, five key ages were used as focal points: the average 3, 4, 5, 6, and 7 year old. Qualitative differences in test performance at these ages may be interpreted in terms of changes in the child's level of functioning as he get older, and changes in what the Indexes measure at various points in the age distribution.

Details about the structure of intellect analysis and factor analysis are presented below. Then each of the six scales is systematically discussed from the vantage points of the abilities it assesses (based on logical and empirical analyses) and the developmental changes across the age range.

### GUILFORD'S STRUCTURE OF INTELLECT APPROACH

Guilford's (1967) three-dimensional model may be used to assign a structure of intellect classification to any cognitive task. By way of summary, the three dimensions are presented below along with definitions of pertinent aspects of the model.

A. Operations: The intellectual processes.
   1. Cognition (C)—Immediate awareness, recognition, or comprehension of stimuli.
   2. Memory (M)—Retention of information in the same form in which it was stored.
   3. Evaluation (E)—Making judgments about information in terms of a known standard.
   4. Convergent production (N)—Responding to stimuli with the unique or "best" answer.
   5. Divergent production (D)—Responding to stimuli where the emphasis is on variety or quality of response (closely associated with creativity).
B. Contents: The type of information to be processed (the nature of the stimuli).
   1. Figural (F)—Shapes or concrete objects.
   2. Symbolic (S)—Numerals, or single letters, or any coded symbol.
   3. Semantic (M)—Words and ideas which have meaning.
   4. Behavioral (B)—Primarily nonverbal, involving human interactions with a stress on attitudes, needs, thoughts, etc.

C. Products: The way the information to be processed is organized. The products are arranged in a hierarchy, extending from Units (U), where the stimuli are perceived singly, to the more complex Classes (C), Relations (R), Systems (S), Transformations (T), and Implications (I).

Meeker (1969) has used Guilford's model as a means of interpreting Wechsler's tests and the Stanford-Binet, providing clinicians engaged in individual assessment with a valuable interpretive approach. Hence, the structure of intellect analysis of McCarthy's tasks presented in this chapter serves a dual function: to describe the abilities measured by the six scales, and to provide a basis for the Meeker-like interpretation of the McCarthy described on pp. 148-152.

Kaufman (1973a) analyzed the McCarthy tests in terms of Guilford's model, but his analysis was substantially modified for this book based on the important comments and suggestions made by Meeker (Personal communication, 1975). The structure of intellect classifications presented for each General Cognitive test in the sections that follow represent a synthesis of Kaufman's (1973a) original analysis and the analysis of McCarthy's tests conducted independently by Meeker and her staff at the S.O.I. Institute in El Segundo, Calif. (Meeker noted that some classifications of McCarthy tasks made by the S.O.I. Institute staff were not clear-cut, and were therefore subject to modification based on clinical judgment.) The explanations of the Guilford factors assessed by the McCarthy, which are presented for each cognitive scale, are based on Meeker's (1975) "Glossary for S.O.I. Definitions."

The Guilford analysis is excluded from the discussion of the Motor Scale because his model pertains to *intellectual* functioning. Guilford (1958) did develop another system for classifying psychomotor tests, but it is not particularly useful for the clinician. The interested reader should consult Kaufman's (1973a) article for a psychomotor analysis of McCarthy's gross and fine motor tests.

## FACTOR ANALYSIS

The factor analytic findings discussed in this chapter for each scale are based on a study by Kaufman (1975b). He divided the standardization sample into five age groups and analyzed the data for each group separately, using the technique of principal factor analysis. The five groups were as follows (sample size is shown in parentheses): $2\frac{1}{2}$ years (102), $3-3\frac{1}{2}$ years (204), $4-4\frac{1}{2}$ years (206), $5-5\frac{1}{2}$ years (206), and $6\frac{1}{2}-8\frac{1}{2}$ years (314).

The separate tests and part-tests were the variables studied, although tests that were too easy or too hard for certain age groups were eliminated from the appropriate analyses. The results of the analyses offer broad support for the six scales chosen by McCarthy, as factors corresponding to *each* scale emerged in at least two of the analyses. Memory, Motor, and Verbal factors were isolated for each of the five groups. At ages $5-5\frac{1}{2}$ and $6\frac{1}{2}-8\frac{1}{2}$, the Verbal factors were sufficiently large to warrant the dual name General Cognitive/Verbal; however, almost all of the highest loading tests were on the Verbal Scale, so these dual factors have been interpreted only as *Verbal* factors in this chapter.

To simplify discussion of the results, *average* factor loadings across the age range are used for each test, rather than separate loadings for each age group. In addition, although the part-tests (e.g., Verbal Memory I and Verbal Memory II) were generally included as *separate* variables in the analyses, only the *average* of the part-test loadings is discussed for the pertinent tests. This "summary" approach does *not* mask developmental trends in the data. The major age-related phenomena concerned the age at which a factor emerged for the first time (e.g., a Quantitative factor was not isolated until ages $5-5\frac{1}{2}$), not the make-up of the factors for different groups.

As will be apparent in the discussions of the factor analytic findings for each scale, the make-up of the factors corresponds closely to the actual composition of the scales themselves. The important implication of this finding is that each McCarthy Index reflects a child's functioning on a "real" and meaningful dimension.

### VERBAL SCALE

*Assesses the child's ability to understand and process verbal stimuli and to express his thoughts vocally.*

The tests constituting the Verbal Scale, and the major abilities assessed by each, are listed below.

3.  Pictorial Memory
    short-term memory (auditory and visual)
    early language development
    attention

4. Word Knowledge
   verbal concept formation
   early language development
   verbal expression (Part II)
7. Verbal Memory
   short-term memory (auditory)
   verbal comprehension
   attention
   concentration (Part II)
   verbal expression (Part II)
15. Verbal Fluency
   verbal concept formation
   logical classification
   creativity (divergent thinking)
   verbal expression
17. Opposite Analogies
   verbal concept formation
   early language development
   verbal reasoning

Short-term memory, language development, verbal concept formation, and vocal expression all enter into competent performance on the Verbal Scale. The creative child can exercise his skills on the Verbal Fluency test, although creativity does not facilitate success on the other (more structured) Verbal tasks.

The stimuli are primarily auditory, ranging from simple pictures and names of common objects (Pictorial Memory, Word Knowledge I) to an entire story read by the examiner (Verbal Memory II). The responses also span a considerable range. The child responds nonverbally to one picture vocabulary item, with the other responses forming a vocal hierarchy ranging from the repetition of the names of pictured objects (Pictorial Memory) to the more mature type of verbal expression required to define concrete and abstract words (Word Knowledge II).

### Structure of Intellect Analysis

The distribution of Guilford factors that underlie the Verbal Scale is evident from the following table. (Explanations of the Guilford factors assessed by the scale are presented beneath the table.)

| Verbal Test | Cogni-tion | Memory | Evalua-tion | Convergent Production | Divergent Production |
|---|---|---|---|---|---|
| 3.  Pictorial Memory | | MMU, MFU | | | |
| 4.  Word Knowledge | CMU | | | | |
| 7.  Verbal Memory | | | | | |
|    I | | MMU, MMS | | | |
|    II | | MMS | | | |
| 15. Verbal Fluency | | | | | DMU |
| 17. Opposite Analogies | CMR | | EMR | NMU, NMR | |

CMU    Vocabulary (Test 4)
CMR    Discovers relations in conceptual, abstract meanings (Test 17)
MMU    Reproduces previously presented ideas or words studied (Test 3; Test 7, Part I, items 1–4)
MFU    Recalls materials learned by visual and auditory presentation (Test 3)
MMS    Remembers order of materials or events presented auditorially (Test 7, Part I, items 5–6; Test 7, Part II)
EMR    Uses logical relationships in testing correctness of a conclusion (Test 17)
NMU    States correct names of concepts and ideas (Test 17)
NMR    Is able to correlate verbal ideas (Test 17)
DMU    Calls up many ideas in a specified class (Test 15)

The Verbal Scale measures *each* of the five mental operations posited by Guilford and includes *semantic* content in all items. As such, the scale provides a broad cognitive basis for assessing the child's skills in verbal comprehension and vocal expression.

### Factor Analytic Findings

Verbal factors emerged for all age groups; the tests with the highest average loadings on the five Verbal factors are shown below. (Tests included on the Verbal Scale are asterisked.)

| | |
|---|---|
| *Opposite Analogies | .54 |
| *Verbal Fluency | .54 |
| *Word Knowledge | .44 |
| *Verbal Memory | .41 |
| Conceptual Grouping | .41 |
| Number Questions | .37 |
| Numerical Memory | .36 |
| Counting & Sorting | .32 |
| *Pictorial Memory | .31 |

A close correspondence between the Verbal factors and the Verbal Scale is clearly evident. The four highest loading tests are included on the Verbal Scale, and Pictorial Memory (the remaining Verbal test) has a respectable average loading of .31. The substantial loadings by Conceptual Grouping and the Quantitative tests are sensible since success on these tasks requires good verbal facility.

### Developmental Trends

The Verbal Index is primarily a measure of early language development in the young child. Verbal comprehension and concrete abilities such as labeling simple objects are the requisite skills for success. With increasing age, the Index becomes more a measure of the maturity and quality of the child's verbal concepts and his facility in expressing his thoughts in words and phrases. By the time the child reaches school age, the ability to handle abstractions, such as defining the word "expert," also enters into the picture.

The 3 year old is extremely limited in verbal expression; most children of this age score 0 on Part II of Verbal Memory, name only one "thing" per category in Verbal Fluency, and are unable to define any of the words in Word Knowledge II. Dramatic improvement in verbal expression occurs between the ages of 3 and 4 years. The average 4 year old recalls some correct (but often unrelated) facts about the Verbal Memory story, gives partially correct definitions of four common concrete nouns, and names *twice* as many "things" in Verbal Fluency as the 3 year old. At age 5, a main developmental accomplishment is the increased ability to decenter, or to get more of an overview of a situation. Thus, the average 5 year old responds in an integrated fashion to the story in Verbal Memory II, recalling the basic "plot" (the wind blew a woman's letters, and a boy picked them up). He also has sufficient perspective to give thorough definitions to the same concrete words that the 4 year old defines incompletely. However, it is not until age 6, on the average, that the child has any real success with the less concrete words.

### PERCEPTUAL-PERFORMANCE SCALE

*Assesses the child's visual–motor coordination and nonverbal reasoning through his manipulation of concrete materials.*

The tests included in the Perceptual–Performance Scale, and the cognitive abilities they presumably assess, are presented below.

1. Block Building
   visual–motor coordination
   spatial relations
2. Puzzle Solving
   visual perception
   nonverbal reasoning
   visual–motor coordination
   spatial relations
6. Tapping Sequence
   short-term memory (primarily visual)
   visual–motor coordination
   attention
8. Right–Left Orientation (for ages 5 and above)
   spatial relations
   verbal concept formation
   nonverbal reasoning
   directionality
12. Draw-A-Design
   visual perception
   visual–motor coordination
   spatial relations
13. Draw-A-Child
   nonverbal concept formation
   visual–motor coordination
   body image
18. Conceptual Grouping
   logical classification
   nonverbal reasoning
   verbal concept formation

Visual–perceptual ability is extremely important for success on the tests in this scale, as is the ability to respond nonverbally to a variety of stimuli. (No speaking is required by the child for any Perceptual–Performance item.) Most tests require perceptual organization (nonverbal intelligence) and visual–motor abilities similar to the ones that characterize Wechsler's Performance Scale. However, unlike Wechsler's Performance tests, speed of responding is not a crucial element in determining the child's Perceptual–Performance Index; only Puzzle Solving includes timed items.

Conceptual Grouping and Right–Left Orientation broaden the dimensions of the Perceptual–Performance Scale by introducing new variables into the test situation. (Note, however, that Right–Left Orientation is only given to children aged 5 and above.) These two tests require multiple modality usage, where auditory–perceptual skills are as crucial as visual–perceptual abilities for successful performance. Manual expression is controlled so that motor coordination plays only a trivial role in the child's nonverbal responses to Conceptual Grouping and Right–Left Orientation items. Furthermore, each of these tests is more conceptual than perceptual, with one measuring the spatial concept of right versus left and the other assessing logical classification skills. The inclusion of these tests in the scale, along with Tapping Sequence, adds diversity to the scope of the nonverbal abilities that are reflected in the Perceptual–Performance Index.

### Structure of Intellect Analysis

The Guilford factors associated with the Perceptual–Performance Scale are presented below in tabular form to provide an overview of the structure of intellect abilities that are reflected in the child's Index. (Explanations of the Guilford factors appear beneath the table.)

| Perceptual–Performance Test | Cognition | Memory | Evaluation | Convergent Production |
|---|---|---|---|---|
| 1. Block Building | CFS | | | NFR |
| 2. Puzzle Solving | CFS, CFT | | EFR | |
| 6. Tapping Sequence | | MFS | | |
| 8. Right–Left Orientation | CFU, CFR, CMU | | | |
| 12. Draw-A-Design | | | | NFU |
| 13. Draw-A-Child | | | | NFS |
| 18. Conceptual Grouping | | | EMR | NFC |

CFS  Perceives spatial patterns and maintains orientation (Tests 1, 2)
CFT  Manipulates or transforms objects into another visual arrangement (Test 2)
CMU  Vocabulary (Test 8)
CFU  Is able to identify objects by name, visually and auditorially (Test 8)

*(Continued)*

CFR    Discovers relations in perceptual material (Test 8)
MFS    Recalls arrangement of objects previously presented (Test 6)
EFR    Evaluates figural relationships (Test 2)
EMR    Uses logical relationships in testing correctness of a conclusion (Test 18)
NFR    Deduces figural relationships (Test 1)
NFU    Comprehends and reproduces an observed bit of behavior (Test 12)
NFS    Reproduces a system of figural design (Test 13)
NFC    Sorts or classifies (Test 18)

Although primarily a measure of *convergent production* ability (especially for young children who are not given Right–Left Orientation), the Perceptual–Performance Scale is also represented by the operations of cognition, evaluation, and memory. The content is predominantly *figural,* befitting a scale that was designed to measure nonverbal skills within the visual–motor modality, and the products span a wide hierarchy ranging from units to transformations.

**Factor Analytic Findings**

Although a Perceptual–Performance factor failed to emerge at age $2\frac{1}{2}$, it did appear at ages $3$–$3\frac{1}{2}$ and at each successive age level. The Perceptual–Performance factors at ages $3$–$3\frac{1}{2}$ and $4$–$4\frac{1}{2}$ were each joined by a Drawing factor, suggesting that Draw-A-Design and Draw-A-Child have a unique component (perhaps fine motor coordination) for preschool children. The tests with the highest average loadings on the four emergent Perceptual–Performance factors are listed below. (Asterisks indicate tests included on the Perceptual–Performance Scale.)

| | |
|---|---|
| *Draw-A-Design | .44 |
| *Puzzle Solving | .42 |
| *Block Building | .41 |
| Counting & Sorting | .38 |
| *Draw-A-Child | .35 |
| *Conceptual Grouping | .30 |
| *Tapping Sequence | .27 |
| Verbal Fluency | .27 |

A close similarity between the theoretical ability underlying the Perceptual–Performance factors and the actual ability reflected in a child's Perceptual–Performance Index is apparent. Of the six tests having an average loading of .30 or more, only Counting & Sorting is not included on the Perceptual–Performance Scale. Yet its inclusion on the Perceptual–Performance factor is quite understandable since the child responds primarily via the nonverbal manipulation of cubes. The .27 loading by Tapping Sequence gives some empirical support for its inclusion on the Perceptual–Performance Scale, although there is no obvious explanation for the identical loading by Verbal Fluency.

Conceptual Grouping is among the six best measures of both the Verbal and Perceptual–Performance factors, suggesting the legitimacy of placing it on either scale. (Including it on both scales was not possible since McCarthy chose to keep the Verbal, Perceptual–Performance, and Quantitative Scales independent of content.) Its inclusion on the Perceptual–Performance Scale is certainly logically defensible since the child is not required to speak for any item, responding instead by manipulating a set of blocks. The same logic justifies the inclusion of Right–Left Orientation on the Perceptual–Performance Scale, although the factor analysis offers absolutely no empirical support for this placement.

### Developmental Trends

Some examiners are surprised by just how difficult many of the Perceptual–Performance tasks are for young children. The seemingly easy Carrot puzzle is not solved by the average child until the age of 5 years. This is also the age at which the child passes the first real sequence (item 2) in Tapping Sequence, earns more than 1 point on the *printed* designs in Draw-A-Design, and draws a reasonably complete child. The growth in the child's logical classification skills (Conceptual Grouping) reflects his ability to manipulate more variables with increasing age and to demonstrate some understanding of the principles of class intension and extension (Inhelder & Piaget, 1969) by age 6. That is to say, the average 4 year old can sort, keeping one variable in mind; the 5 year old can keep 2 or 3 variables in mind (find the "big round red" blocks); and the 6 year old can solve fairly complex classification problems. These developmental findings are consistent with Piaget's theoretical framework.

The Perceptual–Performance Index is largely a reflection of visual–motor coordination in the very young child. His fairly poor performance on the tasks requiring the most conceptual or reasoning ability (Puzzle Solving, Draw-A-Child, Conceptual Grouping) confirms the belief that the Index does not really tap his nonverbal thinking skills. With age, however, perceptual, spatial, and logical reasoning assume much greater importance in determining a child's Perceptual–Performance Index. The role of coordination, per se, becomes less important with age, and is really not a major factor (except on Draw-A-Design) in the overall performance of the *average* school-age child.

## QUANTITATIVE SCALE

*Assesses the child's facility in dealing with numbers and his understanding of quantitative concepts.*

The Quantitative tests are shown below along with the abilities required for success on each task.

    5.   Number Questions
          numerical reasoning
          computational skills
          number facts and concepts
          concentration
          verbal comprehension
  14.   Numerical Memory
          short-term memory (auditory)
          attention
          reversibility (Part II)
  16.   Counting & Sorting
          rote counting
          number concepts
          numerical reasoning

Counting ability, memory, and numerical reasoning are the essential skills needed for capable performance on the Quantitative Scale. Attention and concentration are also important ingredients for success, just as they are for Wechsler's Arithmetic and Digit Span tests. The numbers are kept simple (usually 1–9) and the mental operations are fairly basic to ensure that number *aptitude* rather than arithmetic *achievement* is assessed. Although the child responds vocally to most items, numerous questions in Counting & Sorting require either pointing or manipulation of blocks.

### Structure of Intellect Analysis

The Quantitative tests assess only two of Guilford's operations, Cognition and Memory, as shown in the following table. (Explanations of the Guilford factors are presented below the table.)

| Quantitative Tests | Cognition | Memory |
|---|---|---|
| 5. Number Questions | CMS | MSS, MSI |
| 14. Numerical Memory | | |
| I | | MSU |
| II | | MSS |
| 16. Counting & Sorting | CMU | MSS, MSI, MSC |

CMS   Comprehends or structures problems in preparation for solving them (Test 5)

CMU   Vocabulary (Test 16, items 8, 9)

MSS   Memory for a system of numerals (Test 5, items 1–3; Test 14, Part II; Test 16, items 1, 2, 5, 7–9)

MSI   Memory for well-practiced number operations (Test 5, items 4–12; Test 16, item 3)

MSU   Recalls for immediate production, after one presentation, a series of numerals (Test 14, Part I)

MSC   Memory for number operations needed to group objects (Test 16, items 4, 6)

Based on Guilford's structure of intellect model, the Quantitative Scale emerges as a measure of *symbolic memory*. Immediate recall of numerals and long-term memory of number operations are the skills essential for success. The fact that each test includes symbolic (numerical) content accords well with the scale's name. However, the limited measurement of mental operations indicates that the Quantitative Index is much more narrow in scope than either the Verbal or Perceptual–Performance Index.

### Factor Analytic Findings

Quantitative factors did not emerge for the preschool children; they occurred for the first time at ages 5–5½ and reappeared at ages 6½–8½. Below age 5, the numerical tasks tended to have their highest loadings on the General Cognitive and Verbal factors (Kaufman, 1975b). These results are similar to Thurstone and Thurstone's (1948) finding that the ability to work quickly and accurately with numbers is not distinct from other factors (e.g., verbal ability) in the young child, but emerges gradually in the school-age child.

The tasks with the highest average loadings on the two Quantitative factors are shown below. (Asterisks indicate the tests included on the Quantitative Scale.)

| | |
|---|---|
| *Counting & Sorting | .45 |
| *Number Questions | .38 |
| *Numerical Memory | .31 |
| Right–Left Orientation | .31 |
| Tapping Sequence | .29 |

Like the Verbal and Perceptual–Performance factors, the Quantitative factors correspond closely to the actual make-up of the scale they are presumed to represent. All three tests constituting the Quantitative Scale are among the very best measures of the Quantitative factors. The respectable loading by Tapping Sequence may reflect the fact that older children often use a *numerical* code to store the sequence of notes tapped by the examiner. However, the reason for the substantial loading by Right–Left Orientation is not clear.

### Developmental Trends

The average child who is younger than 5 years old cannot solve the most basic oral arithmetic problem in Number Questions and cannot pass the items in Counting & Sorting that involve the concept of 5. It is therefore not surprising that a quantitative factor failed to emerge for preschool children; numerical ability simply exists at a primitive level in the typical 3- or 4-year-old child. Even the ability to reverse two digits does not occur, on the average, until about age 6. Below age 5, the Quantitative Index does not measure a unitary ability, although success on all three tasks is closely related to *verbal* facility. For ages 5 and above, the Quantitative Index is appropriately named since it assesses the child's ability to reason numerically, understand quantitative concepts, and manipulate numbers.

### MEMORY SCALE

*Assesses the child's short-term memory across a wide range of visual and auditory stimuli.*

The tests constituting the Memory Scale (listed below) are also included on either the Verbal, Perceptual–Performance, or Quantitative Scale; therefore, the abilities assessed by each test have already been delineated above.

3. Pictorial Memory
6. Tapping Sequence
7. Verbal Memory
14. Numerical Memory

To succeed on the Memory Scale, the child must be able to attend closely to the various stimuli, retain them for a brief interval, and reproduce the stored information either vocally or manipulatively. Sequencing ability is important for all tasks *except* Pictorial Memory. For the Verbal Memory and Numerical Memory tests stimuli are presented orally, so good auditory perception is essential for success. Pictorial Memory involves simultaneous presentation of visual and auditory stimuli; attention to both types of cues seems to facilitate performance, although good auditory or visual perception can sometimes compensate for a deficiency in the other modality. Tapping Sequence also provides visual and auditory stimuli at the same time, but success on this task of immediate recall is primarily a function of *visual* memory. The nonmelodious sounds of the xylophone limit the value of the auditory feedback, and may even impede the child's performance on the task by distracting him. Only occasionally will a child attempt to focus primarily (or exclusively) on the auditory aspect of the stimulus.

The tasks in the Memory Scale tend to measure "Level I," or associative memory, abilities (to use Jensen's terminology), and to require responses at the "automatic" level (following the Illinois Test of Psycholinguistic Abilities clinical model). Numerical Memory II (Digits Backward) does not fit into these categorizations, however, because the child must perform the fairly complex operation of reversing the digits before he responds. In addition, Verbal Memory II (repeating a story read by the examiner) is not a prototype of a Level I or automatic task because the stimulus is too long to permit verbatim recall. The child is virtually forced to incorporate the stimulus into his own schemas to be able to respond with the essential ideas (concepts) of the story, since recall of the precise words (percepts) is an awesome task.

Overall, the Memory Scale provides extensive coverage of an important school-related ability that is often overlooked or deemphasized in conventional group and individual intelligence tests. The broad coverage pertains to receptive modality, content to be memorized, and mode of response. Since the content of a short-term memory task is an essential determinant of the child's performance, it is sensible for each Memory test to be included as well on either the Verbal, Perceptual–Performance, or Quantitative Scale.

### Structure of Intellect Analysis

The Guilford factors listed for each Memory task in the preceding sections of this chapter have one important thing in common: memory is the only mental process assessed by each test. The *content*, however, is extremely varied, with semantic, figural, and symbolic items all represented. Thus, from the point of view of the structure of intellect model, McCarthy has certainly realized her goal of measuring short-term memory across a wide variety of stimuli. Note that the Verbal, Perceptual–Performance, and Quantitative Scales are each unified by *content*, whereas Memory is unified by *operation*.

### Factor Analytic Findings

Clearcut Memory factors were isolated for all age levels in the 2½–8½-year-old range. The tests with the highest average loadings on the five Memory factors appear below. (Tests included on the Memory Scale are preceded by asterisks.)

|                     |      |
|---------------------|------|
| *Verbal Memory      | .41  |
| *Pictorial Memory   | .32  |
| Word Knowledge      | .32  |
| *Tapping Sequence   | .27  |
| Puzzle Solving      | .26  |
| *Numerical Memory   | .25  |

The close similarity of the Memory factors to McCarthy's Memory Scale is evident, as all four Memory tests are among the six highest loading tasks. The primary ability assessed is short-term memory, although the inclusion of Word Knowledge and Puzzle Solving in the above list suggests a long-term memory component as well. Both the Picture Vocabulary and Oral Vocabulary portions of Word Knowledge rely on recall of prior associations that the child has made, whereas Puzzle Solving performance is facilitated if the child can visualize (i.e., recall from his experience) an image of the animal or food to be assembled.

### Developmental Trends

The Memory Index measures the same general skill across the age range, although one important dimension does change with age. For very young children, the Index reflects primarily *automatic* level skills. The role of abilities at the *representational* level increases as the child starts to have some success in repeating sentences and a story (ages 4–5) and in reversing digits (age 6). By and large, there is consistency in the average child's *forward span* for digits, words, pictured objects, and musical notes. The average 3 year old has a span of 2; the 4 year old has a span of 3; the 5 and 6 year olds have spans of 3–4; and the 7 year old has a span of 4–5. (Tapping span is a mild exception to this rule below age 5, perhaps because of the motor aspect of the Tapping Sequence task.)

## MOTOR SCALE

*Assesses the child's gross and fine motor coordination.*

The tests included on the Motor Scale, and the motoric skills that each presumably assesses, are presented below.

9.  Leg Coordination
    gross motor coordination
    balance
10. Arm Coordination
    gross motor coordination
    precision of movement
11. Imitative Action
    gross motor coordination
    fine motor coordination
12. Draw-A-Design
    fine motor coordination
13. Draw-A-Child
    fine motor coordination

The Motor Scale includes both cognitive and noncognitive tests, providing fairly broad coverage of the gross and fine motor areas. Measurement of these coordination skills is better for preschool and kindergarten-age children than for school-age children because most gross motor tasks appropriate for assessing the abilities of older children would be impractical to administer in a small testing room. Nevertheless, even for the 6–8½ year olds, adequate measurement is possible in an area of functioning that is not tapped by conventional individually administered test batteries. Furthermore, the well-standardized motor tasks represent a great improvement over the barely normed motor tests that are currently available for young children.

Fine motor coordination is important for competent performance on the two drawing tests, in contrast to the gross motor coordination and general athletic ability needed for success on Arm Coordination. Leg Coordination and Imitative Action also require gross motor ability, with the latter task involving fine motor skills as well. However, unlike Arm Coordination, these tasks are more related to physical and developmental maturation than to athletic prowess or specific experience. As a whole, the Motor Index reflects the child's rate of physical development and, to some extent, his neurological integrity.

### Factor Analytic Findings

Motor factors were identified for each of the five age groups. These factors were "solid," showing much consistency across the age range. The tests having the highest average loadings on the five Motor factors (shown below) clearly identify these factors as noncognitive, with a great stress on gross motor coordination. (Tests included on the Motor Scale are asterisked.)

    *Arm Coordination    .55
    *Leg Coordination    .36
    *Imitative Action    .34
     Tapping Sequence    .25
    *Draw-A-Design       .21

The three gross motor tests belonging exclusively to the Motor Scale have by far the highest loadings on the above factors. Of the two fine motor tests that are shared with the cognitive scales, Draw-A-Design has the fifth highest loading but Draw-A-Child loaded negligibly. No empirical evidence is therefore offered to justify the inclusion of Draw-A-Child on the Motor Scale, perhaps because its scoring system minimizes the influence of coordination. The .25 loading by Tapping

Sequence suggests that the manual dexterity required to manipulate the mallet of the xylophone is one aspect of successful performance.

### Developmental Trends

Of the three gross motor tests, only Arm Coordination is sufficiently difficult to challenge the average child of 6 or above. In contrast, Leg Coordination is the only gross motor test of appropriate difficulty for children below 4 years of age. Hence, the nature of the measurement of gross motor coordination changes with age. For very young children, variability in gross motor performance is due primarily to differences in *balance* and coordination of the *lower* extremities; for the school-age child, variability is primarily a function of differences in *precision of movement* and coordination of the *upper* extremities.

A second developmental trend concerns the degree to which the Motor Index correlates with mental ability across the $2\frac{1}{2}$–$8\frac{1}{2}$-year-old range (McCarthy, 1972, pp. 36–39). At ages $2\frac{1}{2}$–$3\frac{1}{2}$, the Motor Index correlates .60 with the GCI, on the average, even after the influence of the two overlapping tests (Draw-A-Design and Draw-A-Child) is removed. This substantial and highly significant relationship is of the same order of magnitude as the intercorrelations among the Verbal, Perceptual–Performance, and Quantitative Scales.

At ages 4–$5\frac{1}{2}$, however, the corrected correlation between the Motor Index and GCI drops to an average of .27, revealing only a *slight* positive relationship between cognitive and gross motor abilities. At ages $6\frac{1}{2}$–$8\frac{1}{2}$, the average correlation is only .08, suggesting virtual independence between these skill areas. The latter correlation is undoubtedly depressed because of the relatively low reliability of the Motor Index for older children. Nevertheless, one conclusion is clear: the child's gross motor coordination develops in concert with his cognitive abilities at the preschool levels, but the development becomes considerably less synchronous at the kindergarten and school ages.

Sex differences should also be understood to interpret the Motor Index accurately, even though this topic is not very important for most of the McCarthy Scales. Boys and girls did not differ significantly on *any* of the six scales across the $2\frac{1}{2}$–$8\frac{1}{2}$-year-old range, including Motor (Kaufman & Kaufman, 1973b). Furthermore, only four of the separate tests yielded significant sex differences—Verbal

Memory I, Leg Coordination, and Draw-A-Child (all in favor of the girls), and Arm Coordination (in favor of the boys). Since the last three of these tests are all included on the Motor Scale, the importance of considering sex differences when interpreting the Motor Index becomes apparent.

The superiority of the boys on Arm Coordination counter-balances the girls' better performance on Leg Coordination and Draw-A-Child, accounting for the lack of significant sex differences on the Motor Index as a whole. Nevertheless, the fact that boys and girls achieve their Motor Index in different ways is especially pertinent when interpreting a child's relative strengths and weaknesses on the specific tasks (see Chapter 6).

The sex differences on Arm and Leg Coordination deserve comment. The boys' presumed greater experience in catching and throwing might account for their higher scores on Arm Coordination (a test likely to be influenced by prior training). Conversely, the girls' superiority on Leg Coordination probably reflects their more rapid maturation.

## GENERAL COGNITIVE SCALE

*Assesses the child's reasoning, concept formation, and memory when solving verbal and numerical problems and when manipulating concrete materials.*

The abilities measured by the 15 separate cognitive tests have already been listed by the Verbal, Perceptual–Performance, and Quantitative Scales. Some abilities are tapped by several tests and, hence, might be considered the major abilities assessed by the GCI. These skills are listed below with the number of tests assessing each ability shown in parentheses.

verbal concept formation (5)
visual–motor coordination (5)
short-term memory and attention (4)
spatial relations (4)
early language development (3)
verbal expression (3)
nonverbal reasoning (3)

The grouping together of 15 diverse tests to yield an overall index of cognitive functioning affirms McCarthy's belief that there is, in fact, a *g* that is related to successful performance on each task. The implication is that each child possesses a certain measurable amount of this general ability (reflected by his GCI) and applies it to each new problem solving situation. The GCI may be thought of as a kind of IQ, although it represents a far better estimate of the intellectual potential of preschool, kindergarten, and first-grade children than of youngsters at the upper end of the McCarthy age range (see Chapter 1).

It is important to remember that each test in the General Cognitive Scale is also included in one or two of the specific scales. McCarthy's clear message is that her tasks are psychologically complex and that general cognitive ability is but one of several crucial factors that determine a child's demonstrated level of performance on any task. Along this line, McCarthy (1972, p. 6) stated: "The child's GCI is of maximum usefulness when viewed in the context of his Indexes on the other 5 Scales. It is the child's *profile* of scores, rather than any one particular score, that indicates his overall behavioral and developmental maturity in the cognitive and motor domains, as well as his specific strengths and weaknesses." The importance of the implications of her approach for competent assessment of young and potentially learning disabled children cannot be overstated. Furthermore, by deemphasizing the role of the global GCI, the examiner will help avoid the misconceptions that have come to be associated with the term "IQ."

### Structure of Intellect Analysis

The Guilford factors thought to be assessed by each test in the General Cognitive Scale have already been delineated in previous sections of this chapter. To give a capsule overview of the composition of the GCI, we have prepared the following operation-by-content analysis of the 15 cognitive tests. (The "products" dimension was ignored for this analysis.) The percentage of tests assessing each type of ability—e.g., cognition of figural products, memory for semantic products—is indicated in the table.

Content (%)

| Operation | Semantic | Figural | Semantic & Figural | Symbolic | Total* |
|---|---|---|---|---|---|
| Cognition | 26.7 | 13.3 | 6.7 | — | 46.7 |
| Memory | 6.7 | 6.7 | 6.7 | 20.0 | 40.1 |
| Convergent production | 6.7 | 26.7 | — | — | 33.4 |
| Evaluation | 13.3 | 6.7 | — | — | 20.0 |
| Divergent production | 6.7 | — | — | — | 6.7 |

* The sum of the values in the "Total" column exceeds 100% because many of the 15 tests assess more than one operation and/or content.

The operations of cognition and memory are the predominant mental processes assessed by the General Cognitive Scale, although all of Guilford's operations are reflected in the child's GCI. Semantic, figural, and symbolic contents are spread throughout the scale, further attesting to the breadth of the GCI's measurement. The following abilities are assessed by the highest proportion of McCarthy's tests:

1. Cognition of semantic products (immediate awareness, recognition, or comprehension of words and ideas);
2. Convergent production of figural products (responding to shapes or concrete objects with the unique or "best" answer);
3. Memory for symbolic products (retention of numerals, a system of numerals, or well-practiced number operations).

### Factor Analytic Findings

Factors resembling the General Cognitive Scale were found at each age level except 4-4½. However, since general cognitive ability was not distinct from verbal ability for school-age children, it seemed preferable to interpret the large *unrotated* first factor extracted for each of the five groups as the best measure of general cognitive ability. Large unrotated factors are commonly used as estimates of *g* (e.g., Jensen, 1976; Kaufman, 1975a); in the case of the McCarthy, these unrotated factors are clearly the most objective choices for investigating the construct validity of the General Cognitive Scale.

The average loadings on the five unrotated factors are presented below for each of the 18 McCarthy tests. (Asterisks indicate tests included on the General Cognitive Scale.)

| | | | |
|---|---|---|---|
| *Word Knowledge | .69 | *Draw-A-Child | .55 |
| *Number Questions | .67 | *Puzzle Solving | .55 |
| *Opposite Analogies | .66 | *Tapping Sequence | .50 |
| *Verbal Fluency | .66 | *Block Building | .47 |
| *Conceptual Grouping | .63 | *Pictorial Memory | .43 |
| *Counting & Sorting | .58 | Leg Coordination | .42 |
| *Draw-A-Design | .58 | *Right–Left Orientation | .37 |
| *Numerical Memory | .56 | Imitative Action | .36 |
| *Verbal Memory | .56 | Arm Coordination | .36 |

The tests with the highest loadings are the General Cognitive tasks demanding conceptual and reasoning skills; the tests with the poorest loadings tend to be the gross motor tasks, which are excluded from the overall mental scale. The very best measures of general cognitive ability (loadings > .60) all involve verbal ability, with verbal concept formation required for success in four of the five tasks. Nevertheless, the Perceptual–Performance and Quantitative Scales, as well as the Verbal Scale, are represented in the top five tests.

If one arbitrarily chooses .50 as the cutoff point for determining whether a test's loading is satisfactory, then three General Cognitive tests "fail" the criterion: Block Building, Pictorial Memory, and Right–Left Orientation. However, the first two of these tests were included primarily for very young children and they functioned quite well at the early levels; Block Building loaded .58 and Pictorial Memory loaded .55 for children at ages 2½–3½. For Right–Left Orientation, which is only administered to youngsters age 5 and above, there is no adequate explanation for the poor loadings. Empirical findings do *not* support the placement of Right–Left Orientation on the General Cognitive Scale, just as they provide no evidence for its inclusion on the Perceptual–Performance Scale (see pp. 90–91).

### Developmental Trends

The developmental trends indicated in the sections on the Verbal, Perceptual–Performance, Quantitative, and Memory Scales are integrated below in an attempt to define qualitative differences in the functioning of the "typical" child of 3, 4, 5, 6, and 7 years of age.

Remember, these discussions focus on the *average* child at each age, not the bright or dull youngster.

## THE 3 YEAR OLD

The average 3 year old can label his environment quite adequately, but does poorly on tasks requiring reasoning or verbal expression. Thus, he has an excellent picture vocabulary but cannot define words presented orally (Word Knowledge), and he knows color, shape, and size but is unable to classify objects logically (Conceptual Grouping). Furthermore, he solves only one or two Opposite Analogies and names but one "thing" per category in Verbal Fluency.

His quantitative ability is limited to the numbers 1 and 2; he knows how many ears, heads, or noses he has, and he can take 2 blocks, but he does not understand the concept of "3." In the nonverbal sphere, his spatial and visual–motor skills are adequate for handling *simple* stimuli such as building a Tower or Chair, assembling two-piece puzzles, and copying a circle or lines drawn by the examiner. He cannot, however, cope with the more complex items in Block Building, Puzzle Solving, and Draw-A-Design, and he usually scores 0 on Draw-A-Child.

The 3 year old's short-term memory is characterized by the number "two." He is able to recall two of the six objects in Pictorial Memory, he has a forward span of two digits in Numerical Memory, he repeats two of the words in the three-word sequences of Verbal Memory, and he is unable to pass the three-note items in Tapping Sequence.

## THE 4 YEAR OLD

The chief developments over age 3 are the 4 year-old child's emerging conceptual and expressive abilities. Although his level of conceptualization is rather concrete, the 4 year old expresses his ideas with increasing facility. He gives partially correct responses to the first four words (common concrete nouns) of Word Knowledge II, recalls the main point of a story read to him, solves four verbal analogies, and classifies blocks logically so long as only one variable is manipulated.

Improved conceptual ability is also evident in the drawing tests as the child has some success on the first printed design ( ⌐ ) and draws a recognizable picture of a child that usually includes five major body parts (head, eyes, mouth, trunk, legs). He is able to build all four structures in Block Building, an impressive accomplishment; but his improvement in tests requiring abstract reasoning is less pronounced. For example, the 4 year old usually fails the three-piece puzzle (Carrot) and his quantitative skills are still poorly developed (he cannot solve the most elementary addition problem in Number Questions).

In general, the 4-year-old child has a short-term memory span of three; he recalls three objects in Pictorial Memory, repeats three digits in the forward series of Numerical Memory, and copies the three-word sequences in Verbal Memory. He cannot, however, imitate the three-note items in Tapping Sequence.

### THE 5 YEAR OLD

The key developments of the 5 year old, when compared to the child of 4, are increased *complexity* of mental operations and greater thoroughness in his responses. (In Piagetian terminology, the child has *decentered* to some degree.) However, the 5 year old's thinking is still concrete and he is unable to cope with the more abstract items in the battery. In Word Knowledge, the 5 year old gives complete definitions of four common concrete nouns (items 1–4 of Part II), but he has very little success with words that are even slightly abstract. Similarly, his performance on Conceptual Grouping reveals great advances—he can sort blocks even when two or three variables must be kept in mind at once—although he cannot figure out abstract rules of classification. Numerically, he makes great strides in Counting & Sorting (demonstrating knowledge of all skills except ordinal concepts), but his reasoning and computation abilities are inadequate to cope with all but the easiest problem in Number Questions. The 5 year old's relatively thorough and integrated approach to problem solving is illustrated in Draw-A-Child, where he includes all essential body parts, and in Verbal Memory II, where he recalls the basic "plot" of the story.

His short-term memory span ranges from three to four stimuli. He has a tapping span of three notes and a forward span of four digits; he also repeats a four-word sequence in Verbal Memory I and recalls three or four objects in Pictorial Memory.

### THE 6 YEAR OLD

The chief accomplishment of the 6-year-old child is the emergence of his ability to reason abstractly. He is able to generalize logical classification rules (items 7 and 8 of Conceptual Grouping) and he has some success defining the reasonably abstract words "factory" and "shrink." On Puzzle Solving, he often assembles the Pear correctly (a four-piece puzzle), which demands far greater reasoning skills than the two- or three-piece items. Quantitatively, he understands the abstract concepts of "second," "fourth," and "half," and his numerical reasoning skills have improved significantly (he can solve an oral problem involving 3 + 3).

The 6 year old's short-term memory span is essentially the same as the 5 year old's, with one important exception: he is able to reverse two digits. The advent of this skill in the 6 year old is related to the onset of Piaget's concept of reversibility. The rudimentary development of reversibility in the child about to enter the period of concrete operations facilitates his ability to conserve number, and it also allows him to reverse digits in the Numerical Memory task.

THE 7 YEAR OLD

Growth in the 7 year old's spectrum of abilities is most apparent in abstract reasoning skills. Although the 6 year old's development in this area is at a respectable level, it accelerates rapidly during the year between his sixth and seventh birthdays. At age 7, the child does quite well on the difficult six-piece puzzles in Puzzle Solving, has some success defining the abstract word "expert," names the impressive total of five words per category (for a total of 20 words) in Verbal Fluency, and solves seven of the nine Opposite Analogies. Improvement in his visual–motor coordination is also marked; for example, the 7 year old's reproductions of all Draw-A-Design items except the last one resemble the models fairly closely. Growth in numerical reasoning, a skill highly dependent on school learning, is considerably slower. The child of 7 can add and substract with small numbers, but experiences much difficulty with subtraction when large numbers are involved, and with multiplication and division.

The 7 year old has a forward span of five and a backward span of three in Numerical Memory, and he can copy a four-note sequence on the xylophone. This level of performance on the memory tasks involving *nonmeaningful* content reflects a substantial improvement over the level of the 6 year old, and is perhaps related to the 7 year old's improved ability to deal with abstractions. In any event, this degree of improvement was *not* noted in the 7 year old's memory of *meaningful* stimuli.

# Chapter 5

## Interpreting the GCI and the Scale Index Profile

### THE GENERAL COGNITIVE INDEX (GCI)

The GCI's mean and standard deviation of 100 and 16, respectively, are identical to the parameters of the Stanford-Binet IQ and similar to the values for the Wechsler IQs. The various numerical values that the GCI can assume are therefore immediately recognizable and have a built-in meaning to any experienced clinician. (For a discussion of why the GCI may be thought of as an IQ, see pp. 23–28.)

Like the IQ, the meaning of the GCI is more easily communicated to nonclinicians by translating the obtained score to a descriptive classification, a percentile rank, and an age equivalent. Each of these "translations" provides a more meaningful explanation of the child's level of functioning than does a standard score such as the GCI. In addition, to ensure that the child's precise GCI is not overinterpreted, it is desirable to surround it with a band of error of reasonable size. Each of these topics is treated below.

#### Descriptive Classifications

A table of General Cognitive ability levels, highly similar to the descriptive classifications used for the IQ by Terman and Merrill (1973) and Wechsler (1967, 1974), appears on page 25 of the

McCarthy Manual. The classifications are quite familiar (90–109 is Average; 110–119 is Bright Normal, etc.), and should be used to help translate the child's GCI into his *probable* level of ability. However, to use the categorizations for more than *descriptive* purposes would be improper interpretation of the obtained GCI, since actual classification of a child into a specific diagnostic category or educational program should *not* be based on a single score (see Chapter 8).

Therefore, we advocate a change in the names of the classifications currently used to correspond to GCIs or IQs of 69 or below (Mentally Retarded for the GCI, Mentally Defective for Binet IQ, and Mentally Deficient for the Wechsler IQ). No other descriptive classification corresponds to a *diagnostic* category; e.g., the term Very Superior is used rather than the diagnostic term Gifted. An unfortunate consequence of the use of a term like Mentally Deficient or Mentally Retarded to classify a child's IQ or GCI is that it may encourage the examiner to make a clinical decision on the basis of only one score. Since a measure of the child's adaptive behavior is also needed to properly classify a child as being mentally retarded, it is clearly inappropriate to perpetuate the use of a diagnostic category for describing an IQ or GCI. We believe that modifications should be made in the nomenclature of all category systems that include diagnostic classifications; Mercer's (1973) important finding that numerous black and chicano children with low IQs are *not* retarded in their adaptive behavior reinforces the validity of our position.

However, as important as it is for the IQ category systems to use classifications that are not diagnostic, it is even more important for a GCI classification system to exclude a label such as Mentally Retarded. First, McCarthy avoided the term IQ because of the misconceptions associated with it; for consistency, she should have avoided the closely related term Mentally Retarded. Second, research findings suggest that learning disabled children obtain GCIs that are an average of 15 points *below* their IQ (see p. 13). Hence, a number of children who score below 70 on the McCarthy may well obtain IQs in the Borderline or Dull Normal (Low Average) range on the Binet, WPPSI, or WISC-R. Labeling a child Mentally Retarded based on his GCI (without the corroboration of an adaptive behavior scale) may thus mislead a clinician and impel him to formulate an incorrect diagnosis.

We propose that the term *Cognitively Deficient* be used to classify GCIs of 69 and below. The term is not elegant, but it is difficult to find a name that is not already laden with emotional meaning. For example, the analog of Very Superior (Very Inferior) certainly will not do.

### Percentile Ranks

GCIs corresponding to selected percentile ranks ranging from the 1st (GCI = 63) to the 99th (GCI = 137) are presented in a table on page 26 of the McCarthy Manual. The examiner should consult this table (or Table 8-1 on p. 184 of this book) to determine the percentile rank corresponding to the child's obtained GCI. If his precise GCI does not appear in the table, use the percentile rank corresponding to the GCI closest in magnitude to his Index (or, for slightly greater accuracy, interpolate between the tabled values). For GCIs greater than 137 or less than 63, record the percentile ranks as "above the 99th" and "below the 1st," respectively.

A child's percentile rank translates directly into the percent of the group that falls below him. Whenever a percentile rank is used, it is important to define the reference group; for the GCI, the appropriate reference group is the child's *age-mates*. Some individuals who derive little meaning from standard scores or ability classifications relate easily to a statement such as: "Karen obtained a GCI of 113, surpassing the performance of 80 percent of the children her age."

### General Cognitive Age

Age norms are far less precise than standard scores or percentile ranks in a psychometric sense, but they sometimes provide the most effective way of communicating a test score to a parent or teacher. Primarily for this reason, McCarthy (1972, pp. 27, 206–207) developed a table for determining a child's mental age based on his chronological age and GCI. However, the mental ages in her table are derived from the MA/CA × 100 formula and span the range of $1\frac{1}{3}$–$12\frac{1}{2}$ years. Since the children in the standardization sample only spanned the $2\frac{1}{2}$–$8\frac{1}{2}$-year-old range, the extreme mental ages in her table represent extrapolation—the exact type of guesswork that McCarthy tried to avoid when she limited the GCIs to ±3 standard deviations from the mean.

Instead of McCarthy's table of mental ages, Table 5-1 is offered for determining the child's *General Cognitive Age*. The General

Cognitive Age is equivalent to a mental age, but has the advantage of being derived from the standardization data (rather than estimated from a formula). The principle underlying the General Cognitive Age is that the average composite raw score earned by 3 year olds on the General Cognitive Scale reflects typical 3-year-old functioning; the average composite raw score earned by 4 year olds reflects typical 4-year-old functioning; etc.

To develop Table 5-1, the average General Cognitive composite raw scores at each half-year between ages $2\frac{1}{2}$ and $8\frac{1}{2}$ were determined from the normative table on pages 152–201 of the Manual. (The average values are simply the composite raw score(s) corresponding to a GCI of 100 at each age.) These averages were set equal to General Cognitive Ages of $2\frac{1}{2}$, 3, $3\frac{1}{2}$, 4, etc. Then composite raw score values not assigned to any age were set equal to the most appropriate General Cognitive Age. Half-year intervals were used in the table,

**Table 5-1**
General Cognitive Age Equivalents of Composite Raw Scores

| Chronological Age: Less Than 5 | General Cognitive Age | Chronological Age: 5 and Above |
|---|---|---|
| 19–33 | $2\frac{1}{2}$ | 21–36 |
| 34–53 | 3 | 37–57 |
| 54–74 | $3\frac{1}{2}$ | 58–78 |
| 75–95 | 4 | 79–100 |
| 96–112 | $4\frac{1}{2}$ | 101–117 |
| 113–127 | 5 | 118–133 |
| 128–142 | $5\frac{1}{2}$ | 134–149 |
| 143–156 | 6 | 150–163 |
| 157–168 | $6\frac{1}{2}$ | 164–175 |
| 169–180 | 7 | 176–188 |
| 181–193 | $7\frac{1}{2}$ | 189–202 |
| 194–199 | 8 | 203–209 |
| 200–203 | $8\frac{1}{2}$ | 210–213 |

*Note.* Enter the table with the child's *composite raw score* on the General Cognitive Scale to determine his General Cognitive Age. Composite raw scores not included in the table correspond to General Cognitive Ages of either "below $2\frac{1}{2}$" or "above $8\frac{1}{2}$."

The age of 5 should be interpreted as 4 years, 10 months, 16 days for this table, just as it is in the Manual (McCarthy, 1972, p. 83). Right–Left Orientation is *not* administered to children younger than 4 years, 10 months, 16 days.

rather than quarter-years or age equivalents such as 5 years 11 months, to avoid giving the impression of a precision that is unwarranted by any age-norm technique.

To use Table 5-1, remember to enter with the child's *composite raw score* on the General Cognitive Scale (*not* his GCI) in order to determine his General Cognitive Age. Since Right–Left Orientation is only given to children aged 5 and above, separate columns are included in Table 5-1 to accommodate both preschool and school-age children. Note, however, that the General Cognitive Ages of *all* children, regardless of chronological age, can be determined from this single table. This includes children who are younger than $2\frac{1}{2}$ or older than $8\frac{1}{2}$—so long as their *mental ages* are within the $2\frac{1}{2}$–$8\frac{1}{2}$-year-old range. (For a practical application of the age equivalent method, see pp. 123–124 and the case of Elizabeth T. in Chapter 9.)

The fact that General Cognitive Ages cannot exceed $8\frac{1}{2}$ limits their usefulness for bright school-age children, just as the lower bound of $2\frac{1}{2}$ hinders their application to deficient preschoolers. As noted in Chapter 1, the McCarthy does not have an ample ceiling for above average school-age children; examiners who wish to explore the level of functioning of a child with a mental age greater than $8\frac{1}{2}$ are advised to use a different assessment tool. Similarly, children with a mental age below $2\frac{1}{2}$ (including older retarded children) should be tested on an infant scale if a precise age equivalent is desired. Extrapolation of age norms is simply a reckless adventure for a battery that provides less than ideal measurement at its extreme age levels.

Table 5-1 should be used routinely to determine a child's General Cognitive Age, and this information should be incorporated into the case report. A reader who is inexperienced with percentile ranks may have a common-sense understanding of what it means for a 7 year old to "perform as well as the average $4\frac{1}{2}$ year old on the mental ability tasks constituting the McCarthy." The General Cognitive Age also serves the practical function of providing a midpoint for interpreting a child's *relative* strengths and weaknesses on the 18 separate tests (see Chapter 6).

### Bands of Error

The GCI is rather reliable, with coefficients of .90–.96 (mean, .93) obtained for the 10 standardization age groups (McCarthy, 1972). It is also reasonably stable over time, as indicated on page 11 of this book. The standard error of measurement of the GCI is 4 points, which represents greater accuracy than the Stanford-Binet IQ at ages $2\frac{1}{2}$–$5\frac{1}{2}$, but less precision than the WPPSI Full Scale IQ (Sattler, 1974, pp. 431, 452).

Unlike the reliability or stability coefficient, the standard error of measurement is a *practical* statistic that indicates the band of error around the child's test score. With a standard error of measurement of 4 points, the chances are about 2 out of 3 that the child's obtained GCI is within 4 points of his *true* GCI, and chances are about 19 out of 20 that his obtained GCI is within 8 points (2 standard errors) of his true GCI. This information is extremely useful, and shows clearly that one should not place too much emphasis on the *specific* Index that the child obtains. However, a confidence interval of ±4 points (1 standard error) provides an inadequate band of error, while an interval of ±8 points offers more confidence than is needed in most practical situations.

By multiplying the standard error of measurement by different constants ($z$ values) it is possible to compute any confidence interval desired. Table 5-2 shows five confidence levels for the GCI: 68, 85, 90, 95, and 99 percent. These levels, which are the same ones used by Sattler (1974) for several intelligence tests, are provided for each of the 10 standardization age levels and for all ages combined.

*We feel that 85 percent is an appropriate level of confidence for most test purposes.* The examiner should routinely bound a child's GCI by the band of error to avoid overemphasis of the specific value obtained. Since the 85 percent confidence interval for the GCI corresponds to ±6 for 7 of the 10 standardization age groups (see Table 5-2), it is reasonable to use a band of error of ±6 points for all children in the $2\frac{1}{2}$–$8\frac{1}{2}$-year-old range.

The practical implications of the error that is built into all test scores, including reliable global indexes such as the IQ or GCI, should be understood thoroughly by all examiners. Consider the 5-year-old boy who obtains a GCI of 88. His Index classifies him as Dull Normal and ranks him at the 22nd percentile when compared to children his age; his overall performance is equal to that of the average $4\frac{1}{2}$ year old.

The chances are 85 out of 100 that his obtained Index is within 6 points of his true GCI (i.e., his true GCI is likely to be in the 82–94 range). Therefore, with 85 percent confidence, his true ability level may well be Average, not Dull Normal; he may surpass as few as 13

**Table 5-2**
Confidence Intervals for the General
Cognitive Index, by Age

| | Confidence Level (%) | | | | |
|---|---|---|---|---|---|
| Age | 68 | 85 | 90 | 95 | 99 |
| 2½ | ±4 | ±6 | ±7 | ±8 | ±11 |
| 3 | ±4 | ±6 | ±6 | ±7 | ±10 |
| 3½ | ±3 | ±5 | ±6 | ±7 | ±9 |
| 4 | ±5 | ±7 | ±8 | ±9 | ±12 |
| 4½ | ±4 | ±6 | ±6 | ±7 | ±10 |
| 5 | ±4 | ±6 | ±6 | ±8 | ±10 |
| 5½ | ±4 | ±6 | ±7 | ±8 | ±11 |
| 6½ | ±5 | ±7 | ±8 | ±10 | ±13 |
| 7½ | ±4 | ±6 | ±6 | ±8 | ±10 |
| 8½ | ±4 | ±6 | ±7 | ±9 | ±12 |
| All ages combined | ±4 | ±6 | ±7 | ±8 | ±11 |

percent or as many as 35 percent of his age-mates; and his General
Cognitive Age may range from 4 to 5 years. When more stringent
confidence intervals are used, the range of ability levels, percentile
ranks, and age equivalents widens even more dramatically. Whereas
including a band of error around the GCI in a case report is generally
desirable, the examiner's clear and thorough understanding of the
variability inherent in the GCI (and in other global scores such as the
IQ) is essential. The GCI gives a good approximation of the child's
true level of functioning: i.e., his *true* ability classification is almost
certainly within one category of his *obtained* classification. However,
overemphasis on his precise GCI (or ability classification, or
percentile rank, or age equivalent) constitutes misinterpretation of the
band of error and must be avoided.

It is, therefore, inappropriate to "pigeon-hole" a child on the
basis of his specific GCI. For example, placing a child with a GCI of
132 in a class for the gifted and keeping a child with a GCI of 128 in a
regular class is senseless. The probable GCI ranges for these two
children are 126–138 and 122–134, respectively, revealing considerable
overlap. In addition, the term Gifted is not synonymous with Very
Superior; the GCI (or IQ) should be one piece of evidence, along with

tests of creativity and other pertinent measures, for classifying children as Gifted. As indicated earlier (and expanded in Chapter 8), similar arguments apply to the diagnosis of mental retardation and other exceptionalities.

In addition to understanding the band of error and the need for supplementary testing, another way of keeping the GCI in its proper perspective is to consider it as but one of six Indexes yielded by the McCarthy. This attitude shifts the focus from the global to the specific—from an absolute level of performance to relative strengths and weaknesses. The next section discusses issues pertaining to interpretation of the Scale Index profile.

## THE SCALE INDEX

The Scale Index is a $T$ score having a mean of 50 and standard deviation of 10. The table of percentile ranks on page 26 of the McCarthy Manual facilitates understanding of the Scale Index by providing percentile ranks for GCIs *and* Scale Indexes. This information permits the examiner to relate selected Scale Index values to corresponding values of the GCI: e.g., a Scale Index of 43 is comparable to a GCI of 89 since each is equivalent to a percentile rank of 25. (Table 8-1 in this book also permits direct comparison of the GCI and the Scale Index.)

To further aid the examiner's task of relating the Scale Index to the GCI (with its more familiar mean of 100 and standard deviation of 16), Table 5-3 is presented. In this table, Scale Index values have been grouped to correspond to the well-known ability level classifications used for the GCI and IQ. The following thumbnail overview of Table 5-3 should be committed to memory by the examiner to provide a quick frame of reference for interpreting any Scale Index:

    70   Very Superior
    60   Bright Normal (High Average)
    50   Average
    40   Dull Normal (Low Average)
    30   Deficient

### Bands of Error

The Verbal Index is the most reliable (internally consistent) of the separate Indexes (mean $r$ = .88), followed by the Perceptual–Performance Index ($r$ = .84), Quantitative Index ($r$ = .81), Memory

**Table 5-3**
Ability Levels on the Verbal, Perceptual–Performance,
Quantitative, Memory, and Motor Scales

| Scale Index | Descriptive Classification | Percentile Range | Corresponding GCI Range |
|---|---|---|---|
| 69 and above | Very Superior | 97th and above | 130 and above |
| 63–68 | Superior | 90th–96th | 120–129 |
| 57–62 | Bright Normal (High Average) | 75th–89th | 110–119 |
| 44–56 | Average | 26th–74th | 90–109 |
| 38–43 | Dull Normal (Low Average) | 11th–25th | 80–89 |
| 32–37 | Borderline | 4th–10th | 70–79 |
| 31 and below | Deficient (cognitively or motorically) | 3rd and below | 69 and below |

Index ($r = .79$) and Motor Index ($r = .79$) (McCarthy, 1972, p. 31). Although the values for each Index across the age range fluctuate around the mean, few age trends are evident. The only trend of note involves the Motor Index, which is more reliable at ages $2\frac{1}{2}$–$5\frac{1}{2}$ ($r = .82$) than at ages $6\frac{1}{2}$–$8\frac{1}{2}$ ($r = .68$).

The average standard errors of measurement for all age groups are about 4 points for each of the five scales, ranging from 3.4 for Verbal to 4.7 for Motor. Using the same statistical technique described above for the GCI, confidence intervals at five levels of precision were computed for each specific scale (Table 5-4). The overall values of the intervals are *numerically* the same as the corresponding values for the GCI. Despite the numerical equivalence, the confidence intervals for the Scale Indexes reflect *less precision* than the same intervals for the GCI. For example, 4 points equals 40 percent of a standard deviation for the Scale Index ($SD = 10$), but only 25 percent of a standard deviation for the GCI ($SD = 16$).

The 85 percent level of confidence is reasonable to use for the Scale Indexes as well as for the GCI. For convenience, an interval of $\pm 6$ points may be considered characteristic of all five specific scales, although the examiner certainly has the option of using $\pm 5$ for Verbal and $\pm 7$ for Motor. For those who desire even greater precision, the various confidence intervals for the five scales may be computed

**Table 5-4**
Confidence Intervals for the Five Scale
Indexes (All Ages Combined)

| Scale | Confidence Level (%) | | | | |
| --- | --- | --- | --- | --- | --- |
| | 68 | 85 | 90 | 95 | 99 |
| Verbal | ±3 | ±5 | ±6 | ±7 | ±9 |
| Perceptual–<br>Performance | ±4 | ±6 | ±7 | ±8 | ±10 |
| Quantitative | ±4 | ±6 | ±7 | ±8 | ±11 |
| Memory | ±4 | +6 | ±7 | ±9 | ±12 |
| Motor | ±5 | ±7 | ±8 | ±9 | ±12 |
| Average | ±4 | ±6 | ±7 | ±8 | ±11 |

separately by age level using the reliability coefficients in the Manual and the statistical technique described by Sattler (1974, pp. 431).

The band of error around each Scale Index is considerable and precludes reaching definitive conclusions about a child's absolute level of functioning in any of the specific cognitive or motor areas. As an example, suppose a 3-year-old girl obtains a Memory Index of 57, which represents a Bright Normal level of functioning and ranks her at the 75th percentile for children her age. Her true Memory Index is likely to be in the 51–63 range (55th–90th percentile), which spans the categories of Average to Superior. This relative lack of precision in the child's obtained Indexes virtually demands that none of the Scale Indexes be treated in isolation. Instead, the most meaningful way to interpret the McCarthy is to evaluate the *profile* of Indexes and to focus on the overall picture that emerges by considering each Index in the context of the child's other abilities.

### Interpreting the Profile of Scale Indexes

Understanding the child's approximate level of ability (relative to his peers) in each of the five specific skill areas is useful; this evaluation is facilitated by Tables 5-3 and 5-4. However, the crux of profile interpretation is not based on any absolute comparison to the normative sample; it involves, instead, a consideration of the child's *relative* strengths and weaknesses. Comparisons are made in reference to the child's *own* level of performance, so he becomes, in effect, his own norm. The GCI adequately describes the child's level of functioning in a norms-referenced sense. Effective profile interpretation uses that level as a point of departure, and then seeks to determine the skill areas that are well developed or poorly developed in relation to the child's *overall* functioning. The fact that a dull child's relative strengths may not measure up to a bright child's relative weaknesses is irrelevant for profile analysis.

McCarthy (1972, p. 35) provides one table that may be used to determine a child's relative abilities on the five specific scales. It presents the size of the differences required for statistical significance (.05 level) when comparing a child's Indexes on any pair of scales. These differences range from about 10 to 13 points depending on the particular pair of Indexes. Values were not computed for three pairs (Verbal versus Memory, Quantitative versus Memory, Perceptual–Performance versus Motor) because of the substantial content overlap in each pair.

Ysseldyke and Samuel (1973) argued that McCarthy was wrong not to report values for the three pairs of overlapping scales, stating that the conventional formula is applicable to *all* possible pairs of Indexes. However, Ysseldyke and Samuel neglected to take into account that when a test is included on two scales, scores on that test do not contribute to the *difference* between the two Indexes. Consequently, they do not contribute to the *reliability* of that difference. To use the pertinent formula for overlapping scales, the standard errors of measurement of each scale must be based *only* on the nonoverlapping portions. McCarthy was aware of this problem and made the appropriate correction before computing the value for Perceptual–Performance versus Memory (which overlap slightly). However, the values reported by Ysseldyke and Samuel (1973) for the pairs of scales with overlapping content are incorrect and should not be used by the clinician.

The pairwise technique of profile interpretation has been commonly used with multiscore batteries such as Wechsler's scales. It is therefore natural for Ysseldyke and Samuel (1973) to propose this method for identifying diagnostic strengths and weaknesses on the McCarthy, and for McCarthy (1972) to promote this type of interpretation by providing a pertinent table. There are, however, several impractical aspects of the pairwise approach that cause even more difficulties than the overlapping content of some scales.

Comparing numerous pairs of scores is simply an unwieldy process. For the McCarthy, the examiner must systematically determine the significance of a number of different Index pairs; for the WISC-R or WPPSI, the number of subtest combinations is voluminous. When he is through, the examiner is left with a series of statements about the child's abilities (in the form "A less than B," "C greater than D," etc.) that would challenge the transitive reasoning ability of a skilled logician. An *overview* of the child's relative strengths and weaknesses is thus not easily obtained.

A common misuse of the pairwise technique is for the examiner to compare the significance of only the extreme Indexes or scaled scores. When the pairs are not chosen systematically (or randomly), but are selected because they are extreme, the role that chance errors play increases greatly and there is danger of overinterpretation.

A different technique for determining relative strengths and weaknesses is needed, one without the pitfalls of the pairwise approach. Such a procedure is available by making use of one of F. B. Davis' (1959) valuable formulas for interpreting differences among averages and separate test scores. Based on equation (1) in Davis' article, it is possible to determine significant strengths and weaknesses *relative to the child's own mean Scale Index*. The values presented in Table 5-5 were computed for each scale using data from the standardization sample. Each value equals the difference required for statistical significance when comparing a child's Index on one scale with his average Index on all five scales. (For technical details of Davis' approach, see his 1959 article along with Kaufman's, 1975a, note applying the formula to the McCarthy.)

Overall, differences of about 7–8 points from the child's own mean are significant at the .05 level, with differences of about 9–10 points significant at the .01 level. For most practical purposes, the 5 percent significance level offers an ample degree of confidence when interpreting a child's profile. Although the precise values shown in Table 5-5 for each age may be used, the examiner should feel free to use the following rule of thumb to determine significant strengths and weaknesses at the 5 percent level:

Differences of ±7 points from the child's mean are significant for Verbal, Perceptual–Performance, and Quantitative Indexes.

Differences of ±8 points are significant for Memory and Motor Indexes.

**Table 5-5**
Differences Required for Significance When Comparing a Child's Index on One Scale with His Average Index on All Five Scales

| Age | Verbal | | Perceptual-Performance | | Quantitative | | Memory | | Motor | |
|---|---|---|---|---|---|---|---|---|---|---|
| | 5% Level | 1% Level | 5% Level | 1% Level | 5% Level | 1% Level | 5% Level | 1% Level | 5% Level | 1% Level |
| 2½ | 6.2 | 8.1 | 8.2 | 10.8 | 8.4 | 11.0 | 8.0 | 10.5 | 7.2 | 9.4 |
| 3 | 6.0 | 8.0 | 6.6 | 8.6 | 7.3 | 9.6 | 8.4 | 11.0 | 7.3 | 9.6 |
| 3½ | 5.4 | 7.1 | 5.9 | 7.7 | 7.2 | 9.4 | 7.0 | 9.3 | 7.0 | 9.3 |
| 4 | 6.1 | 8.0 | 6.6 | 8.7 | 8.9 | 11.7 | 7.1 | 9.3 | 7.9 | 10.4 |
| 4½ | 6.4 | 8.5 | 6.2 | 8.2 | 7.9 | 10.4 | 8.4 | 11.1 | 7.2 | 9.5 |
| 5 | 6.5 | 8.6 | 6.6 | 8.8 | 6.6 | 8.8 | 8.3 | 10.9 | 7.4 | 9.8 |
| 5½ | 6.5 | 8.5 | 7.0 | 9.2 | 6.7 | 8.8 | 8.9 | 11.7 | 7.8 | 10.2 |
| 6½ | 7.1 | 9.4 | 8.2 | 10.7 | 7.6 | 10.0 | 7.3 | 9.6 | 9.2 | 12.2 |
| 7½ | 6.2 | 8.2 | 7.2 | 9.5 | 7.2 | 9.5 | 7.1 | 9.3 | 8.6 | 11.3 |
| 8½ | 7.0 | 9.2 | 8.7 | 11.4 | 7.6 | 10.0 | 7.7 | 10.2 | 10.3 | 13.5 |
| All ages combined | 6.4 | 8.4 | 7.1 | 9.4 | 7.5 | 9.9 | 7.8 | 10.3 | 8.0 | 10.5 |

The steps to follow to determine a child's relative strengths and weaknesses are simple, straightforward, and objective.

*Step 1.*   Compute the *mean* of the child's five Scale Indexes. (If one or two of the Indexes are "below 22," or "above 78," compute the *median* Index.)

*Step 2.*   Take each of the scales in turn to see if the child's Index is significantly above or below his mean Index. Use either the specific values shown in Table 5-5 or the rule of thumb indicated above.

*Step 3.*   Indexes significantly above the child's mean reflect *relative strengths,* whereas Indexes significantly below reflect *relative weaknesses.* These should be labeled "S" and "W," respectively.

*Step 4.*   Interpret all other discrepancies from the mean as *chance fluctuations.*

This technique provides an overview of the child's abilities by using his own average level of performance as the "pivot" point. The use of empirical criteria ensures that *real* deviations will be interpreted, but that *apparent* peaks and valleys will be ignored. In addition, it is all right to average the five Indexes despite the overlap in content between some pairs of scales. Whereas the overlap presents interpretive problems with the pairwise method, no such problem arises when using F. B. Davis' techniques. According to F. B. Davis (Personal communication, 1974), the overlapping errors of measurement are properly taken into account in his formula.

We recommend that this procedure for interpreting a child's profile of abilities be applied routinely when the McCarthy is given, just as Sattler's (1974) application of Davis' formulas to Wechsler's tests should be used whenever a clinician interprets a profile of WPPSI or WISC-R scores.

*Example.*   Jill, a 6 year old, obtained the following composite raw scores and Indexes on the McCarthy:

| Scale | Composite Raw Score | Scale Index |
|---|---|---|
| Verbal | 78 | 57 |
| Perceptual–Performance | 44 | 36 (W) |
| Quantitative | 30 | 50 |
| General Cognitive | 152 | 97 |
| Memory | 46 | 60 (S) |
| Motor | 50 | 53 |

The average of Jill's five Scale Indexes is 51.2 (the GCI does not enter into this analysis). Her Perceptual–Performance Index is significantly (7 points or more) below her own mean, indicating weakness in her non-verbal skills. However, Jill has a relative strength in short-term memory since her Memory Index of 61 is significantly (8 points or more) above her average Index. The apparent peak in Jill's profile created by her Verbal Index of 57 should be ignored and considered a chance deviation from her own average.

Some examiners may only be interested in determining the child's *cognitive* strengths and weaknesses and may wish to exclude the Motor Index from the computations. We do not encourage this practice: nevertheless, the differences required for significance when comparing a child's cognitive Index on one scale to his average cognitive Index are shown below for the entire standardization sample. (The child's average cognitive Index equals the mean of his Verbal, Perceptual–Performance, Quantitative, and Memory Indexes.)

|          | Verbal | Perceptual–Performance | Quantitative | Memory |
|----------|--------|------------------------|--------------|--------|
| .05 level | 5.7    | 6.4                    | 6.8          | 7.0    |
| .01 level | 7.5    | 8.4                    | 8.9          | 9.3    |

### Communicating the Level of a Strength or Weakness

A child's strengths and weaknesses may be extreme (e.g., $\pm 20$ points from his mean) or they may barely reach statistical significance. It is important to communicate the *level* of a strength or weakness since this information provides a more complete picture of the child's profile. In the preceding example, merely stating that the child obtained a Memory Index of 61 and a Perceptual–Performance Index of 36 does not adequately communicate the levels of her strength and weakness. As indicated above, the $T$ scores that are used to define the Scale Indexes are not commonly understood.

Communicating strengths and weaknesses can be done effectively by using the ability categories in Table 5-3 and/or percentile ranks. The case report for Jill (in the above example) might have included the following statements: "Jill evidenced a relative strength on the Memory Scale and a relative weakness on the Perceptual–Performance Scale. That is to say, she displayed a High Average short-term memory (85th percentile), but achieved only a Borderline level in her nonverbal skills (8th percentile)."

Another useful means of describing the child's strengths and weaknesses is with *age equivalents*. Table 5-6 presents Scale Ages corresponding to composite raw scores on the five specific scales. (This table was developed in the same manner as Table 5-1, which provides General Cognitive Ages; see pp. 109–111 for an explanation.) In the above example, Jill's composite raw scores on the Memory and Perceptual–Performance Scales correspond to Scale Ages of 7½ and 5, respectively. Thus, an alternate way of explaining Jill's strength and weakness would be to contrast her 7½-year-old level in short-term memory tasks with her 5-year-old nonverbal abilities.

The age equivalent technique has the advantage of being universally understood. Despite the problems associated with age norms

**Table 5-6**
Scale Age Equivalents of Composite Raw Scores on the
Five Specific Scales

| Scale Age | Verbal | Perceptual–Performance Chron. Age: Less Than 5 | Perceptual–Performance Chron. Age: 5 and Above | Quantitative | Memory | Motor |
|---|---|---|---|---|---|---|
| 2½ | 11–16 | 7–11 | 9–14 | 3–5 | 4–7 | 7–11 |
| 3 | 17–27 | 12–17 | 15–21 | 6–9 | 8–12 | 12–16 |
| 3½ | 28–38 | 18–23 | 22–28 | 10–13 | 13–18 | 17–23 |
| 4 | 39–47 | 24–30 | 29–35 | 14–17 | 19–24 | 24–30 |
| 4½ | 48–55 | 31–37 | 36–43 | 18–20 | 25–28 | 31–36 |
| 5 | 56–62 | 38–43 | 44–49 | 21–23 | 29–32 | 37–41 |
| 5½ | 63–67 | 44–48 | 50–55 | 24–27 | 33–36 | 42–45 |
| 6 | 68–72 | 49–53 | 56–60 | 28–31 | 37–40 | 46–49 |
| 6½ | 73–77 | 54–57 | 61–64 | 32–34 | 41–43 | 50–54 |
| 7 | 78–81 | 58–60 | 65–68 | 35–38 | 44–45 | 55–58 |
| 7½ | 82–85 | 61–63 | 69–72 | 39–41 | 46–47 | 59–61 |
| 8 | 86–88 | 64–65 | 73–75 | 42–44 | 48–49 | 62–64 |
| 8½ | 89–91 | 66–67 | 76–77 | 45–47 | 50–51 | 65–67 |

*Note.* Composite raw scores not included in the table correspond to Scale Ages of either "below 2½" or "above 8½."

The age of 5 should be interpreted as 4 years, 10 months, 16 days when determining a child's Perceptual–Performance Age. See the note to Table 5-1 for explanation.

*Caution:* Enter the table with **composite raw scores**, not Scale Indexes.

(see pp. 128-131), Scale Ages will often help highlight the level of a child's significant strengths and weaknesses when other approaches do not communicate. In psychoeducational diagnosis, particularly, the test results are often intended for teachers whose experience with preschool and primary-grade children may render age norms more meaningful than other statistics.

Regardless of which method the examiner selects to communicate a child's strengths and weaknesses, he should exercise one caution. It is best not to include in a report the age equivalent, percentile rank, or ability level for Scale Indexes that do *not* deviate significantly from the child's own mean. The inclusion of many numbers in a case report often clutters, rather than clarifies, the interpretation. In addition, the reader may be misled into believing that a nonsignificant deviation is meaningful. In the above example, the child's Verbal Index was *not* significantly higher than her average Index. However, if all of her scores are translated into percentile ranks, her Verbal Index (75th percentile) might give the erroneous impression of being considerably higher than her GCI (42nd percentile).

### The Use of Scale Ages for Retarded and Gifted Children

The Scale Ages in Table 5-6 are useful for more purposes than communicating strengths and weaknesses. They also enable the examiner to interpret the profiles of retarded children who score "below 22" on most or all scales, and of gifted youngsters who score "above 78." An examiner who uses Table 5-6 in conjunction with Table 5-1 (General Cognitive Ages) is able to determine an extremely retarded or gifted child's level on each of the six scales, thereby salvaging a differential test profile for a low- or high-scoring youngster.

If two 7 year olds obtain GCIs "below 50" and five Scale Indexes "below 22," they appear to be equally deficient and to have no relative strengths or weaknesses. However, one may be functioning at a 3-year-old level and the other at a 4½-year-old level; this information can be determined from Table 5-1. Furthermore, the child with a General Cognitive Age of 3 may have a Verbal Age of 2½ and a Perceptual–Performance Age of 5, whereas the other retarded youngster may perform at a 4-4½-year-old level on all five scales. The latter analysis is made possible by Table 5-6.

One of the limitations of the McCarthy is the fact that the Indexes range only 3 standard deviations from the mean; the Scale Age technique provides a partial solution to this problem. However, a differential Scale Age profile can only be obtained for extremely retarded children age 5 years and above, and for highly gifted children below 5 years of age. (The McCarthy does not have enough "bottom" for very retarded young children, or enough "top" for older gifted youngsters.) In addition, age norms are far less efficient psychometrically than standard score norms (see Thorndike & Hagen, 1977, chap. 4). *Consequently, a Scale Age profile cannot substitute for a Scale Index profile without a loss of precision.*

Nevertheless, the information yielded by Scale Indexes is extremely valuable for understanding the strengths and weaknesses of children who score below or above the norms, as illustrated by the case study of Elizabeth T. in Chapter 9. The alternative is a profile of indeterminate Indexes, which tends to frustrate an examiner, particularly one who routinely tests retarded children. As a rule, a child's Scale Age profile should be interpreted when he obtains *three or more* Indexes "below 22" or "above 78." If only one or two Indexes fall outside the 22–78 range, then interpretations of strengths and weaknesses should be based on the Scale Index profile. (As indicated on page 120, use the median rather than the mean Index as the child's average level of performance.) Although Indexes may be computed only for children in the 2½–8½-year-old range, composite raw scores on the six scales may be computed for *any* individual, regardless of age. *Consequently, the Scale Age interpretive technique may be used for retarded children older than 8½ so long as their mental ages fall somewhere within the 2½–8½ year-old range.* The technique may be used as well for very bright children below age 2½ who reach the ceiling of an infant scale. Tables 5-1 and 5-6 thus extend the usefulness of the McCarthy for extreme populations by easing the chronological age limitations.

### Evaluating the Scatter in a Profile

For years, clinicians have been interpreting the amount of "scatter" (intertest variability) in an individual's profile of scaled scores on a Wechsler battery. A common stereotype has persisted that normal children have "flat" profiles. Consequently, diagnostic significance has traditionally been attached to profiles exhibiting much scatter (e.g., Clements, 1966), despite the unavailability of data on "normal scatter." When a study finally was conducted with the WISC-R (Kaufman, 1976b), the results indicated that normal children exhibit *considerable* scatter in their profiles—probably much more than many examiners realized. One important implication of these findings for diagnosis of an exceptionality is apparent: the variability in a child's profile should be compared to a *basal* (normal) level of scatter before concluding that it is abnormal.

To help ensure that clinicians interpret scatter on the McCarthy with appropriate caution, Kaufman (1976a) examined the amount of variability in the Scale Index profiles of normal children. As with the WISC-R, considerable interscale variability proved to be the norm. The average child in the $2\frac{1}{2}$-$8\frac{1}{2}$-year-old range had a difference of 14.4 points ($SD = 6.0$) between his highest and lowest Scale Index. Even a range of 20 points on the five specific scales (e.g., 40–60, 35–55) may be considered normal. The inclusion of the Motor Index in the computations does not account for the sizable fluctuations in the average child's Index profile. The mean difference between the child's highest and lowest *cognitive* Index (excluding Motor) was still a very substantial 11.9 ($SD = 5.4$) for the standardization sample.

Slight fluctuations in the mean Scale Index ranges (both with and without the Motor Index) were evident across the age range, but no developmental trends were observed. Consequently, one set of norms for evaluating scatter has been provided (Table 5-7), based on data for the entire sample of $2\frac{1}{2}$-$8\frac{1}{2}$-year olds. Table 5-7 was developed by defining normal scatter as the mean Index range $\pm 1$ standard deviation, with the two extremes defined as "flat profile" and "marked

**Table 5-7**
Norms for Determining the Amount of Scatter in a
Child's Profile of Scale Indexes

| Amount of Scatter | Difference Between the Child's Highest and Lowest Scale Indexes | |
| --- | --- | --- |
| | All 5 Scales | 4 Cognitive Scales (Excluding Motor) |
| Marked Scatter | 21+ | 18+ |
| Normal Scatter | 8–20 | 6–17 |
| Flat Profile | 0–7 | 0–5 |

scatter," respectively. To evaluate the amount of scatter in a child's profile, subtract his lowest Scale Index from his highest one. Then consult Table 5-7 to determine whether the fluctuations in his profile are unusual when compared to the amount of scatter in the profiles of normal children. The examiner may evaluate the scatter among all five Scale Indexes, or among the four cognitive Indexes, depending upon his preference or purpose.

Another method for determining the amount of scatter in a child's mental and motor profile is to consider the significant strengths and weaknesses relative to his own mean. In the standardization sample, 38 percent had no significant deviations ($p < .05$) from the mean of his five Scale Indexes, 30 percent had one significant deviation, 23 percent had two, and only 9 percent had three or more (Kaufman, 1976a). Therefore, a child who exhibits 0, 1, or 2 relative strengths and/or weaknesses is evidencing normal scatter. *Three or more Indexes must deviate significantly from a child's own mean to constitute marked scatter.*

Both of these methods for evaluating scatter are equally acceptable. If a profile reaches *either* criterion of marked scatter, then it is reasonable to conclude that the child has an unusual amount of variability in his spectrum of abilities.

The fact that normal children exhibit a good deal of scatter in their profiles does not minimize the importance of understanding each child's relative strengths and weaknesses. Only by gaining a complete overview of the child's integrities and areas of deficit is it possible to make appropriate educational recommendations (see Chapter 8). However, *diagnosis* of an exceptionality must be performed with extreme caution. The child's Index profile should be evaluated empirically to see if there is marked scatter. If the child exhibits marked fluctuations in his ability profile (i.e., an amount of scatter that is not usually found in normal children), only then should the interscale variability be used as evidence for a possible exceptionality. *Apparent* scatter (i.e., normal variability that may *seem* like considerable scatter) has educational but *not* diagnostic implications.

# Chapter 6
## Interpreting Specific Areas of Strength and Weakness

Determining the child's relative strengths and weaknesses on the five scales is only the beginning of McCarthy interpretation. Effective psychoeducational diagnosis demands more than an assessment of a child's global areas of integrity and deficiency. Adequate descriptions of his specific skills are necessary for the test information to be maximally useful.

The fact that a child may have a relative strength on the Perceptual–Performance Scale and a relative weakness on the Memory Scale provides an important starting point for understanding the make-up of his ability spectrum; but are his Perceptual–Performance abilities equally well developed on spatial and conceptual tasks? Is his short-term memory just as weak when dealing with meaningful stimuli as when recalling nonmeaningful stimuli? Is his average Verbal Index (relative to his own mean) really just the midpoint of his exceptional verbal concept formation and inadequate auditory memory? These and similar questions should be raised by any clinician who desires a meaningful overview of a child's specific skills. The purpose of this chapter is to provide a systematic method of obtaining such an overview.

CONVERTING TEST SCORES TO
A COMMON UNIT

The weighted raw scores for all 18 tests are entered on the back of the child's record form as an intermediate step in the computation of his Indexes. However, these scores are not directly interpretable; they do not communicate the *level* of the child's performance, and they certainly are not comparable from test to test.

Table 17 in the Appendix of the McCarthy Manual presents means and standard deviations of raw scores on the 18 tests. This table facilitates test interpretation, but it is difficult to use. For example, the table includes means of the *unweighted* raw scores, whereas the back of the record form lists the *weighted* raw scores. Consequently, Table 6-1 (which is very similar to Table 3-1 in the chapter on prorating) was developed to enable the examiner to convert the weighted raw scores on the back of the record form to a common unit—the *test age*.

Before using Table 6-1, create a column labeled "Test Age" on the back of the record form, just to the left of the test names. Then enter Table 6-1 with the child's weighted raw score on each test, and determine its corresponding test age. Finally, enter each test age in the newly created column on the record form. (Note that separate test ages are obtained for each part of Verbal Memory and Numerical Memory.) Figure 6-1 on page 135 presents an illustration of what the back of a child's record form should look like after following this procedure.

Obtaining test ages in the above manner is an easy process. Even though a number of other conversion techniques are preferable to age norms for *psychometric* reasons (see Thorndike & Hagen, 1977, chap. 4), they tend to be impractical. For example, the test scores could have been converted to standard score units such as stanines. However, that would have necessitated the development of a different conversion table for each age, and it would have increased the examiner's clerical work. The test age method has several *practical* advantages: (1) a single table is applicable for all children in the McCarthy age range; (2) the technique may be used to assess the relative strengths and weaknesses of retarded children who are older than 8½ years of age (see pp. 123–124); and (3) age equivalents communicate meaning to virtually anyone reading a case report, and they are commonly used in both school and clinical settings.

**Table 6-1**

Test Age Equivalents of *Weighted* Raw Scores on the McCarthy Tests

| Test | 2½ | 3 | 3½ | 4 | 4½ | 5 | 5½ | 6 | 6½ | 7 | 7½ | 8 | 8½ |
|---|---|---|---|---|---|---|---|---|---|---|---|---|---|
| 1. Block Building | 4-5 | 6 | 7 | 8 | — | 9 | — | 10 | — | — | — | — | — |
| 2. Puzzle Solving | 0 | 1 | 2 | 3 | 4 | 5 | 6 | 7 | 8 | — | 9 | 10 | 11 |
| 3. Pictorial Memory | 1 | — | 2 | — | 3 | — | — | 4 | — | — | — | — | 5 | — |
| 4. Word Knowledge (I + II) | 7-8 | 9-10 | 11 | 12-13 | 14-15 | 16 | 17 | 18 | 19 | 20 | 21 | 22 | 23 |
| 5. Number Questions | 2 | 4 | — | 6 | — | 8 | — | 10 | 12 | 14 | 16 | 18 | 20 |
| 6. Tapping Sequence | 1 | — | 2 | — | 3 | — | 4 | — | — | 5 | — | — | 6 |
| 7. Verbal Memory | | | | | | | | | | | | | |
|     Part I | 2-3 | 4-5 | 6-7 | 8-9 | 10 | 11 | 12 | — | — | 13 | — | — | 14 |
|     Part II | 0 | 1 | 2 | 3 | 4 | 5 | 6 | 7 | 7 | 8 | 8 | — | 9 |
| 8. Right–Left Orientation | 2 | 3 | 4 | 5 | — | 6 | — | 7 | — | 8 | — | 9 | 10 |
| 9. Leg Coordination | 3-4 | 5-6 | 7-8 | 9 | 10 | 11 | — | 12 | — | — | — | — | — |
| 10. Arm Coordination (I+II+III) | 1 | 2-3 | 4 | 5-6 | 7 | 8 | 9-10 | 11-12 | 13-14 | 15-16 | 17 | 18 | 19 |
| 11. Imitative Action | 2 | — | 3 | 4 | — | 4 | | | | | | | |
| 12. Draw-A-Design | 1 | 2 | 3 | 4 | 5-6 | 7 | 8 | 9-10 | 11 | 12 | 13 | 14 | 15 |
| 13. Draw-A-Child | 0 | 1 | 2-3 | 4-6 | 7-8 | 9 | 10 | 11 | — | 12 | 13 | 14 | 15 |
| 14. Numerical Memory | | | | | | | | | | | | | |
|     Part I | 2 | 3 | 4 | — | 5 | — | 6 | — | 7 | — | 8 | — | 9 |
|     Part II | — | — | 0 | — | — | 2 | — | 4 | — | 6 | — | 8 | — |
| 15. Verbal Fluency | 2-3 | 4-5 | 6-7 | 8-9 | 10-11 | 12-13 | 14-15 | 16-17 | 18-19 | 20 | 21-22 | 23 | 24 |
| 16. Counting & Sorting | 1 | 2 | 3 | 4 | 5 | 6 | 7 | — | 8 | — | 9 | — | — |
| 17. Opposite Analogies | 0 | 2 | 4 | 6 | 8 | — | 10 | — | 12 | — | 14 | — | 16 |
| 18. Conceptual Grouping | 1-2 | 3 | 4 | 5 | 6 | 7 | 8 | — | 9 | — | 10 | — | 11 |

*Note.* Weighted raw scores not included in this table correspond to Test Ages of "below 2½" or "above 8½."

129

Nevertheless, the well-known limitations of age norms should be understood by any McCarthy examiner who uses age equivalents for interpreting the 18 tests, as well as for interpreting the six Indexes (see Chapter 5). For one thing, a year's growth has a different meaning during the preschool period (where development is rapid) than during the school-age years. In addition, the abilities assessed by the scales and the separate tests undoubtedly develop at somewhat different rates. Finally, an age equivalent of, say, 5 years cannot mean the same thing for a 2½ year old, a 5 year old, and an 8 years old. Cautious interpretation is therefore essential to avoid overstepping the bounds of the McCarthy age norms. One type of caution is the avoidance of placing too much stock in the precise age level a child obtains on any particular task, especially when it is very discrepant with the child's "norm." A second safeguard against overinterpretation is the use of the profile of test scores as a means of formulating hypotheses about the child's abilities, rather than reaching bold conclusions about his strengths and weaknesses.

## DETERMINING STRENGTHS AND WEAKNESSES
## ON THE 18 TESTS

A child's profile of test ages will evidence numerous fluctuations, with some deviations due solely to chance and others due to real differences in the child's abilities. To distinguish between meaningful and chance fluctuations, it was necessary to develop a set of empirical guidelines. Sattler's (1974, pp. 142–146) standard deviation method for determining specific strengths or weaknesses on the Stanford-Binet seemed to be particularly relevant to the problem at hand and was therefore adapted to the McCarthy.

Sattler's basic premise is that fluctuations in test performance which occur within a specified band of age levels may be considered as normal (or chance, or expected) variability. With his ±1 standard deviation method, the "normal band" for any given age is obtained by determining the mental age of children who score 1 standard deviation *above* the mean and the mental age of children who score 1 standard deviation *below* the mean. These two extremes define the range of normal functioning. On the Stanford-Binet, successful performance at levels exceeding the upper bound of the normal band signifies well-developed abilities ("strengths"), whereas failure at levels below the lower bound denotes poorly developed abilities ("weaknesses").

The normal bands may be constructed with reference to the child's *chronological* or his *mental* age. To illustrate the application of Sattler's standard deviation method to McCarthy's General Cognitive Scale, the steps for computing a normal band of functioning for a chronological age of 4 years are listed below:

1. A GCI of 116 corresponds to performance 1 standard deviation *above* the mean (+1 *SD*). From the normative table in the McCarthy Manual, a GCI of 116 is found to correspond to composite raw scores of 108–110. (Pages 164–165 in the Manual present the norms for age 4).
2. Table 5-1 in the preceding chapter permits the conversion of composite raw scores to *General Cognitive Ages*. Values of 108–110 equal a General Cognitive Age of 4½.
3. A GCI of 84 corresponds to performance 1 standard deviation *below* the mean (−1 *SD*) and is equivalent to composite raw scores of 61–62.
4. Values of 61 and 62 may be shown to equal a General Cognitive Age of 3½.
5. The normal band for age 4 is therefore 3½–4½. Hence, test ages of 3 and below denote weaknesses, whereas test ages of 5 and above reflect strengths. Test ages of 3½ and 4½, however, should be treated as chance deviations from 4.

For psychoeducational diagnosis, knowledge of a child's *relative* strengths and weaknesses is crucial. Hence, the normal band should usually be computed around the child's General Cognitive Age (i.e., mental age) rather than his chronological age. Since the technique for determining a band of normal variability around the mental age is the same as obtaining a band around the chronological age (see Sattler, 1974, p. 143), a second illustration is not necessary. In the preceding example, the same five steps would be followed to calculate a normal band around a General Cognitive Age of 4 years (regardless of the child's chronological age).

When the ±1 standard deviation procedure is applied to the McCarthy at each half-year of age between 2½ and 8½ years (i.e., 2½, 3, 3½, etc.), certain consistencies become apparent. For the younger groups (below age 5), the normal band is ±½ year. For the older ages the normal band is ±1 year, reflecting the slower rate of development during kindergarten and the primary ₌rades. Although there are slight exceptions to these overall findings (e.g., at age 4½ the normal band is

4-5½), the consistencies are striking enough to warrant the general procedures indicated below.

To determine the child's relative strengths and weaknesses on the 18 McCarthy tests:

*Step 1.* Obtain the General Cognitive Age from Table 5-1 (p. 110).

*Step 2.* Compute the normal band using the following rules: (1) For General Cognitive Ages of 2½-4½, the band equals General Cognitive Age ±½ year. (2) For General Cognitive Ages of 5-8½, the band equals General Cognitive Age ±1 year.

*Step 3.* Treat all test ages within the normal band as chance fluctuations from the child's own mean.

*Step 4.* Consider all test ages that are outside the normal band to reflect relative strengths or weaknesses in the child's ability profile.

Some examiners prefer to calculate a child's strengths and weaknesses on the 18 tests using the chronological age as a baseline. This approach involves similar procedures to the ones listed above. Step 1 requires rounding off the child's chronological age to the nearest half-year, whereas Steps 2, 3, and 4 are essentially the same. It makes little difference which baseline is used for children with average or near-average intelligence. For superior or deficient children, however, we have a decided preference for the use of General Cognitive Age. It is redundant to learn that an extremely bright youngster has strengths on most cognitive tests (or that a retarded child has many weaknesses) compared to his chronological age. But with the General Cognitive Age as a baseline, children tend to have about an equal number of integrities and deficiencies, regardless of their ability level. The latter picture of the child's abilities is more balanced, and therefore has greater clinical and educational value.

It is generally a good idea to use both General Cognitive Age *and* chronological age as baselines for the gross motor tests (Leg Coordination, Arm Coordination, Imitative Action). Since performance on these tests is closely related to one's physical development, the child's chronological age represents a meaningful yardstick. However, his General Cognitive Age is also an appropriate baseline because a comparison of the child's specific motor skills to his overall cognitive ability completes the picture of his *relative* integrities and deficiencies.

One point is worthy of note before presenting an illustration of the method for determining strengths and weaknesses on the 18 tests. Some tests, most notably Block Building and Imitative Action, are easy for older children. A child may obtain a perfect score on an easy task and earn a test age of only 5 or 6. Should this test age be below the child's baseline age (either chronological age or General Cognitive Age), it is to be ignored.

**ILLUSTRATION**

Randi, a 4-year-old girl, obtained the composite raw scores and Indexes shown below.

|  | Composite Raw Score | Index |
|---|---|---|
| Verbal | 49 | 53 |
| Perceptual–Performance | 36 | 60 |
| Quantitative | 19 | 58 |
| General Cognitive | 104 | 112 |
| Memory | 29 | 57 |
| Motor | 30 | 53 |

By entering Randi's General Cognitive composite raw score in Table 5-1 (p. 110), she is found to function at the level of the average 4½ year old. In addition, none of her Scale Indexes differ significantly from her own mean (using the procedure described in Chapter 5), suggesting that her cognitive and motor abilities are all about equally developed.

However, a look at Randi's test ages on the 18 tasks reveals some clear strengths and weaknesses. Figure 6-1 shows the back page of her record form with a column of "Test Ages" added to the left of the test names. These ages, which were obtained from Table 6-1, range from 2½ to 7 years. To determine her normal band of functioning, her General Cognitive Age of 4½ years was used as the baseline. Following the general rule of 4½ ±½ year, all of Randi's test ages in the 4–5-year-old range were considered to be consistent with her overall functioning.

Her relative strengths and weaknesses, indicated by an "S" or "W" in Figure 6-1, are listed below. (Test ages are in parentheses.)

Strengths
Tapping Sequence       (7)
Pictorial Memory       (6)
Draw-A-Design          (6)

Weaknesses

| | |
|---|---|
| Arm Coordination | (2½) |
| Puzzle Solving | (3) |
| Conceptual Grouping | (3½) |
| Imitative Action | (3½) |

Randi's strengths in both Tapping Sequence and Pictorial Memory suggest a well-developed short-term memory when visual stimuli are paired with auditory stimuli. Her 6½-year-old level in these tasks, compared with her 4½-year-old performance on the purely auditory memory tests (Verbal and Numerical Memory), suggests that visual stimuli enhance her ability to recall.

The fact that Randi has a strength in one Motor Test (Draw-A-Design) and weaknesses in two others (Arm Coordination and Imitative Action) indicates that her Motor Index merely represents the midpoint of a wide range of skills. Further examination reveals that she evidenced strong (5½-year-old level) fine motor ability on the drawing tests, particularly when compared to her relatively weak (3–3½-year-old level) gross motor coordination. Note, however, that Arm Coordination was her only gross motor skill to fall significantly below her *chronological* age of 4.

Randi's strengths and weaknesses also reflect some variability on the Perceptual–Performance Scale. Her 7-year-old performance on Tapping Sequence probably represents a synthesis of her well-developed visual memory and fine motor skills. In contrast to these integrities is an apparent weakness in her nonverbal reasoning, indicated by 3–3½-year-old performance on the two best measures of this ability—Puzzle Solving and Conceptual Grouping.

Therefore, Randi's profile was not as "flat" as her Indexes would suggest. She displayed a good short-term memory when visual and auditory stimuli were paired together, and her fine motor coordination was well developed. Her gross motor coordination was relatively weak, however, as was her ability to reason nonverbally. These inferences about her strong and weak areas will aid the examiner in making any educational recommendations that may be necessary.

## FORMULATING HYPOTHESES FROM THE TEST PROFILE

Competent test interpretation requires the ability to integrate the findings from numerous tasks to generate hypotheses about the child's

1. Enter the *weighted raw scores* which are in the shaded boxes on pages 2-7 of the record form. For each test, enter the score in the box(es) bearing that test's number. (For example, the score for Test 3 is entered in 2 boxes.)
2. Sum the scores in each of the 5 columns. Enter the totals in the *composite raw score* boxes at the foot of the page.
3. Transfer the *composite raw scores* to the front cover. (Open the booklet and turn it over so that the front and back covers are side by side.) Enter the scores in the Composite Raw Score column in the box labeled "Composite Raw Scores and Scale Indexes."
(For more detailed directions on the completion of the record form, see Chapter 7 of manual.)

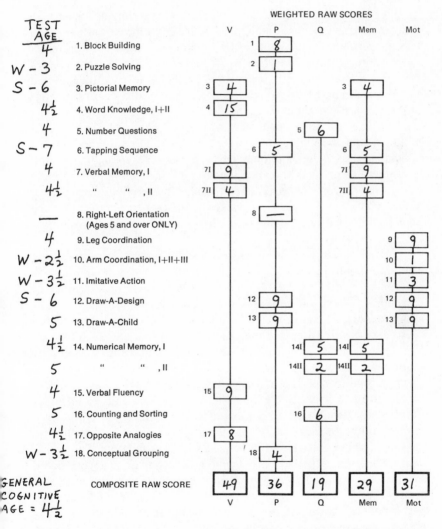

Fig. 6-1. The back page of 4-year-old Randi's record form, illustrating the test age method of determining relative strengths and weaknesses on the 18 tests.

135

skills. As in the above illustration, the *pattern* of test ages is far more important than any particular strength or weakness. Various test ages have to be grouped together in different ways (two at a time, three at a time, etc.) to formulate defensible hypotheses. The strengths and weaknesses serve as useful starting points, but are not ends in themselves.

For example, if a child's test age on Puzzle Solving indicates a significant strength, this finding may reflect well-developed nonverbal reasoning, understanding of spatial relations, visual perception, or visual–motor coordination (see p. 88). His test ages on other reasoning tests, spatial tests, etc., need to be evaluated (even if they are not significant strengths) to isolate the possible area of integrity. If none of the various hypotheses is supported, then mere knowledge of a significant strength in a single test such as Puzzle Solving makes a minimal contribution to understanding the child's abilities. The 18 individual tests were not intended to be reliable enough to permit interpretation of their so-called unique abilities. The only legitimate way to infer strong or weak areas (besides interpreting the profile of Scale Indexes) is to garner evidence from two or more tasks; the greater the consistency across tests, the more confidence the examiner can have in his hypothesis.

Before attempting to interpret a child's test age profile, the examiner should be thoroughly familiar with the kinds of abilities that presumably underlie successful performance on each separate test (see Chapter 4). Then, the test ages that qualify as significant strengths and weaknesses, relative to the child's General Cognitive Age, should be studied briefly to enable the examiner to formulate some "loose" hypotheses and to get a clinical feel for the child's ability profile. If more than one strength or weakness occurs on tests in the *same* specific cognitive or motor scale, the examiner then has a logical "lead" to investigate. Sometimes the investigation leads to information that is already known. For example, if a child has a significantly low Quantitative Index, it is not surprising to discover that his test ages on Number Questions and Numerical Memory II are also significant weaknesses. However, new hypotheses also may be uncovered by this process, especially if a few strengths or weaknesses are found on a scale whose Index did *not* differ significantly from the child's average performance. The simultaneous occurrence of a strength *and* a weakness on the same scale is also a good bet to yield information that is not evident from the Scale Index profile.

Sometimes a single deviant test age can be quite meaningful. For example, if a child's Verbal Index reflects a significant *strength,* then the finding of a *weakness* on any Verbal test is of interest. The implication is that the child's verbal strength may be fairly specific rather than a broadly defined integrity in verbal comprehension and expression; the examiner should investigate this possibility.

There are no hard and fast rules for deciding whether a hypothesis should be accepted or rejected. Probably the most objective method is to compute the average test age for the two or more tests that the examiner groups together, and see if this average differs substantially from the child's baseline age. If the average test age falls outside the normal band of functioning computed for the child, then it is certainly reasonable to accept the hypothesis of a strong or weak skill area. However, final decisions about the validity of hypotheses rest on the examiner's clinical judgment.

To formulate and investigate various hypotheses, the clinician needs a good deal of open-minded flexibility along with insight into the multifaceted dimensions of each test. Effective "detective" work requires translating a "hunch" to a hypothesis, checking it out, and then generating alternative hypotheses if the first one is not validated. Some reasonable explanations for the variability in a child's test age profile are offered in the sections that follow. First, combinations and groupings of tests *within* each of the five specific scales are discussed. Then, the tests constituting the General Cognitive Scale are subdivided in novel ways, using classification systems adapted from Bannatyne (1971, 1974), Meeker (1969), and Sattler (1965, 1974). The various subgroupings of tests within the six scales are not meant to be exhaustive; the creative examiner will be able to deduce a variety of other hypotheses based on his particular background, clinical experience, and knowledge of the specific child in question.

### Verbal Scale

The Verbal tests may be divided on the basis of two important variables: (1) the nature of the task (memory versus conceptualization), and (2) the amount of verbal expression required to answer the items. These two divisions are shown below.

| Memory | *versus* | Conceptualization |
|---|---|---|
| 3.  Pictorial Memory | | 4.  Word Knowledge |
| 7.  Verbal Memory I | | 15.  Verbal Fluency |
| Verbal Memory II | | 17.  Opposite Analogies |

| Much Expression Required | *versus* | Little Expression Required |
|---|---|---|
| 4. Word Knowledge | | 3. Pictorial Memory |
| 7. Verbal Memory II | | 7. Verbal Memory I |
| 15. Verbal Fluency | | 17. Opposite Analogies |

It is not unusual for a child to do better on the memory tests than on the conceptual tasks, or vice versa. Similarly, a child who has difficulty expressing his ideas in words may do well when only one word is required for an answer (Opposite Analogies) or when mere repetition of words is demanded, but perform markedly more poorly when much verbalization is involved.

Suppose a child has a strength in Pictorial Memory and a weakness in Word Knowledge. These findings may reflect more basic and generalized integrities and deficits. The child may perform considerably better on semantic memory tasks than on the verbal tests requiring conceptualization; or, he may score higher on tasks with limited verbal expression than on those requiring much verbalization. These hypotheses may be "screened" by quick inspection of Verbal test ages, and checked out by computing averages of the pertinent groups of test ages. Perhaps one of these hypotheses will be supported by the data; if not, then other combinations of tests (either within the Verbal Scale or cutting across several scales) should be investigated in a similar manner.

Verbal Memory II occasionally does not coordinate with the other semantic memory tasks because it is more complex and requires more than just good rote recall. A child with well-developed verbal concepts may compensate for a poor rote memory and do quite well on Part II of Verbal Memory. Conversely, a child with an excellent rote memory may do poorly when recalling the story because he lacks a conceptual understanding of the sequence of events. The fact that Verbal Memory II may be considered either a conceptual or a memory task, depending on the cognitive make-up of the specific child, affirms the examiner's need for flexibility when analyzing the test profile.

Verbal Fluency is the only McCarthy test measuring a creative ability and, hence, the child's test age may be discrepant with his performance on the other conceptual or expressive Verbal tasks. However, before speculating about a possible strength or weakness in creativity, at least two other hypotheses should be investigated. Verbal Fluency assesses categorical thinking (logical classification skills), so the child's test age should be compared to his test age on Conceptual

Grouping. If *both* test ages are consistently high or low, then the child's strength (or weakness) may be related to his abstract classification skills. Verbal Fluency also demands the ability to solve intellectual problems *quickly*, and may be correlated to the child's performance on Puzzle Solving. Only when competing hypotheses have been exhausted should an examiner conclude that a discrepant test age on Verbal Fluency may be due to a strength or weakness in creative ability. However, decisions based on a single test must remain tentative pending supplementary testing.

### Perceptual-Performance Scale

The tests on the Perceptual–Performance Scale may be subdivided in two main ways:

| Visual–Motor Coordination | *versus* | Verbal Concept Formation |
|---|---|---|
| 1. Block Building | | 8. Right–Left Orientation |
| 2. Puzzle Solving | | 18. Conceptual Grouping |
| 6. Tapping Sequence | | |
| 12. Draw-A-Design | | |
| 13. Draw-A-Child | | |

| Imitation | *versus* | Thinking |
|---|---|---|
| 1. Block Building | | 2. Puzzle Solving |
| 6. Tapping Sequence | | 8. Right–Left Orientation |
| 12. Draw-A-Design | | 13. Draw-A-Child |
| | | 18. Conceptual Grouping |

The five tests in the visual–motor coordination category are classical tests of performance ability (nonverbal intelligence). Coordination is an important aspect of each task, and little verbalization by the examiner is needed to communicate the nature of the items. In contrast, Right–Left Orientation and Conceptual Grouping demand a minimal amount of motor coordination for the child to respond, while depending heavily on verbal comprehension skills. A child with a visual–motor deficit may thus do quite well on two of the Perceptual–Performance tests. Conversely, poor verbal ability may depress the Perceptual–Performance Index of a child with exceptional nonverbal intelligence.

In the imitation–thinking dichotomy, "thinking" refers to mental processes that are at a higher level than mere repetition or copying skills. Within the thinking category, Draw-A-Child assesses nonverbal concept formation, whereas the other three tests measure reasoning.

In addition, the type of reasoning required for success on Right–Left Orientation is often task specific and not generalizable to other kinds of problems. Consequently, the examiner should not be surprised by variability in the child's scores on the "thinking" tests.

Two additional clusters of Perceptual–Performance tests are discussed in the section on the General Cognitive Scale and are listed below. The spatial grouping is derived from Bannatyne's (1971) model and includes tests requiring spatial orientation and the understanding of spatial relations. The tasks labeled "convergent production of figural products" are grouped according to Guilford's structure of intellect model; each test requires the child to find the one best answer to a problem involving shapes or concrete objects.

Spatial
   1.  Block Building
   2.  Puzzle Solving
   8.  Right–Left Orientation
  12.  Draw-A-Design
Convergent Production of Figural Products
   1.  Block Building
  12.  Draw-A-Design
  13.  Draw-A-Child
  18.  Conceptual Grouping

Numerous other categorizations of Perceptual–Performance tests are possible. For example, a child who has greater ability dealing with meaningful than with abstract stimuli (pictures of people or things versus designs) is likely to score higher on Puzzle Solving and Draw-A-Child than on Draw-A-Design and Conceptual Grouping. A child who has visual perception problems is likely to perform very poorly on the two tests that depend the most heavily on visual–perceptual skills—Puzzle Solving and Draw-A-Design.

### Quantitative Scale

The Quantitative tasks may be divided into the groupings shown below.

| **Number Concepts** | *versus* | **Memory** |
|---|---|---|
| 5.  Number Questions | | 14.  Numerical Memory I |
| 16.  Counting & Sorting | |        Numerical Memory II |

This division should be investigated routinely for children below 5 years of age because the Quantitative Index does not measure a distinct unitary ability at the young age levels (see pp. 93–94). Even among older children it is not uncommon to see discrepant levels of functioning in the areas of computational skills and short-term memory.

When one of the Quantitative tasks is discrepant with the other three, the deviant test age should be related to the child's scores on other General Cognitive tests. Counting & Sorting is the only Quantitative task involving visual stimuli and motoric responses; a strength or weakness in Counting & Sorting should therefore be related to the child's Perceptual–Performance Index. Number Questions resembles Wechsler's Information and Arithmetic tests, so a discrepant score on this Quantitative task may well be consistent with the child's Verbal Index.

Numerical Memory I involves simple rote recall, whereas the other three Quantitative tasks each involve some mental manipulation of numbers. This distinction may account for a relative strength or weakness in repeating digits forward, and should be corroborated with performance on other tests of rote memory.

### Memory Scale

The six Memory tasks may be grouped in the logical ways indicated below.

| Meaningful Content | versus | Nonmeaningful Content |
|---|---|---|
| 3. Pictorial Memory | | 6. Tapping Sequence |
| 7. Verbal Memory I | | 14. Numerical Memory I |
| Verbal Memory II | | Numerical Memory II |

| Visual & Auditory Stimuli | versus | Auditory Stimuli Only |
|---|---|---|
| 3. Pictorial Memory | | 7. Verbal Memory I |
| 6. Tapping Sequence | | Verbal Memory II |
| | | 14. Numerical Memory I |
| | | Numerical Memory II |

| Simple Rote Memory | versus | Complex Memory |
|---|---|---|
| 3. Pictorial Memory | | 7. Verbal Memory II |
| 6. Tapping Sequence | | 14. Numerical Memory II |
| 7. Verbal Memory I | | |
| 14. Numerical Memory I | | |

The division according to meaningfulness of content is sometimes altered slightly, with Verbal Memory I joining the nonmeaningful grouping. Some children repeat word series (and even sentences) in a stimulus–response fashion with little or no attention paid to the meaning of the words. An item such as "after–color–funny–today," which includes abstract terms not easily visualized, deemphasizes meaning. In contrast, successful repetition of the story demands comprehension of its meaning, as does the ability to recall pictures of common concrete objects that are named by the examiner.

Older children occasionally solve Tapping Sequence items by coding the taps *numerically*. Therefore, the meaningful versus nonmeaningful split may have an alternative interpretation for some youngsters—namely, verbal versus numerical ability. This hypothesis is easily checked out because verbal–numerical discrepancies are reflected more globally in the difference between the child's Verbal and Quantitative Indexes.

When the child's scores on Pictorial Memory and Tapping Sequence are discrepant with his test ages on the four auditory–vocal memory tasks, a number of hypotheses are suggested. High scores on the two tests may indicate a good visual memory or the beneficial effects of multisensory stimulation; low scores may reflect a deficient visual memory or a problem with intersensory integration (see pp. 161–162).

A child with a good rote memory is sometimes unable to cope with the more complex and conceptual demands of tasks such as retelling a story or repeating digits backward. It is far less common for a child to score higher on the two complex tasks than on the ones requiring simple rote memory, but it does happen. Such a child apparently has difficulty maintaining the stimulus trace when responding automatically, but can compensate if requirements of the memory task virtually "force" him to rely on higher level cognitive processes.

A child's test age on Tapping Sequence occasionally differs significantly from his ability level on other memory tasks, perhaps because it is the only one requiring a motor response. Therefore, unusually good or poor performance on Tapping Sequence is likely to be congruent with his performance on other visual–motor tests. Similarly, Pictorial Memory is the only memory test that does not involve sequencing, which may account for a significant discrepancy with all other memory tests.

### Motor Scale

The main division of the Motor tests is gross versus fine motor coordination:

| Gross Motor | *versus* | Fine Motor |
|---|---|---|
| 9. Leg Coordination | | 12. Draw-A-Design |
| 10. Arm Coordination | | 13. Draw-A-Child |
| 11. Imitative Action | | |

A child's test ages often cluster in the above manner, although one cannot immediately attribute the disparity to gross versus fine motor ability. The gross motor tests are noncognitive, whereas the fine motor tests are cognitive, so the difference may simply be a function of the child's intelligence. If his test ages on the fine motor tests are consistent with his General Cognitive Age, then the latter hypothesis is most likely true. Also, the fine motor tests both involve drawing. In order to conclude that a child has a global strength or weakness in fine motor coordination, his performance in Draw-A-Design and Draw-A-Child must be related to his ability on other tasks with a fine motor component such as Tapping Sequence and Puzzle Solving. Inconsistent findings would suggest that the child's strength or weakness may be specific to paper-and-pencil coordination. A child's performance on Imitative Action may diverge from his performance on Leg and Arm Coordination. This may be due to the fine motor component of some Imitative Action items or to the relative simplicity of the task for most young children. Therefore, it may be necessary to eliminate Imitative Action from consideration when examining hypotheses concerning coordination.

The gross motor–fine motor dichotomy is also analogous to Gesell's distinction between Motor and Adaptive skills (Gesell & Amatruda, 1947). McCarthy's gross motor tests bear a clear resemblance to the motor tasks developed by Gesell in his New Haven laboratory. In addition, Draw-A-Design and Draw-A-Child are analogous to Gesell's Copy Forms and Incomplete Man tasks, which are among the best measures of adaptive development. Copy Forms and Incomplete Man are also the crux of Ilg and Ames' (1972) Gesell School Readiness Tests and exemplify their hypothesized construct of "behavioral maturity." Therefore, from the theoretical viewpoint of Gesell and his colleagues, a disparity between the child's gross and fine motor abilities may reflect maturational differences in the child's rates of physical and behavioral development.

Sometimes a child will obtain quite different scores on the two drawing tests. This contrast may be related to the more conceptual nature of Draw-A-Child and, in particular, to the scoring systems of each test. Coordination is emphasized when scoring Draw-A-Design items, but is minimized for Draw-A-Child. For example, a child who draws crude representations of arms and hands earns the same credit as one who draws well-proportioned upper extremities. When test ages on the two drawing tests are highly discrepant, the examiner should check for a corresponding difference between the GCI and Motor Index. High Draw-A-Child and low Draw-A-Design scores, for example, suggest good conceptualization but poor coordination. A *qualitative* evaluation of the human figure drawn by a child with the above pattern will undoubtedly reflect poor motor coordination and, possibly, visual–perceptual problems.

Children also occasionally score at very different levels on Leg and Arm Coordination. Most Leg Coordination items are not specifically taught or trained, so the task offers insight into the child's physical development. The Arm Coordination tasks, however, are commonly practiced; the child's test age may reflect either much training or a complete lack of prior experience. Consistent with the above statements are empirical findings regarding sex differences: girls (who mature faster) scored higher on Leg Coordination, whereas boys did better on Arm Coordination (Kaufman & Kaufman, 1973b). Therefore, any interpretation of differences between a child's test ages on Leg and Arm Coordination should take into account these research findings.

Since Leg Coordination is very dependent on balance while Arm Coordination demands precision of movement, differences in these tasks may mirror discrepant development in the child's musculature and may suggest possible neurological involvement. Markedly different test ages in Leg and Arm Coordination might be followed up with supplementary neurological testing, as long as one or both test ages are significantly below the child's *chronological* age.

### General Cognitive Scale

McCarthy's grouping of the 15 General Cognitive tests into Verbal, Perceptual–Performance, Quantitative, and Memory Scales has both rational and empirical support, and represents a clinically valuable division. However, other groupings are also logically defensible and may provide extra insight into the test age profile of some children. Three supplementary approaches to categorizing the General Cognitive tests are presented below, adapted from the techniques of Bannatyne (1971, 1974), Meeker (1969), and Sattler (1965, 1974).

These approaches are most useful when the analysis of the child's Scale Indexes and the subsequent investigation of test age fluctuations within the separate scales lead to unclear or ambiguous hypotheses about the child's strengths and weaknesses. The application of one or more of the supplementary approaches may provide the reorganization needed to reconcile apparent contradictions, tie together "loose ends," or uncover hidden areas of integrity or deficit.

## BANNATYNE'S APPROACH

Bannatyne (1971, pp. 591–592, 1974) suggested a procedure for reanalyzing WISC subtests that he found useful for diagnosing dyslexic children. He grouped the subtests into four categories: Spatial Ability (Picture Completion, Block Design, Object Assembly); Verbal Conceptualization Ability (Comprehension, Similarities, Vocabulary); Sequencing Ability (Digit Span, Arithmetic, Coding), and Acquired Knowledge (Information, Arithmetic, Vocabulary).

We have reorganized McCarthy's General Cognitive tests to conform to Bannatyne's four-way division of the WISC. Pictorial Memory and Draw-a-Child are the only tasks omitted from the regrouping (shown below); Word Knowledge, similar to the WISC Vocabulary subtest, appears in two categories.

Spatial Ability
1. Block Building
2. Puzzle Solving
8. Right–Left Orientation
12. Draw-A-Design

Verbal Conceptualization Ability
4. Word Knowledge
15. Verbal Fluency
17. Opposite Analogies
18. Conceptual Grouping

Sequencing Ability
6. Tapping Sequence
7. Verbal Memory I
   Verbal Memory II
14. Numerical Memory I
    Numerical Memory II

Acquired Knowledge
4. Word Knowledge
5. Number Questions
16. Counting & Sorting

Table 6-2 permits the examiner to compute age equivalents for each of the four categories. Sum the *weighted* raw scores of all tests

**Table 6-2**

Age Equivalents of Sums of *Weighted* Raw Scores on Tests Grouped into Bannatyne's Four Categories

| Age Equivalent | Spatial Ability | | Verbal Conceptualization Ability | Sequencing Ability | Acquired Knowledge | Age Equivalent |
|---|---|---|---|---|---|---|
| | Without R–L Orientation | With R–L Orientation | | | | |
| $2\frac{1}{2}$ | 5–7 | 6–10 | 7–16 | 3–7 | 8–12 | $2\frac{1}{2}$ |
| 3 | 8–10 | 11–14 | 17–22 | 8–11 | 13–16 | 3 |
| $3\frac{1}{2}$ | 11–13 | 15–18 | 23–29 | 12–16 | 17–20 | $3\frac{1}{2}$ |
| 4 | 14–16 | 19–22 | 30–36 | 17–21 | 21–25 | 4 |
| $4\frac{1}{2}$ | 17–19 | 23–25 | 37–42 | 22–25 | 26–29 | $4\frac{1}{2}$ |
| 5 | 20–22 | 26–28 | 43–47 | 26–29 | 30–32 | 5 |
| $5\frac{1}{2}$ | 23–25 | 29–31 | 48–51 | 30–32 | 33–35 | $5\frac{1}{2}$ |
| 6 | 26–27 | 32–34 | 52–57 | 33–36 | 36–38 | 6 |
| $6\frac{1}{2}$ | 28–29 | 35–37 | 58–60 | 37–39 | 39–41 | $6\frac{1}{2}$ |
| 7 | 30–31 | 38–40 | 61–65 | 40–41 | 42–44 | 7 |
| $7\frac{1}{2}$ | 32–33 | 41–42 | 66–68 | 42–43 | 45–47 | $7\frac{1}{2}$ |
| 8 | 34 | 43–44 | 69–71 | 44–45 | 48–50 | 8 |
| $8\frac{1}{2}$ | 35 | 45–46 | 72–73 | 46 | 51–52 | $8\frac{1}{2}$ |

*Note.* The McCarthy tasks grouped into each of Bannatyne's categories are listed on page 145. Sum the weighted raw scores on the component tests in each category. Then enter the table with the sums to determine the age equivalents.

included in each grouping; then enter the table with the totals and determine the age equivalents. Note that age norms for Spatial Ability are presented both with and without Right–Left Orientation.

## SATTLER'S APPROACH

Since the McCarthy mental tests bear a close resemblance to the Binet tasks (see pp. 24–25), long-time Binet examiners may find it useful to interpret the McCarthy from a Binet-like perspective. Sattler's (1965, 1974) division of the Stanford-Binet tasks into seven rationally determined categories has provided a useful framework for interpreting a child's areas of strength and weakness on the Binet. We have therefore divided McCarthy's cognitive tests in accordance with Sattler's model, as shown below. Each McCarthy test has been assigned to only *one* category, to be consistent with Sattler's method of classifying the Binet tasks. Sattler (Personal communication, 1976) agreed with our classifications of McCarthy tests, although he pointed out that Right–Left Orientation might justifiably be classified as Visual–Motor instead of Reasoning.

Language (maturity, extent, and quality of vocabulary)
    4.  Word Knowledge
  15.  Verbal Fluency

Memory (meaningful, nonmeaningful, and visual memory)
    3.  Pictorial Memory
    6.  Tapping Sequence
    7.  Verbal Memory I
       Verbal Memory II
  14.  Numerical Memory I
       Numerical Memory II

Conceptual Thinking (abstract thinking and utilizing a categorical attitude)
  17.  Opposite Analogies
  18.  Conceptual Grouping

Reasoning (nonverbal and spatial reasoning)
    2.  Puzzle Solving
    8.  Right–Left Orientation

Numerical Reasoning (arithmetic ability)
    5.  Number Questions
  16.  Counting & Sorting

Visual–Motor (manual dexterity, eye-hand coordination, and perception of spatial relations)
1.   Block Building
12.   Draw-A-Design
13.   Draw-A-Child

Social Intelligence (social maturity and social judgment)
None

Sattler's definitions of the Language, Conceptual Thinking, and Reasoning categories are broader than the ones presented above for the McCarthy. The more restricted definitions shown here reflect the specific abilities measured by the McCarthy tasks in each category, rather than the more heterogeneous set of Binet skills. For children below age 5, the Reasoning category includes only the Puzzle Solving test because Right–Left Orientation is not administered. It would be sensible to combine the Reasoning and Numerical Reasoning categories for these youngsters (a suggestion made by Sattler, Personal communication, 1976).

Determining the child's level of ability (age equivalent) in each of Sattler's categories is a straightforward process and does not require a separate table. The age equivalent for Memory equals the child's Memory Age, as determined from Table 5-6 on page 122. The other categories contain only two or three tasks, so an average test age may be computed quite easily. The profile of age equivalents can then be examined to detect any sizable deviations from the child's General Cognitive Age.

## MEEKER'S STRUCTURE OF INTELLECT TECHNIQUE

Meeker's approach to interpretation has one important factor in common with Bannatyne's and Sattler's methods—the tasks are grouped according to their presumed mental process or operation. Each technique provides a valuable supplementary aid for interpreting the General Cognitive Scale since McCarthy, like Wechsler, divided the tasks primarily on the basis of *content;* only the Memory Index reflects a unitary mental operation. One advantage of Meeker's procedure over other supplementary approaches is the theoretical basis (Guilford's structure of intellect model) for her choice of mental processes.

Meeker analyzes the WISC-R, WPPSI, and Stanford-Binet by

determining a child's level on each separate Guilford factor (e.g., cognition of semantic units, evaluation of figural relations). Such an approach involves placing templates over a record form, and requires differential classification of items within some subtests. This method is fine for a person deeply involved in Meeker analysis, but it is generally too time consuming for a supplementary interpretation of the McCarthy. We therefore suggest focusing primarily on Guilford's five operations.

The McCarthy tests are shown below, grouped by operation. (The specific Guilford factors measured by each task are listed in Chapter 4.) Tests tend to appear in more than one category because most tasks in conventional ability tests are not "pure" measures of a single Guilford operation. Counting & Sorting is excluded from the Cognition category because only the last two items require this operation.

Cognition (immediate awareness, recognition, or comprehension)
1. Block Building
2. Puzzle Solving
4. Word Knowledge
5. Number Questions
8. Right–Left Orientation
17. Opposite Analogies

Memory (retention of information in the form it was stored)
3. Pictorial Memory
5. Number Questions
6. Tapping Sequence
7. Verbal Memory I
   Verbal Memory II
14. Numerical Memory I
    Numerical Memory II
16. Counting & Sorting

Evaluation (Making judgments in terms of a known standard)
2. Puzzle Solving
17. Opposite Analogies
18. Conceptual Grouping

Convergent Production (responding with the unique or "best" answer)
1. Block Building
12. Draw-A-Design

13.   Draw-A-Child
17.   Opposite Analogies
18.   Conceptual Grouping

Divergent Production (Responding to stimuli where the emphasis
is on variety or quality of response)
15.   Verbal Fluency

Table 6-3 permits the examiner to compute age equivalents for
Guilford's mental operations by summing the weighted raw scores of
the component tests in each category. Divergent production is not
included because only Verbal Fluency assesses this process; the test
age for Verbal Fluency (see Table 6-1) equals the age equivalent for
divergent production. Since divergent production of semantic units is
the only creative ability measured by the McCarthy, a significant
deviation on Verbal Fluency precludes generalization to other
divergent skills.

The examiner who wants to look beyond the global operations
may compute average test ages for various subgroupings of the
McCarthy tasks. Cognition can be broken down into semantic and
figural groups. (Right–Left Orientation is not listed below because it
measures *both* Semantic and Figural Cognition.)

Semantic Cognition
4.   Word Knowledge
5.   Number Questions
17.   Opposite Analogies

Figural Cognition
1.   Block Building
2.   Puzzle Solving

The tasks that measure memory according to Guilford's system
may be divided into three groups.

Semantic Memory
3.   Pictorial Memory
7.   Verbal Memory I & II

Figural Memory
3.   Pictorial Memory
6.   Tapping Sequence

**Table 6-3**
Age Equivalents of Sums of *Weighted* Raw Scores on the Tasks Measuring Guilford's Structure of Intellect Operations

| Age Equivalent | Cognition | | Memory | Evaluation | Convergent Production | Age Equivalent |
| --- | --- | --- | --- | --- | --- | --- |
| | Without R-L Orientation | With R-L Orientation | | | | |
| 2½ | 11–19 | 12–22 | 4–12 | 0–4 | 5–11 | 2½ |
| 3 | 20–26 | 23–30 | 13–20 | 5–8 | 12–18 | 3 |
| 3½ | 27–33 | 31–37 | 21–27 | 9–12 | 19–25 | 3½ |
| 4 | 34–39 | 38–44 | 28–35 | 13–16 | 26–33 | 4 |
| 4½ | 40–45 | 45–50 | 36–43 | 17–19 | 34–38 | 4½ |
| 5 | 46–50 | 51–56 | 44–48 | 20–23 | 39–43 | 5 |
| 5½ | 51–54 | 57–61 | 49–53 | 24–25 | 44–48 | 5½ |
| 6 | 55–59 | 62–66 | 54–60 | 26–27 | 49–52 | 6 |
| 6½ | 60–63 | 67–71 | 61–65 | 28–29 | 53–56 | 6½ |
| 7 | 64–68 | 72–76 | 66–69 | 30–31 | 57–59 | 7 |
| 7½ | 69–72 | 77–81 | 70–73 | 32–33 | 60–61 | 7½ |
| 8 | 73–76 | 82–86 | 74–76 | 34–35 | 62–63 | 8 |
| 8½ | 77–80 | 87–90 | 77–80 | 36–37 | 64–65 | 8½ |

*Note.* The McCarthy tasks measuring each of the above structure of intellect operations are listed on pages 149–150. Sum the weighted raw scores on the component tests in each category. Then enter the table with the sums to determine the age equivalents.

151

Symbolic Memory
   5.  Number Questions
 14.  Numerical Memory I & II
 16.  Counting & Sorting

Evaluation and convergent production each contain only one main subgroup. For evaluation, a very specific ability is measured by the subgroup of Opposite Analogies and Conceptual Grouping—*evaluation of semantic relations*. In contrast, the subgroup of convergent production tasks measures a broad ability (*convergent production of figural products*), spanning four different products:

  1.  Block Building (NFR)
 12.  Draw-A-Design (NFU)
 13.  Draw-A-Child (NFS)
 18.  Conceptual Grouping (NFC)

We have not dwelled upon the study of *specific* Guilford factors (operation–content–product) because more reliable hypotheses may be generated from the McCarthy tasks by grouping factors together. Most of the specific factors are measured by only one McCarthy task or by a few items in two or more tasks. Notable exceptions are evaluation of semantic relations (mentioned above), cognition of a semantic unit (Word Knowledge, Right–Left Orientation, and two Counting & Sorting items), and cognition of a figural system (Block Building, Puzzle Solving). Examiners who choose to conduct a thorough Meeker analysis of the McCarthy and evaluate specific Guilford factors may wish to investigate the merits of the remedial programs developed by Meeker (e.g., Meeker & Shadduck, 1973).

# Chapter 7
## Interpreting the McCarthy Qualitatively

The clinical information that may be derived by observing a child's behavior during a test-taking session, and by interpreting the *qualitative* aspects of his test performance, is at least as important as the scores themselves. Children are often tested because of a suspected learning or behavioral disorder; effective diagnosis demands the ability to interpret cognitive and motor tests both quantitatively *and* qualitatively. The *nature* of a perceptual problem is not evident in a child's Perceptual–Performance Index or in his scores on the separate tests, but requires careful analysis of his errors. Similarly, motor problems due to possible neurological dysfunction may be detected by observing *how* the child holds a pencil, stands on one foot, or taps a xylophone, regardless of his scores on the gross and fine motor tests. In addition, behavioral characteristics such as impulsivity, perseveration, immaturity, and distractibility are often evidenced in many ways (both obvious and subtle) during the course of a test battery; a clinician needs to be keenly observant and he should be aware of the specific tasks that are likely to elicit different behaviors in young children.

Just as the picture stimulus cards in the Children's Apperception Test (CAT; Bellak & Bellak, 1971) are not all equally effective in eliciting a child's feelings and motivations, such as need for nurturance or aggression, the McCarthy tasks differ in the types of behaviors they are likely to evoke and in the kinds of clinical informa-

153

tion they yield. One CAT card will typically elicit problems over sibling rivalry; another focuses attention on toilet training; while a third evokes feelings of aggression. Similarly, some McCarthy tasks are particularly vulnerable to the effects of distractibility, whereas others seem to elicit aggressive or perseverative behavior.

The 18 McCarthy tests may be viewed as a set of stimuli which are differentially effective in eliciting various perceptual, motor, or emotional responses from the young child. The aims of this chapter are to point out which tasks are the most useful for observing different behavioral characteristics and to show how qualitative evaluation of some tests can provide valuable supplementary information about the child's cognitive and perceptual–motor abilities.

Probably the most clinically valuable tests are Draw-A-Design and Draw-A-Child. Design-copying and human figure-drawing tests provide an abundance of stimuli for evaluating perceptual ability, motor development, neurological integrity, school readiness, intelligence, and emotional disturbance. Both types of tasks have value as projective tools, with human figure drawings proving especially useful for gaining insight into the child's body image, attitudes, fears, and preoccupations.

The clinical, developmental, and diagnostic importance of design-copying tests have been researched and elaborated for the Bender-Gestalt (Koppitz, 1963, 1975), Gesell Copy Forms (Ilg & Ames, 1972), and for many other similar tests (e.g., Beery & Buktenica, 1967). Koppitz, in particular, provides numerous guidelines and clues for evaluating a child's method of copying designs and for interpreting qualitative aspects of his products. Since many of her suggestions and insights are not limited to Bender designs, they may be generalized and applied as well to McCarthy's Draw-A-Design test. Similarly, the clinical interpretations of human figure drawings discussed by DiLeo (1973), Hammer (1958, 1960), Harris (1963), Koppitz (1968), and Machover (1949, 1953, 1960) may be used to evaluate the child's product in McCarthy's Draw-A-Child test. Examiners who are particularly interested in the issues of immaturity and school readiness should be able to find in Ilg and Ames' (1972) approach much that is applicable to McCarthy's two drawing tests.

Because of the impressive amount of interpretive information that is already available on drawing tests, McCarthy's Draw-A-Design and Draw-A-Child tasks are not featured in this chapter. (They are, however, integrated with the Bender-Gestalt and Draw-A-Man tests, respectively, in Chapter 8.) The examiner is strongly advised to consult the literature in this area and to apply the pertinent perceptual–motor, conceptual, emotional, and neurological interpretations to the McCarthy. Instead, the focus of this chapter is on the four McCarthy tests (other than Draw-A-Design and Draw-A-Child) that we have found to be rich sources of clinical information: Puzzle Solving, Tapping Sequence, Arm Coordination, and Verbal Fluency. In the course of the discussions of these four tests, we have incorporated at least some qualitative interpretation of *all* 18 McCarthy tests, and of the hand dominance rating that is obtained during the administration of the Motor Scale. Although numerous kinds of behaviors are discussed below, particular attention is given to variables that are often associated with learning disabled children, such as impulsivity, distractibility, and inability to tolerate frustration.

## PUZZLE SOLVING

The Puzzle Solving test affords the examiner numerous opportunities for making important perceptual, motor, and behavioral observations. Perceptual errors, for example, can be categorized into three of the groupings used by Koppitz (1963) for evaluating the Bender designs: distortions, integration errors, and rotations. Knowledge of these kinds of errors gives the examiner insight into the qualitative nature of the child's perceptual and spatial functioning. Comparison of the types of errors made on Puzzle Solving with the errors made on design-copying tests (see pp. 188–189) can reveal consistent deficiencies and may identify pervasive problems.

A distortion error results when the child's product resembles the animal or food he is trying to construct, but he seems unaware of any errors in the puzzle. This problem may occur when the child reverses the two outside pieces of the Carrot, interchanges some of the pieces of the Bear (or Pear), or constructs a Bird with only four or five of the puzzle pieces. Errors of integration occur when the child correctly assembles portions of a puzzle but is unable to put them together to form a whole. Although rotations are not scored as errors on the Puzzle Solving test, it is important to note whenever a child orients a puzzle improperly. Several clear rotations may reflect perceptual or spatial problems for a school-age child if these observations are corroborated by other evidence such as rotations in Draw-A-Design, mirror images on items 2 and 3 in Block Building, and lack of knowledge of right versus left. The same type of errors for a preschool child are more likely to reflect developmental level rather than perceptual-spatial impairment.

As a rule, preschool children do not solve enough puzzles correctly to permit a thorough interpretation of their visual perceptual abilities. Nevertheless, their errors have to be scrutinized to deduce whether the problem is perceptual, conceptual, or motoric. A child who connects two wrong pieces is different from a child who lines the pieces up to make a "train," and both are quite different from a child who puts the appropriate pieces together but fails because of a misalignment. Even though it is not always possible to determine whether an error is due to perception or conception, it is usually easy to spot failure that results from poor motor coordination.

In general, the Puzzle Solving items afford good opportunities to detect motor difficulties, including subtle problems in older children. Whereas most McCarthy visual or motor tasks demand the use of one hand at a time, success on Puzzle Solving is facilitated by the ability to integrate and coordinate both hands simultaneously. (Block Building and the two-hand catches in Arm Coordination also require this ability.) A child who uses only one hand to solve the puzzles, or whose hands synchronize poorly, may be experiencing neurologically related motor difficulties, regardless of his success or failure on the items. The examiner should be especially aware of children who use their left hand to manipulate pieces to the left of their midline and their right hand for pieces to the right of their midline. This behavior, which may also occur during Block Building, Counting & Sorting, and Conceptual Grouping, implies a possible failure to integrate the functions of the two sides of the body (Ayres, 1972a, pp. 111–112). Other evidence of this problem may be observed during the administration of the Motor Scale: e.g., the failure to establish hand dominance (see pp. 164–166) or to hold down a shifting piece of paper with one hand while drawing with the other hand (Ayres, 1972a, pp. 138–140).

Alignment of the puzzle pieces presents particular difficulty to a child with motor problems. Some children have a hard time getting the pieces to align properly and simply cannot succeed within the time limits; others align the pieces adequately, but then find it virtually impossible to "let go" of the puzzle without pushing at least one piece out of position. The examiner has to be alert to all kinds of motor abnormalities to help detect neurological dysfunction in children.

*However, clinical experience with children, especially preschoolers, is essential in order to distinguish between abnormal behavior and reasonably normal motor development.*

In addition to the perceptual and motor insights that can be gained from observing the child's Puzzle Solving performance, the examiner can derive other qualitative information from this test. The nature of the task permits an assessment of the child's approach to problem solving. Whereas most of the other tasks in the battery are either imitative or require mental problem solving, Puzzle Solving allows the examiner to observe the child's thought processes in action. As the child manipulates the colorful materials he will reveal many important characteristics to the perceptive examiner. Some children will be observed using a purely random trial-and-error approach, whereas others will use a more systematic and insightful approach. A child's specific method is certainly related to age and ability level (with younger and duller children more likely to apply a trial-and-error approach), but it is also a function of *cognitive style.* Kagan's (1965) impulsive–reflective dichotomy, for example, relates to problem-solving style. An impulsive child will tend to assemble pieces without much forethought, and probably will resort to a trial-and-error approach. The more reflective child, however, is likely to plan his moves carefully and use an insightful method.

Although impulsivity may be observed throughout the Puzzle Solving test, an impulsive child almost invariably falls prey to item 3 (Carrot). The pieces are set before the child in a manner that often promotes a mere pushing together of the three pieces, without rearranging their order. A truly impulsive child is not likely to reflect about his completed product and notice the error in the shape of his carrot, thereby failing the item. If a lack of impulse control is noted on other puzzles as well, and in additional tasks such as Conceptual Grouping and Opposite Analogies (where the impulsive child may immediately begin to select blocks, or complete the analogy, without reflecting on all pertinent aspects of the examiner's statement), then conclusions can be reached about the child's behavior which may have diagnostic and educational significance. For example, curricular materials can be selected with this variable in mind to help avoid pitfalls common to the impulsive child (see Strauss and Lehtinen, 1947). The fact that the impulsivity may depress some of the child's Indexes also merits the examiner's consideration. However, note that an extremely reflective child may also be penalized on Puzzle Solving because of the time limits imposed on all items and the bonus points for quick performance that may be earned on the last three items.

Observation of the child's problem-solving approach also permits evaluation of his abilities to benefit from feedback and to tolerate frustration. The objects to be constructed are common and colorful; errors are usually quite obvious to children with adequate visual perception. When errors are made, it is interesting to observe children's responses. Do they evidence rigid behavior and persist in trying to connect the same wrong pieces? Do they demonstrate flexibility of thought and try many new combinations until they achieve some success? Are they so easily frustrated by failure that their emotions either interfere with their performance or cause them to give up? Do they evidence goal-oriented and persevering behavior, continuing to work until told to stop or even working slightly beyond time limits? Are they so compulsive that they continue long after the time limits expire, resisting the examiner's efforts at redirection? Do they blame the examiner for deceiving or tricking them—e.g., leaving a piece out or giving them an impossible task? Are they aware of the meaning of the stopwatch and, if so, how do they cope with the potentially stressful and anxiety-producing situation? Are they mature enough to understand that *all* puzzle pieces must be used to solve an item correctly? The answers to these questions and others like it may offer more information about the child than his test age on Puzzle Solving; this point underscores both the clinical value of an ability test such as the McCarthy and the necessity that an examiner be a prudent observer.

The nature of the Puzzle Solving *materials* often evokes reactions from the children. For example, a fearful child may become truly frightened by the Bear. Immature and regressive behavior, in particular, often accompany the visual stimulation of the puzzle pieces. Children who can behave at an age-appropriate level during most of the McCarthy tasks may be unable to control their regressive tendencies when solving the puzzles. "Eating" the Carrot and Pear, or "growling" at the Bear are not uncommon occurrences for young or immature children.

Finally, Puzzle Solving, like Draw-A-Child, usually elicits spontaneous verbalization from the child. These informal remarks sometimes provide a wealth of projective information about the child's attitudes, preoccupations, fears, interests, and anxieties. The Wechsler tests and the Stanford-Binet include many emotionally laden stimuli (e.g., several Picture Arrangement and Verbal Absurdity items involve considerable violence) which are effective for evoking projective data. However, McCarthy avoided items with emotional content to diminish the inhibiting effect of negative emotions on a young child's test performance. Consequently, it is incumbent upon the McCarthy examiner to be carefully attuned to all spontaneous comments made by the child and to record them for subsequent clinical evaluation.

## TAPPING SEQUENCE

The xylophone and mallet seem to arouse many spontaneous behaviors in young children. After being given the mallet, a child may treat the equipment as a toy and begin banging away merrily, with little thought to the task at hand, demonstrating immature or regressive behavior. Conversely, a hostile child may see the mallet as a weapon and start to bang on the xylophone with considerable aggression.

Children who comply with the examiner's instructions and copy the correct sequence sometimes perseverate and continue to tap notes, thereby failing the item. A similar type of perseverative behavior may be evidenced on other McCarthy tasks: during Block Building, several blocks may be placed on the bases of items 2–4, instead of just one; in copying the stimuli in Draw-A-Design, horizontal lines may extend the entire width of the page, circles may wrap around several times, etc; after correctly taking two or three blocks in Counting & Sorting, several additional blocks may be added to the pile; and after selecting all the correct blocks in Conceptual Grouping (e.g., the squares), the left over blocks may suddenly be added to the group ("There are the squares . . . and here come the circles!"). Children who perseverate on Tapping Sequence and on other tasks, including verbal ones (see p. 168), are revealing important diagnostic and clinical information about themselves. The examiner must not forget, however, that a certain amount of perseverative behavior is normal for preschool youngsters. Also, perseveration can lead to failure on many items, rendering a child's scores on several tests (and on some Indexes) invalid as estimates of his true ability in the affected areas. The qualification should be noted along with the numerical score.

Tapping Sequence, like the other short-term memory tasks in the McCarthy, is vulnerable to the effects of distractibility and anxiety. With the exception of item 1 in Tapping Sequence, *none* of the items in the Memory Scale may be repeated; consequently, the child who has a short attention span, is distractible, or suffers from anxiety tends to perform rather poorly on the McCarthy tests of immediate recall. However, determining whether poor performance on Tapping Sequence, Pictorial Memory, Verbal Memory, or Numerical Memory is due to a behavioral variable such as distractibility or to an inadequate memory requires considerable skill and experience. Observation of a child's test-taking behavior, coupled with scrutiny of his wrong responses, helps an examiner understand the probable cause of failure on memory tasks. For example, a child who tends to repeat the correct notes (or digits, or words) in the wrong order most likely has a *sequencing*, rather than an attentional, problem.

Since low scores on memory tests usually have important diagnostic and educational implications, the examiner should try to determine as accurately as possible whether the problem is due to distractibility, a short attention span, a poor short-term memory, inability to sequence, anxiety, a more general difficulty with "automatic" tasks, or some other variable. In order to generate hypotheses, to facilitate the choice of appropriate supplementary tests (if necessary), and to make pertinent educational suggestions, it is important for the examiner to note the child's test behaviors (including compensating mechanisms such as "humming" the tune that is tapped or mouthing digits spoken by the examiner) and to record all incorrect responses.

The clinician should be aware that the average 4-year-old child is successful on item 1 of Tapping Sequence but is not able to reproduce any other items. Item 1 is an introductory item that is demonstrated three times, if necessary; the child earns full credit for successful performance on any of the three trials. As a result, Tapping Sequence is not really a memory test for many young children. Poor performance is more likely to be due to motor coordination problems or an inability to understand what is expected of them than to any type of attentional deficit. This consideration does *not* hold true for any of the other memory tests, although a similar phenomenon occurs for Number Questions. Typically, tests of mental arithmetic join memory tasks as being the most susceptible to distractibility (Cohen, 1959; Wender, 1971, pp. 88–93). However, most of the early items in Number Questions involve number facts or concepts such as "half" rather than mental computations. Thus, distractibility, or any kind of attentional deficit, is *not* likely to be a primary cause of poor performance on this test for children below school age since they are not expected to solve the oral arithmetic problems.

In addition to the usefulness of Tapping Sequence for observing regressive, aggressive, perseverative, and distractible behaviors, the task has two additional features that enhance its clinical value. One is the motor coordination that is required for successful responding; the other is the fact that two types of stimuli—visual and auditory—are received simultaneously.

For many young children the motor act of tapping a xylophone is difficult. Even if a child with a motor problem has learned to compensate for his lack of coordination when manipulating a pencil or a rubber ball, he is likely to evidence motor abnormalities (and experience frustration) during Tapping Sequence. Coordination difficulties suggestive of possible neurological involvement usually are reflected in the child's ability to make contact with the keys of the xylophone. Some children repeatedly miss the keys; others abruptly stop the movement of their arm in a jerky uncoordinated fashion just before striking a key and then require a second movement to make contact. Observations of these and other motor behaviors should be viewed as supplementary information, along with observations of the child's coordination during the other gross and fine motor tests, to be interpreted in conjunction with his Motor Index.

The simultaneous presentation of visual and auditory stimuli may affect a child's performance on Tapping Sequence, just as it may on Pictorial Memory and Conceptual Grouping. Children with a deficit in one modality may be able to compensate by selectively attending to stimuli in their preferred modality. Conversely, children who function adequately in both the visual and auditory channels of communication may have a problem with intersensory integration (Ayres, 1972a, especially Chapter 3; Birch & Lefford, 1963), and their performance on the multisensory tasks may suffer as a result. Although multisensory presentation of stimuli can enhance performance for some children, the extra modality can serve as "noise" for youngsters with poor intersensory integration and disrupt their ability to respond appropriately. One should never *infer* inadequate intersensory integration from McCarthy test scores. However, one may *suspect* a problem and test out the hypothesis with an informal test of intersensory integration (e.g., Birch & Belmont, 1965) if: (1) observations of the child's expressions and behaviors during the entire test battery suggest a possible problem with multisensory tasks, or (2) scores on Tapping Sequence, Pictorial Memory, and perhaps Conceptual Grouping tend to be low when compared with scores on primarily visual tests (e.g., Block Building, Puzzle Solving, Draw-A-Design) or primarily auditory tests (e.g., Number Questions, Verbal Memory, Opposite Analogies).

## ARM COORDINATION

The gross motor tests offer the examiner more than just an extra dimension for assessing young children. These tests, especially Arm Coordination, are clinically rich and permit numerous kinds of observations that are not possible during other portions of the battery. Unlike the formal and structured cognitive testing that takes place at the table, the administration of most gross motor items occurs under informal and recesslike conditions.

The unstructured nature of Leg and Arm Coordination unleashes some children, reducing the examiner's control of the situation. Manipulative children who may have attempted only half-heartedly to take control during the sit-down testing sometimes seize the opportunity to try to set the rules for the games and test the examiner's limits. For example: "I don't want to walk on the line. Watch me hop." "Now *you* catch the beanbag with only one hand." "Watch me hit the target with my eyes closed." "Anyone can bounce a ball. Look how far I can throw it." "I'm not in the mood to skip, but I will if you hop all the way to the wall."

The freedom of movement also allows observation of the hyperactive child, who may have limited his movement to excessive squirming during the first portion of the battery. The immature child as well is given the opportunity to engage in much silly behavior (and usually does) when he is asked to perform various body movements or to play games with toys; sometimes the immature or regressive behavior continues during Imitative Action, as the child brings the tube to his mouth or forehead instead of his eye. Overconcern about bodily harm is also observed as some children are afraid to walk backward or fear the Beanbag Catch Game. Determination of whether the latter behaviors reflect insecurity about motor ability, a generalized fearfulness, paranoic tendencies, or some other variable depends upon the examiner's perceptiveness in interpreting these and related test behaviors.

Some very aggressive children perceive the ball and beanbag as weapons, rather than toys, and give examiners legitimate cause for concern about their own bodily harm. (On projective drawings, "balls" are considered symbols of the "forces" between people, and the manner of play is interpreted as establishing what type of relationship exists between the ball possessor and others; see Burns and Kaufman, 1972, pp. 46–74.) Whereas Tapping Sequence permits observation of aggression against objects, the Arm Coordination tasks may elicit aggression against either objects (such as windows) or people. The fact that Arm Coordination may evoke aggressive behaviors enhances its clinical value. However, the examiner should always be aware of potential dangers to person or property and be cautious while administering the test—especially when testing children suspected of behavioral disorders.

Sometimes aggressive behavior occurs as a response to extreme frustration. Since the Ball Bouncing and Beanbag Target Games are fairly difficult for many children, especially younger ones, the ability to tolerate frustration is almost a built-in requirement of the test. (For example, the average 3 year old earns only about 1 point on each of the three parts of Arm Coordination.) In addition, failure on all three Arm Coordination tasks is almost always quite obvious to the child; even a child who hits the target with the beanbag does not know he earns half-credit, and may perceive his inability to make a bull's-eye as failure. Children who cannot cope with unsuccessful performance may become aggressive or extremely withdrawn, which may disrupt rapport and require tactful intervention by the examiner. Defense mechanisms are also commonly used in the face of frustration. Rationalization ("My arm hurts." "I missed it because I don't like playing catch.") and projection ("Your throw was awful.") are frequent defenses used by children during Arm Coordination.

Deception and cheating are also occasionally noticed during Arm Coordination, again adding to the clinical usefulness of the test. Children reveal much about their sense of ethics as they inch forward (usually when the examiner is apparently not looking) to get closer than the prescribed distance for catching the beanbag; as they "accidentally" step well over the foul line in the target game; as they argue strenuously that a toss that missed the target really went through the hole; or as they furtively switch to their preferred hand for catching or throwing when the examiner turns his head for a moment. The way to deal with occurrences such as these is discussed in Chapter 2. However, the clinical value of the observations should not be lost because of the examiner's possible preoccupations with correct administration and scoring of the items.

The unstructured motor break also provides a good opportunity to note a child's *affect*. Despite the frustration children may encounter, the gross motor tasks are still gamelike and are mostly fun. Children with dull affect during the more mundane cognitive items are often seen to undergo metamorphosis and liven up dramatically during the "intermission." The children who maintain a dull affect even during the recesslike activities are of particular concern and require careful clinical evaluation. Emotionally labile youngsters, who may vacillate from one extreme emotional state to another and display volatile behavior during the motor tests, also merit special attention.

Problems with impulse control are sometimes observed during the beanbag games. An impulsive child may throw the beanbag at the target without aiming, as if it were a "hot potato." He may also have a difficult time keeping one hand behind his back while attempting to catch the beanbag with his other hand. As the beanbag approaches, the hidden hand will emerge and sometimes help out to make the catch.

The examiner has to be extremely perceptive and knowledgeable to discern whether an emergent hand is caused by behavioral or neurological variables. It may be due to motor overflow (Roach & Kephart, 1966, pp. 44–47) or motor impersistence (Ayres, 1972a, p. 173), which are among the many neurological "soft" signs that may be observed during the administration of the Motor Scale. Regardless of a child's success at the various coordination items, his style of responding may reveal unusual awkwardness, poor muscle tone, or other evidence of possible neurological involvement. Wavering while standing on one foot, awkward movements with one or both arms when throwing the beanbag, or other visible coordination difficulties with balance or precision of muscle movements—if corroborated with other soft signs—may suggest neurological dysfunction. When a child evidences several motor abnormalities, the possibility of developmental apraxia (Ayres, 1972a, chap. 11) should be considered.

A different type of soft sign concerns the establishment of hand dominance. During the administration of Arm Coordination, the examiner notes the child's preferred hand for each task. These preferences, along with the hand the child uses for the drawing tests, determine whether the child is classified as having established hand dominance. Since lateral dominance usually develops between the ages of about 5 and 9 years (Belmont & Birch, 1963; Crawford, 1966), failure to establish a consistent hand preference is of little concern for children below age 5. For older children, mixed hand dominance should be regarded as a soft sign that is worthy of interpretation *only if the child evidences other soft signs as well.* Hence, the examiner should investigate the pattern of behaviors of an older child who has not established hand dominance for evidence of any spatial, perceptual, or motor problems. The results of numerous research studies on lateral dominance (many of which are discussed by Ayres, 1972a, and Bannatyne, 1971) yield conflicting results about its clinical, diagnostic, and educational value. The positive research findings suggest the potential value of this variable for some purposes; the negative findings underscore the need for keeping the child's hand dominance rating on the McCarthy in perspective and not interpreting it in isolation. In addition, Bannatyne's (1971, p. 212) emphatic criticism of laterality items which "utilize activities such as hammering or writing for which a particular hand has been *deliberately trained*" applies to McCarthy's measure of hand dominance and is worthy of careful consideration.

A study of McCarthy's hand dominance rating for the normal standardization sample found that children aged 5–8½ who had established hand dominance (either right or left) did significantly better on Right–Left Orientation than those with mixed dominance (Kaufman, Zalma, & Kaufman, in preparation). The same study showed that 8½ year olds who had established dominance obtained a significantly higher Motor Index than age-mates with mixed dominance. Finally, the study revealed that preschool children who established hand dominance obtained GCIs and Motor Indexes that were one-third of a standard deviation *higher* than the Indexes obtained by preschoolers with mixed dominance. One implication of the findings of this study is that it indeed makes sense to integrate the child's hand dominance rating with other variables such as motor coordination and spatial orientation (knowledge of right versus left). Another implication is that precocious establishment of dominance in young children may be a sign of a developmental or neurological integrity in their functioning.

Since the measure of hand dominance is based on only four independent observations, the examiner may wish to supplement the rating
by recording the hand the child uses to hold the mallet in Tapping
Sequence and the tube in Imitative Action, and the predominant hand
used to handle the blocks in Counting & Sorting and Conceptual
Grouping. The thumb placed on top in the clasping hands item of Imitative Action might also be noted; this type of item requires no training and is therefore ideal for assessing laterality, according to Bannatyne (1971). In addition, it may be of interest to determine whether
the child *performs* better with one hand or the other. Comparisons of
the number of catches made with each hand or the number of points
earned with each hand in the target game would provide this information. However, differences must be large (e.g., three catches with the
left hand and none with the right hand) to infer a meaningful discrepancy. This type of right–left comparison may also be applied to
the Standing on One Foot item in Leg Coordination if supplementary
data on laterality are desired. Eye preference is recorded during Imitative Action, but this laterality information is of dubious value. First,
the measurement is based on a single item; second, it is questionable
whether children are evidencing true eye preference or simply trying to
imitate the eye used by the examiner in the demonstration.

The above discussion of lateral dominance is based on conventional definitions and usage of this concept. However, the exciting
findings of the split-brain research, concerning differentiation of function of the right and left hemispheres (Bakan, 1971; Kinsbourne &
Smith, 1974; Ornstein, 1972, 1973), have revolutionized the notion of
cerebral dominance. Unfortunately, virtually all of the research has
been conducted on adults, so little is known about the development of
hemisphere dominance. As new studies are carried out with young
children, topics such as hand dominance may be viewed from a different perspective, perhaps subsumed by a more global and comprehensive approach to dominance. (Ayres, 1972a, chap. 16, offers some
insights on the relationship of hand dominance to the split-brain findings.) At that time, research findings, such as those mentioned above
concerning McCarthy's hand dominance rating, may need to be reinterpreted, and the clinical and neuropsychological applications of
laterality may acquire new and different dimensions.

One final comment about Arm Coordination merits attention:
namely, the many clinical observations and qualitative interpretations
afforded by it (and by Leg Coordination) are, in part, dependent on its

relatively *unstructured* nature. Although the examiner has to maintain control of the situation in the face of manipulation, aggression, or immaturity, it is important to remember the benefits of avoiding the imposition of too much structure. The child needs the break and the easing, at least temporarily, of the teacher–student type of relationship that often pervades individual tests of mental ability. Furthermore, the examiner needs to retain the opportunities to observe the multifaceted behaviors that are often elicited during the motor break. Even with a child who has no soft signs or behavioral problems, the gross motor tests are a showplace for his energy level, athletic ability, spirit of competition, and his basic drive and motivation for success.

## VERBAL FLUENCY

The competitive spirit and achievement motivation that may emerge during Arm Coordination usually reappear during the highly speeded Verbal Fluency test. Many children accept the challenge of this word game and try to bombard the examiner with appropriate responses in rapid-fire succession. Others may become highly anxious because of the stopwatch and the demands of the task and simply panic on one or more of the items. Still others, particularly younger or immature children, may be oblivious to the timing and respond as quickly as the fireman in the Stanford-Binet item who smoked a cigar before putting out the fire.

It is not uncommon for an immature youngster to start talking about something irrelevant once the timing has begun. For example, a child may say "a dog" for the animal naming item and then start telling the examiner about the pet dog he received as a Christmas gift. Occasionally, a manipulative child, sensing the *examiner's* slight increase in tension level during the competitive Verbal Fluency test, may give one or two responses and say—in a calm, emotionless man-ner—"I don't want to finish now. We'll do this one later." The examiner needs to be perceptive to be able to distinguish between immaturity, manipulativeness, and simple reflectiveness. Some youngsters respond quite deliberately because of a reflective cognitive style. As is true for Puzzle Solving, a reflective child is often penalized on Verbal Fluency because of the time limits that are imposed. However, this problem is not nearly as severe for the McCarthy as it is for the WPPSI and WISC-R, which include numerous timed items.

Perseveration is sometimes noted during Verbal Fluency, as illustrated by the following responses to "things to wear:" pants, short pants, long pants, black pants, red pants, pretty pants. Perseveration may also span two or more items: e.g., a child who has just finished the second item (animals), may include a few animals among his responses to item 3 (things to wear). Perseveration on verbal tasks may also be noted during Opposite Analogies and Verbal Memory. A child who responds correctly to the analogy "cotton is *soft,* and rocks are _____," for example, sometimes answers "hard" to the next few analogies as well. On Verbal Memory, a youngster may incorporate details from the sentences in Part I while telling the story in Part II. Children who perseverate on the verbal tests may exhibit some perseverative tendencies on nonverbal tasks as well. Their responses to the Perceptual–Performance tests that are most susceptible to perseveration (see p. 159) should be evaluated to assess the pervasiveness of the behavior.

The specific responses given by children to the various Verbal Fluency items may be analyzed qualitatively. Some responses provide information about the child's background, culture, or socioeconomic level (e.g., naming things to eat or wear that are extremely expensive, or that are associated closely with a particular ethnic group or subculture). A child's answers to Things to Wear may indicate a preoccupation with sex (bra, panties), although more evidence would be needed—such as the drawing of genitals in Draw-A-Child—before formulating any hypotheses. Some children may give sex-related responses to impress or shock the examiner, just as they may blurt out "ants" or "snails" for things to eat.

Children who give responses that seem weird or bizarre may be evidencing loose thinking or schizophrenic thought patterns. However, unless the child exhibits additional signs of a behavioral disorder on other tasks, the examiner should place little emphasis on a few weird answers. Apparent bizarre responses may result from a child's attempt to bluff when he runs out of correct answers. Furthermore, the seeming illogic of a child's categorization may be logical from the perspective of his own level of cognitive development. Logical classification skills are in the process of rapid development for children in the 2½–8½ age range. Even a 7 or 8 year old who seems to be able to group objects may not yet be a true classifier in the Piagetian sense (Inhelder & Piaget, 1969). Consequently, the examiner should consider the child's performance on Conceptual Grouping before evaluating any unusual categorizations in Verbal Fluency.

One of the most valuable assets of Verbal Fluency is that the child's responses may be evaluated for their creativity. Even though fluency is one aspect of divergent thinking, or creativity, the mere number of responses in a given category does not offer enough qualitative information about the breadth and scope of the child's creative potential. Besides fluency, Guilford (1967) describes other important aspects of creativity such as originality, flexibility, and elaboration. Originality refers to the unusualness (infrequency of occurrence) of a correct response; flexibility concerns the number of different *kinds* of responses (e.g., does a child only name dessert foods for Things to Eat, or does he name meats and vegetables as well); and elaboration involves the amount of novelty that is spontaneously added to a stimulus.

Elaboration is not pertinent to the Verbal Fluency test. However, this aspect of creativity may be assessed informally by evaluating the child's product in Draw-A-Child. Youngsters who respond to the instruction of drawing a boy or girl by adding jewelry and several articles of clothing, or by showing the human figure engaged in an activity, would be rated highly on the creative variable of elaboration.

Originality and flexibility may be assessed by evaluating a child's responses to the Verbal Fluency items. Originality may be determined statistically be delineating the number of times each correct response is given by a large normal population. Original responses may be defined arbitrarily as those responses which are given by fewer than 5 of 100 children at any particular age. However, a formal approach to studying originality makes it more of a quantitative than a qualitative venture and would involve a cumbersome set of tables for each age group. Instead, the examiner should informally evaluate a child's responses to the Verbal Fluency items. Common sense plus experience with the McCarthy will enable the examiner to label various responses as original. A child who names "limes, radishes, and yogurt" for things to eat is obviously more original than the youngster who says, "meat, corn, and eggs"—even though both are equally fluent. Similarly, bees and pelicans are more unusual animals than dogs and tigers; mittens and a poncho show greater originality as things to wear than socks and pants; and a helicopter and slide are more original things to ride than a car or a train.

To determine a child's flexibility, a system is needed to group responses to each Verbal Fluency item into subcategories. A proposed system developed by N. Kaufman (1973) to facilitate the assessment of a child's flexibility is presented in Figure 7-1. The responses given by two children to the animal naming item are listed below:

*Carl:* tiger, zebra, monkey, goat, cow, elephant
*Kay:* bird, cow, squirrel, lion

Carl's six animals fit into only two of the categories shown in Figure 7-1 (Zoo, Barnyard), whereas *each* of Kay's four animals represents a separate category (Birds, Barnyard, Wildlife, Zoo). Therefore, even though Carl was more *fluent* on the animal item, Kay evidenced greater *flexibility*. Figure 7-1 offers a suggested way of categorizing responses, but it is by no means definitive. Examiners are encouraged to use their creativity to modify Figure 7-1 or to develop an entirely new classification system.

No empirical guidelines are available to determine how flexible or original a child's responses must be to qualify as "very creative," and none are needed. The examiner should use subjective judgment to estimate whether the child's responses to Verbal Fluency and Draw-A-Child are suggestive of good creative potential. Observations of the child's behaviors during other portions of the battery may also be helpful. For example, a 3½-year-old girl was observed pretending that the large square blocks in Conceptual Grouping were bread, and the large round blocks were balogna. She then made a balogna sandwich and used the small round blocks as money to buy it!

When creative ability is suggested, the examiner may consider administering comprehensive tests that are specifically geared for assessing creativity (nonverbal as well as verbal) in children. The Torrance Tests of Creative Thinking (Torrance, 1974b) are useful supplements for an evaluation of the school-age child's creativity; for preschool youngsters, the examiner may wish to administer the research edition of Thinking Creatively in Action and Movement (Torrance, 1976). Although the creative aspects of intelligence are not measured by conventional intelligence tests and are rarely assessed in psychoeducational diagnosis, this aspect of functioning is worthy of thoughtful consideration. N. Kaufman (1973) found that many of the 22 minimally brain dysfunctioned children she tested exhibited considerable fluency, flexibility, and originality. In addition, the group as a whole tended to give more original responses than their matched

## "FLEXIBILITY" CATEGORIES

| 1. Things to Eat | 2. Animals | 3. Things to Wear | 4. Things to Ride |
|---|---|---|---|
| A. Meat, Poultry, Fish | A. Zoo (found predominantly in the zoo, not wild in U.S.: e.g., lion, giraffe, hippopotamus) | A. Regular outfits (e.g., pants, shirt, dress, skirt, sneakers) | A. Land vehicles—motorized (e.g., car, truck, train, motorcycle, tractor) |
| B. Fruits | | B. Undergarments, Nightwear | B. Land vehicles—self-propelled (e.g., bike, sliding board, skates, scooter) |
| C. Vegetables | B. Wildlife (found wild in U.S., although they may also be in zoo: e.g., chipmunk, squirrel, deer, fox, mouse) | C. Outerwear (e.g., coat, sweater, hat, gloves) | C. Air vehicle |
| D. Desserts, Candy | | D. Accessories (e.g., jewelry, tie, belt, wig) | D. Water vehicle |
| E. Dairy & eggs | | E. Special occasion clothes (e.g., swim trunks, smock, Halloween mask) | E. Animals |
| F. Condiments | C. Barnyard | | F. Amusement ride (e.g., ferris wheel) |
| G. Flour products (breads, cereals, macaroni) | D. Birds (excluding barnyard fowl) | | |
| | E. Reptiles, Amphibians, Fish | | |
| | F. Insects | | |

Fig. 7-1. List of "flexibility" categories for classifying responses to each Verbal Fluency item.

controls. Even though her study is inconclusive, it is clear that some children with learning problems may have an untapped and unknown integrity in creative intelligence—one which may have important consequences for their remedial program.

One major pathway toward remediating learning disabilities is to focus on available strengths. Whereas raising the child's deficit level is always an educational goal, it cannot be reached without help from the child's assets and capabilities. Perhaps making use of the learning disabled's creative verbal abilities could further his language functioning by freely associating the two. Stressing the stimulation and inclusion of originality and flexibility in language style may very well facilitate the desired improvement in performance. One study that attempted to incorporate this consideration into the instructional plan for the learning disabled was undertaken by Zamm (1973), who developed a language arts program which focused on meaning and creativity. Another program designed to make use of the learning disabled child's creativity for his remediation is found in the report by Kaslow (1972). In addition, it would be so potentially helpful if the currently boring linguistic readers could be infused with greater interest and creative value. An example of a set of books designed for creative content interest is *Books for Young Explorers* published by the National Geographic Society (see Bannatyne, 1973, pp. 105–106, for an evaluation of this series). Other curriculum and instructional materials that are intended to facilitate creative thinking are summarized by Torrance (1974a).

Because of the potential educational value of creativity, clinicians are advised to be alert for evidences of creative talent in the child's responses to Verbal Fluency and Draw-A-Child and in the child's behaviors during the testing session, and to administer a formal measure of creativity when appropriate.

# PART III

# Integration of the McCarthy
# with Other Tests

Parts I and II dealt exclusively with the McCarthy Scales. Part III extends the scope of McCarthy interpretation by integrating the Indexes and test scores with data obtained on other tests. Since examiners usually administer more than one test to a child referred for a learning or behavioral disorder, the ability to interpret the McCarthy scores in the context of other test scores is essential for a competent clinician.

Chapter 8 relates the McCarthy to other instruments and discusses the different types of supplementary measures that are desirable under various circumstances. The two main reasons for using multitest assessment—diagnosis and educational planning—are also treated in this chapter.

Finally, Chapter 9 presents nine case studies of preschool and primary-grade children who were referred to a clinic for psychological evaluation. Each child was administered the McCarthy along with assorted other tests. The case reports reflect the integration of test data, background information, and behavioral observations, and represent an application of the principles discussed in Chapter 8 and all of Part II.

# Chapter 8
## Using the McCarthy as Part of a Larger Test Battery

The days of using a single instrument for making a diagnosis or for planning an educational program should be over, or at least numbered. Even a test battery as diverse as the McCarthy should be treated as a rich source of clinical hypotheses, but not as a 1-hour diagnostic tool or as an indicator of specific areas to be remediated. Elsewhere we have proposed a variety of studies that would enhance the McCarthy's value to the test user (Kaufman & Kaufman, 1977). If some of these studies are conducted, the results may support the diagnostic importance of certain McCarthy profiles and the value of educational programs geared specifically to the child's performance on the McCarthy. Until then, the McCarthy—like the WPPSI, WISC-R, ITPA, and Stanford-Binet—should be used to help understand the child's pattern of functioning and to make appropriate educational *suggestions* based on the findings. The more complex issues of diagnosis, remediation, and selecting a preschool curriculum demand the integration of McCarthy results, data yielded by other instruments, clinical observations, and specific histories.

The aim of this chapter is to enable the examiner to integrate a child's McCarthy scores with his scores on other tests. Too often several tests are given to a child only to have the examiner interpret each in isolation. Regardless of whether an instrument is called a test of ability, intelligence, language, or perceptual–motor development, it shares certain commonalities with virtually all other tests in the cognitive domain. Davis and Walker (1976), for example, obtained substantial intercorrelations of about .80 among the following diverse variables: McCarthy GCI, Stanford-Binet IQ, overall score on the ITPA, and overall score on Carrow's (1973) Test for Auditory Comprehension. Knowledge of the commonalities between the McCarthy and other tests is essential since it facilitates both test selection and test interpretation.

The type of tests often needed to supplement the information yielded by the McCarthy is discussed below, as is the psychoeducational diagnostic technique of selecting additional measures based on hypotheses generated from a McCarthy administration. The use of McCarthy short forms for screening is treated to address a practical issue—the need to identify rapidly those children who are likely to benefit most from a complete psychoeducational evaluation. Finally, a section is devoted to the use of selected portions of the McCarthy to serve as supplements when a different intelligence test, such as the WPPSI, WISC-R, or Stanford-Binet, is chosen as the featured ability measure in a neuropsychological battery.

The topics of diagnosis and educational planning are also discussed in this chapter, at the beginning and end, respectively. The goal is to put the other topics (pertaining to the integration of the McCarthy with various instruments) into a meaningful context and, hence, into better perspective. Therefore, the diagnostic and educational issues are handled globally rather than in depth.

The fact that competent diagnosis and remediation demand multitest assessment does not imply that the McCarthy has to be routinely supplemented with other instruments. The McCarthy provides a broad profile of abilities that is quite ample for many testing purposes. Indeed, the limited availability of testing time, coupled with a backlog of cases to be tested, often makes it impossible for an examiner to devote more than about 1 hour to each child. Hence, this chapter is intended primarily for examiners who are engaged in psychological or psychoeducational assessment, and whose schedules permit the administration of several tests. However, the chapter should also be useful for examiners who are called on to diagnose and/or plan remediation, but who are not permitted the freedom to do extensive testing. These examiners need to be reminded of the limitations in the coverage of the McCarthy, or of any conventional intelligence test, and of the *tentativeness* of any diagnosis or educational plan based on a single test battery.

Many tests are mentioned in this chapter. Since the focus of the book is on the McCarthy, an effort was made *not* to evaluate the other measures critically. Examiners are advised to consult Buros' (1972) *Mental Measurements Yearbook,* as well as pertinent test manuals, to determine the suitability of any particular instrument for their purposes. From our perspective, each test that is mentioned has psychometric properties adequate enough to be used in the manner described in the sections that follow.

### DIAGNOSTIC ISSUES

Effective psychological diagnosis, like effective medical diagnosis, takes time and requires multifaceted measurement. One key to being a good diagnostician is maintaining an up-to-date and thorough repertoire of available instruments for assessing a variety of mental, perceptual, language, motor, and emotional processes in children. Knowledge of these measurement tools allows the examiner latitude when selecting supplementary tests for a comprehensive psychological evaluation.

Sometimes the examiner can select additional tests in advance, based on the reasons for the child's referral. Other times, supplementary measures can only be chosen in light of the child's performance on the McCarthy. When a second testing session is feasible, the examiner can choose extra measures leisurely, after studying the McCarthy profile in depth. If only one session is possible, decisions about additional testing have to be made on the spur of the moment based on clinical hunches and subjective judgments of the child's integrities and deficits. Thorough understanding of the typical performance of children at different points in the McCarthy age range (see Chapter 4) greatly facilitates these on-the-spot judgments. An intuitive understanding of what is measured by other available instruments, along with the flexibility that permits fragmentation of longer batteries to ensure that only *pertinent* subtests are administered, is also essential.

When diagnosing a child suspected of a learning or behavioral disorder there are some fairly straightforward procedures to follow. If the child's GCI or IQ is in the deficient or borderline ranges, then a measure of adaptive behavior should be administered to determine the child's level of social functioning. Mercer and Lewis' (in press) or Lambert et al.'s (1975) instruments for assessing adaptive behavior are excellent supplements to the GCI or IQ for school-age children; the Vineland Social Maturity Scale (Doll, 1965) may be used for preschool youngsters as well. (Note that all three instruments require interviews with the parent or teacher.) A primary diagnosis of mental retardation may then be made if *both* the cognitive and adaptive measures yield a consistent picture of subnormal functioning.

If retardation can be eliminated as a suspected diagnosis, and if there is no evidence of sensory loss, a more severe neurological impairment merits consideration. A thorough neuropsychological battery, such as the type proposed by Lerner (1976) or Bush and Waugh (1976) is advised. Whereas the McCarthy provides measurement in several of the areas that need evaluation—notably academic potential, gross and fine motor coordination, and memory—a comprehensive battery will also include formal assessment of speech, language, school achievement (where relevant), and additional perceptual–motor functions.

Chalfant and Scheffelin (1969) and Clements (1966) have provided definitions of learning disabilities (minimal brain dysfunction) which offer a valuable set of guidelines for reaching a logical diagnosis. The operational definition outlined by Chalfant and King (1976) represents an even greater step in the direction of objective diagnostic procedures. Since virtually all definitions of learning disabilities emphasize differential performance in skill areas, the McCarthy profile should contribute much toward the ultimate diagnosis. Significant scatter among a child's Scale Indexes (Chapter 5) or performance on the drawing tests that is significantly below his overall age of functioning (Chapter 6) raises the odds of a diagnosis of learning disabilities. However, other pertinent criteria must be met as well before reaching even a tentative conclusion; diagnoses such as emotional disturbance or brain damage are also possible (and not uncommon) explanations of a discrepancy between ability and achievement.

Emotional disturbance is particularly difficult to distinguish from learning disabilities as a primary diagnosis of children who have poor academic achievement despite normal or near-normal intelligence. Learning disabled children usually manifest behavioral characteristics that are similar in kind (but not in severity) to the traits of some emotionally disturbed youngsters. In addition, learning disabled children often have an overlay of emotional disturbance resulting from their school failure, further complicating the task of the diagnostician. Supplementary projective measures, such as drawing tests, the Children's Apperception Test, or the Rorschach, should be administered to facilitate differential diagnosis (e.g., DiLeo, 1973; Haworth, 1966; Koppitz, 1963, 1968; Rabin & Haworth, 1960).

The procedures discussed above apply, in general, to the differential diagnosis of both preschool and school-age children. However, diagnosis of preschool children is particularly difficult. For one thing, the test performance of preschool youngsters tends to be variable from one occasion to the other. A low GCI (or IQ) may show a striking increase, and a dynamic profile may flatten out considerably, based on a second evaluation. Many factors can account for this variability including an uneven rate of development, delayed language, motivational differences, or situational changes in emotional behavior. Further complicating the diagnostic process in very young children is the possibility that deficient functioning may be due to a developmental lag or to a sensory loss that has escaped detection.

One of the salient characteristics of learning disabled children is poor school achievement. For preschool youngsters, this criterion cannot be evaluated for obvious reasons. Nevertheless, preschoolers may be diagnosed as having neurological impairment and as being good candidates for encountering school failure in the future if they manifest many of the test-related and behavioral symptoms of the learning disabilities–minimal brain dysfunction syndrome. Here again, a problem arises. Most of the typical behavioral traits of learning disabled children—e.g., emotional lability, impulsivity, low frustration tolerance, distractibility—are also characteristic of very young children. Determining when these behaviors reach abnormal proportions, perhaps to a degree that will warrant a primary diagnosis of emotional disturbance, requires considerable experience with preschool children and a thorough understanding of the growing child from both a developmental perspective (Mussen, Conger, & Kagan, 1973) and a clinical perspective (Shirley, 1963).

Because of the variability in the test performance of young children, the rapidity of growth at some points in the developmental cycle, and the difficulty in reaching clearcut diagnoses, the wisest course of action is *periodic retesting* of preschool youngsters. Whenever feasible, reevaluations should be undertaken within 6–12 months of the previous testing, depending on the child's age and the apparent severity of the symptoms. In general, younger children and children with more serious problems require the most frequent follow-up testing.

The McCarthy is thus proposed for inclusion in neuropsychological batteries. For children aged 3–6½ years it should be given strong consideration as the major cognitive and motor instrument in a comprehensive evaluation. For older children, the examiner may prefer to administer the WISC-R as the featured tool in a neuropsychological battery. (The limitations of the McCarthy for school-age youngsters are discussed in Chapter 1.) However, even when a different intelligence test is used, the examiner may consider using portions of the McCarthy for supplementary information or for following up clinical hypotheses.

In short, the McCarthy is not a diagnostic tool unless used in conjunction with other measures. When used alone, the McCarthy provides valuable information about a child's approximate level of mental and motor functioning; it yields data concerning his relatively strong and weak areas of functioning; it promotes the generation of hypotheses about specific skills that may be evaluated with subsequent testing; it includes a set of stimuli which permit the qualitative observation of numerous important behaviors; and it produces a profile which lends itself to suggestions for educational planning. However, future research notwithstanding, the McCarthy profile does not lead directly to a diagnostic conclusion.

Examiners who are interested in improving their skill at differential diagnosis are advised to consult Bakwin and Bakwin (1966), Kessler (1966), or Wolman (1972), who discuss attributes, etiologies, and distinguishing characteristics of various childhood psychopathologies. In addition, the following references deal more specifically with the diagnosis of learning disorders and should be valuable resources for the clinician: Bannatyne (1971); Berry (1969); Carrow (1972); Frierson and Barbe (1967, Part III); Hellmuth (1968); Khanna (1973); Kirk & Kirk (1971); Lerner (1976, chap. 5); Natchez (1968, Part II); Sapir and Nitzburg (1973, Section V); Bush and Waugh (1976). The film *Why Billy Couldn't Learn* (distributed by the California Association for Neurologically Handicapped Children, P.O. Box 604, Los Angeles, Calif. 90053) shows psychoeducational diagnosis in action and illustrates the principles discussed in many of the above books. Also of interest to the diagnostician working with young children is Palmer's (1970) approach to clinical assessment,

Sattler's (1974) broad coverage of intellectual assessment, Copel's (1967) treatment of the differential diagnosis of various psychopathologies, and Wisland's (1974) application of psychoeducational diagnosis to numerous exceptionalities. Finally, McCarthy's (1952, 1954, 1966, 1971) own treatment of the diagnosis of speech- and language-related disorders (e.g., developmental aphasia, childhood schizophrenia) has much to offer the clinician.

## SUPPLEMENTING THE INFORMATION
## YIELDED BY THE McCARTHY

An extra 15 or 20 minutes of testing time and a similar increment in scoring time can embellish the picture of a child that emerges from an administration of the McCarthy. Whenever feasible the examiner should consider supplementing the McCarthy with a measure of sociocultural knowledge and with the Bender-Gestalt test; subsequent evaluation of a child's drawing of a boy or girl by a more comprehensive scoring system is also desirable. (The administration of the Bender and the evaluation of the human figure drawing are applicable primarily to children aged 5 and above.) When ample testing time is available, the Illinois Test of Psycholinguistic Abilities (ITPA) sometimes merits attention as an adjunct measure. The McCarthy and ITPA complement each other quite nicely. The commonalities between the instruments permit more reliable assessment of a child's verbal and nonverbal abilities, while the uniqueness of each sometimes justifies the administration of both comprehensive batteries. The integration of the McCarthy with social and cultural measures, drawing tests, and the ITPA, is treated below.

### Social and Cultural Measures

Disadvantaged children are sometimes penalized on intelligence tests by the inclusion of culturally loaded and socially oriented items. Their IQs may slip into the Borderline or Mentally Deficient categories, suggesting subnormal potential, because they did not acquire enough facts from their environment or because of subcultural differences in social customs. In this sense, it is advantageous that the child's GCI on the McCarthy is not heavily dependent on social and cultural knowledge.

However, the failure of the McCarthy to measure sociocultural skills leaves a gap in the examiner's understanding of the child's total ability spectrum. The problem may be remedied for children aged 4 and above by administering the WPPSI or WISC-R Information and Comprehension subtests. The Stanford-Binet tasks categorized by Sattler (1974, p. 139) as measuring social intelligence may also be administered as a supplement to the McCarthy. This category comprises tasks such as Response to Pictures, Comprehension, Picture Absurdities, and Problem Situations, and measures both social judgment and social maturity. The diversity of tasks is appealing and they are suitable for all children in the 2½–8½-year-old range; unfortunately, the lack of a *score* makes these tasks more of a qualitative than a quantitative supplement. However, the age level of the hardest task passed by the child may be used as a crude estimate of his level of sociocultural functioning.

Another means of measuring the social knowledge of children aged 3 and above is to administer the two Social Adjustment subtests of the Detroit Tests of Learning Aptitude (Baker & Leland, 1967). Whenever appropriate, both subtests should be given since they measure different skills. Social Adjustment A resembles the Binet or Wechsler Comprehension tasks, and Social Adjustment B assesses understanding of socially relevant information and vocabulary.

For children aged 4 and above, Wechsler's Information and Comprehension subtests provide the best supplement to the McCarthy due to the excellence of the WPPSI and WISC-R normative samples and the availability of reliable scaled scores for each subtest. However, the Wechsler, Binet, and Detroit measures of sociocultural abilities all add a great deal to the information yielded by the McCarthy, and all are worthy supplements. One important side effect of using the McCarthy along with a separate measure of social and cultural knowledge is that the latter skills are assessed without influencing the child's estimate of academic potential (i.e., his GCI).

The advantages of administering any of the abovementioned tasks in conjunction with the McCarthy actually go beyond the measurement of sociocultural skills. The McCarthy is also fairly limited in its assessment of verbal expression and reasoning (see p. 18) and the Guilford operation of evaluation (see p. 102). Most social and cultural items require all of these skills for success. Consequently, by administering a few selected portions of a different test battery, the McCarthy examiner can enhance his understanding of the child's functioning in several key areas.

When the Wechsler Information and Comprehension subtests are administered, the child's scaled scores may be compared to his GCI and Verbal Index. Since the standard scores for the Wechsler subtests, the GCI, and the Scale Indexes all have different means and standard deviations, Table 8-1 was developed to facilitate direct comparisons. This table also includes the ITPA standard scores and the Wechsler IQs to enable the examiner to compare a child's level of functioning on a variety of measures. Enter the table with the child's scores on two different tests, and convert the scores to a common metric such as a percentile rank or the number of standard deviations from the mean. *As a rule of thumb, two scores should be more than one standard deviation apart to be considered significantly different.*

*Example:* Suppose a child earns a scaled score of 7 on WPPSI Comprehension and a McCarthy Verbal Index of 54. From Table 8-1, his Comprehension score is found to be 1 standard deviation *below* the mean, whereas his Verbal Index (when rounded to the nearest Index in the table) is $\frac{1}{2}$ standard deviation *above* the mean. The difference of $1\frac{1}{2}$ standard deviations between them may be considered significant, suggesting that his ability on the Comprehension subtest is more poorly developed than his overall verbal skills, as assessed by the McCarthy.

To interpret differences between scores on the McCarthy and on sociocultural measures, the examiner should consider the entire McCarthy profile. Unusually high or low scores on the supplementary tasks may be related to social and cultural variables, but they may also be a function of the child's expressive or reasoning abilities. These competing hypotheses should be checked out, using the investigative approach described in Chapter 6, before reaching any conclusions about the child's sociocultural knowledge.

Let us assume that a disadvantaged child scores significantly higher on the McCarthy GCI and Verbal Index than on the adjunct sociocultural tasks. If an examination of his McCarthy profile reveals adequate reasoning and verbal expression, then the best explanation of the depressed scores is the impact of the child's culturally disadvantaged or culturally different environment. The fact that he did relatively well on the McCarthy suggests that he has potential despite his limited exposure to socially relevant information. With proper intervention, the prognosis would be good.

High scores on the sociocultural tasks are also of interest, especially when they do not seem to be a function of well-developed prob-

**Table 8-1**

Comparability of the Standard Scores Yielded by the
McCarthy and by Other Individual Ability Tests

| Number of SDs from the Mean | McCarthy GCI, Binet IQ | McCarthy Scale Index | Wechsler V, P, or FS IQ | Wechsler Scaled Score | ITPA Scaled Score | Per- centile Rank |
|---|---|---|---|---|---|---|
| +3 | 148 | — | 145 | 19 | 54 | 99.9 |
| +2¾ | 144 | 78 | 141 | 18 | 52 | 99.7 |
| +2½ | 140 | 75 | 138 | — | 51 | 99.4 |
| +2¼ | 136 | 72 | 134 | 17 | 50 | 99 |
| +2 | 132 | 70 | 130 | 16 | 48 | 98 |
| +1¾ | 128 | 68 | 126 | 15 | 46 | 96 |
| +1½ | 124 | 65 | 122 | — | 45 | 93 |
| +1¼ | 120 | 62 | 119 | 14 | 44 | 89 |
| +1 | 116 | 60 | 115 | 13 | 42 | 84 |
| +¾ | 112 | 58 | 111 | 12 | 40 | 77 |
| +½ | 108 | 55 | 108 | — | 39 | 69 |
| +¼ | 104 | 52 | 104 | 11 | 38 | 60 |
| 0 | 100 | 50 | 100 | 10 | 36 | 50 |
| −¼ | 96 | 48 | 96 | 9 | 34 | 40 |
| −½ | 92 | 45 | 92 | — | 33 | 31 |
| −¾ | 88 | 42 | 89 | 8 | 32 | 23 |
| −1 | 84 | 40 | 85 | 7 | 30 | 16 |
| −1¼ | 80 | 38 | 81 | 6 | 28 | 11 |
| −1½ | 76 | 35 | 78 | — | 27 | 7 |
| −1¾ | 72 | 32 | 74 | 5 | 26 | 4 |
| −2 | 68 | 30 | 70 | 4 | 24 | 2 |
| −2¼ | 64 | 28 | 66 | 3 | 22 | 1 |
| −2½ | 60 | 25 | 62 | — | 21 | 0.6 |
| −2¾ | 56 | 22 | 59 | 2 | 20 | 0.3 |
| −3 | 52 | — | 55 | 1 | 18 | 0.1 |
| Mean | 100 | 50 | 100 | 10 | 36 | |
| SD | 16 | 10 | 15 | 3 | 6 | |

lem-solving or expressive skills. These relatively high scores may suggest the effects of an enriched socially aware environment, a high need for achievement, or a strong (perhaps too strong) parental push. However, another possibility should be considered. Tests such as Information and Comprehension correlate quite substantially with IQ (e.g., Wechsler, 1967, pp. 26–32). Therefore, it is feasible that children who perform well on sociocultural tests would obtain IQs much higher than their GCIs. Since two groups of learning disabled children were found to obtain IQs that were about 15 points higher than their GCIs (DeBoer et al., 1974; Kaufman & Kaufman, 1974), the discrepancy between social intelligence and the McCarthy scores may be related to a possible learning disability. If several other pieces of evidence suggest the same diagnosis, then additional neuropsychological testing is advised.

Research is needed to compare the sociocultural skills and McCarthy Indexes of different groups of children. One such study has been performed. Shellenberger and Lachterman (1976) found that a group of 30 school-aged Puerto Rican children from Pennsylvania scored poorly (about the 10th percentile) on *both* the Information–Comprehension combination and the McCarthy Verbal Index. In contrast, they scored at the 40th percentile on the Perceptual–Performance Index. Thus, their nonverbal skills were much better developed than their verbal abilities. Furthermore, about an equal amount of deficiency was evidenced in the verbal areas of memory, concept formation, and sociocultural knowledge. Similar studies with other distinct groups are highly desirable.

### Bender-Gestalt (Koppitz Scoring System)

Despite the inclusion of the Draw-A-Design test in the McCarthy, the Bender-Gestalt is still a valuable supplement for children aged 5 and above. Since McCarthy's designs are generally quite different from the Bender designs, there is little overlap of specific content. By doubling the number of design-copying items, the reliability of the measurement of the child's ability in this extremely important area is greatly increased.

The differences between the tasks are noteworthy. The McCarthy designs comprise lines and curves and are very similar to the designs in countless other drawing tasks (e.g., Ilg & Ames, 1972; Wechsler, 1967). The Bender-Gestalt designs tend to be unique, particularly the figures that include dots or small circles. The ability to juxtapose dots to produce various patterns depends on somewhat different perceptual organization and visual–motor skills than does the ability to copy the more standard "whole" designs.

Other distinctions between McCarthy's Draw-A-Design test and the Bender-Gestalt concern the format for administering the items. The McCarthy items are presented each on a separate page in a booklet; the Bender designs are presented one at a time on separate cards, with the child expected to copy all designs on one (or two) sheets of paper. Thus, the Bender requires the child to organize the designs with appropriate maturity, or else the placement of the earlier designs may influence performance on the later ones. Indeed, the mere presence of other designs on the response page may affect the child's later reproductions. With the McCarthy, the use of the booklet eliminates the organizational aspects of the task, although children with figure–ground difficulties sometimes encounter problems; that is, the paper in the booklet is not completely opaque, so faint images of other designs can be seen next to (or superimposed on) the design to be copied. Normal children ignore the slight interference, but a child with visual perceptual problems may be distracted by it.

Thus, children may perform much better on one or the other of these design-copying tests, depending on the specific nature of their perceptual–motor impairment. It is beneficial to give the Bender as a supplement to help ensure that children with various types of perceptual or developmental problems are "flagged." Furthermore, an abundance of research has shown the relationship of the Bender to various neurological, academic, intellectual, and emotional variables (Koppitz, 1963, 1975). One cannot assume that Draw-A-Design—by virtue of its status as a design-copying test—necessarily relates in a meaningful way to all of these important areas; research is needed to explore these relationships and to estimate the contribution of supplementary perceptual–motor tests such as the Bender. For now, the Bender-Gestalt rates as a high priority supplement to the McCarthy for assessing kindergarten and primary-grade children. Besides the reasons indicated above, the Bender also has a long history as a clinically valuable projective tool (Clawson, 1962; Koppitz, 1963).

Table 8-2 is provided to enable the examiner to determine whether a child's performance on the Bender-Gestalt is consistent with his Draw-A-Design performance. For each weighted raw score on Draw-A-Design, comparable *error* scores on the Bender-Gestalt (using

**Table 8-2**
Relationship of Draw-A-Design Scores to Error Scores
on the Bender-Gestalt (Koppitz System)

| Draw-A-Design Weighted Raw Score | Comparable Error Score on Bender-Gestalt | Normal Range of Errors on Bender-Gestalt |
|---|---|---|
| 17+ | 0 | 0-3 |
| 16 | 1 | 0-5 |
| 15 | 2-3 | 0-6 |
| 14 | 4 | 1-8 |
| 13 | 5 | 2-9 |
| 12 | 6-7 | 2-10 |
| 11 | 8 | 3-12 |
| 10 | 9 | 5-13 |
| 9 | 10 | 6-14 |
| 8 | 11-12 | 7-15 |
| 7 | 13 | 9-17 |
| 6 | 14 | 10-18 |
| 5 | 15-16 | 11-19 |
| 4 | 17 | 12-20 |
| 3 | 18 | 13-21 |
| 2 | 19 | 15-23 |
| 1 | 20-21 | 17-25 |
| 0 | 22 | 18-26 |

Koppitz' scoring system) were determined. This was accomplished by equating the means and standard deviations of the Draw-A-Design scores (McCarthy, 1972, p. 205) and the Bender-Gestalt error scores (Koppitz, 1963, p. 188) for children aged 5–8½ years. Table 8-2 shows the direct correspondence between scores on the two tasks, and it also indicates the normal (or expected) number of errors on the Bender for each possible score on Draw-A-Design.

For example, Table 8-2 reveals that a score of 13 on Draw-A-Design is comparable to 5 errors on the Bender; furthermore, a child may make anywhere from 2 to 9 errors on the Bender and still perform consistently on both design-copying tests. (To be inconsistent, the Bender and Draw-A-Design scores have to differ by more than one standard deviation.) If the child's performance on the two tasks is inconsistent, the examiner should try to account for the discrepancy by evaluating the types of errors made on each test and by considering carefully the differences between the tasks. Even when a child performs consistently on the Draw-A-Design and Bender-Gestalt tests, the examiner should go beyond the quantitative approach of Table 8-2 and analyze the child's performance qualitatively.

Koppitz (1963) groups errors into four categories: distortion, integration, perseveration, and rotation. These categories, which help the examiner gain insight into the specific nature of the child's per-ceptual–motor functioning, have been found to be differentially related to various childhood difficulties. For example, children with *reading* problems tend to make an excessive number of rotation and distortion errors, whereas children with *number* problems are more likely to commit perseveration or integration errors (Koppitz, 1963, p. 66). Since knowledge of the type of design-copying errors the child makes may have diagnostic significance, the examiner should analyze errors on Draw-A-Design by the same four categories to evaluate the consistency of the child's perceptual–motor functioning.

To facilitate the examiner's task, various errors on the Draw-A-Design items that are penalized by McCarthy's scoring system are categorized below into Koppitz' four groupings. The specific errors included here pertain to both the minimum and additional criteria used by McCarthy (1972, pp. 97–111) and are meant to illustrate rather than exhaust the possibilities.

1. Distortion
   Any 0-point drawing for item 1 (O), item 4 (⌐), item 7 (⊠), item 8 (◹), or item 9 (⬧).
   Disproportion between the size of the two circles in item 6 (⊕).
2. Integration
   An asterisklike pattern for item 5 (✳) that is *not* constructed from three intersecting lines.
   Any error relating to the area of overlap of the two intersecting circles in item 6 (⊕).
   Any error involving the connection of one or both intersecting lines to the outline of item 7 (⊠) or item 9 (⬧).
3. Perseveration
   Vertical or horizontal line (items 1 and 2) which is too long and extends to the end of the page.
   Any asterisklike drawing for item 5 (✳) containing more than eight rays.

4. Rotation
   Vertical or horizontal line (items 1 and 2) that is straight, but fails because it is drawn at too much of an angle.
   A passable reproduction of item 4 (⎵) that is not positioned approximately like the model.
   Mirror images of the model for item 7 (▨ ) or item 8 (◻).

When a child who makes certain types of errors on the Bender designs (e.g., distortions and rotations) also makes the same kind of errors on Draw-A-Design (and perhaps even on Puzzle Solving—see pp. 155-156), the examiner has a broad base for making inferences about a child's perceptual–motor functioning. If there is considerable disagreement in the type of errors made, then the examiner should try to reconcile the discrepancy with further qualitative analysis of the child's responses.

### Comprehensive Evaluation of Draw-A-Child

McCarthy's system for scoring Draw-A-Child is short and objective and emphasizes the child's *concepts* to a greater extent than his coordination. McCarthy (1972, p. 11) acknowledged that this type of system was functional, but advised the skilled clinician "to make a more qualitative and complete interpretation of the drawing." Her advice makes sense to anyone who knows the value of the projective aspects of children's drawings and derives meaning from comprehensive scoring of their products.

However, supplementary analysis of Draw-A-Child is far more important for youngsters aged 5 and above than for preschool children. The drawings of preschoolers are usually of limited complexity (DiLeo, 1973; Koppitz, 1968) and may be evaluated quite satisfactorily by McCarthy's system. In addition, the role of developmental and coordination factors is so important for preschoolers that it is often difficult to infer unequivocal projective meaning from their drawings. Indeed, about four of five 3-year olds score 0 on Draw-A-Child, and 4-year olds typically include only a few body parts in their drawings. It is not until age 5 that virtually all the basic parts of the body are drawn.

Harris' (1963) modification and expansion of Goodenough's scoring system for the Draw-A-Man Test represents a valuable means of evaluating children's pictures of males and females. Although norms are presented for children as young as 3 years old, the Goodenough-Harris scoring system should typically be used as a supplementary Draw-A-Child scoring procedure for children aged 5 and older. Besides the reservations indicated above, Harris (1963, p. 294) cautions the reader about the validity of the norms for 3- and 4-year-old children.

The Goodenough-Harris scoring of a drawing takes about 5–10 minutes after a little practice (and considerably less time with much practice) and is well worth the effort for school-age children. McCarthy's system does not treat pictures of girls and boys separately, although the products of older children often show distinct sex-related features; Harris (1963) provides separate procedures for evaluating drawings of males and females. Furthermore, the Goodenough-Harris system offers a thorough and comprehensive method for analyzing virtually every aspect of a child's drawing. Credit is given for including various types of clothing in the drawing, showing appropriate detail and proportion of numerous body parts, portraying the figure in profile, exhibiting good motor coordination (pencil control), and using mature drawing techniques. Consequently, the Goodenough-Harris scoring system does a far better job of assessing the true quality of an older child's product than does the McCarthy system; it is particularly valuable for distinguishing among drawings that earn virtually perfect scores on McCarthy's system. Finally, the standard score on the Draw-A-Man or Draw-A-Woman test may be used as an estimate of intellectual potential for children who have a *language* problem (since their McCarthy Indexes probably underestimate their true ability).

Koppitz (1968) provides two different objective systems for evaluating Human Figure Drawings: Developmental Items, which are related primarily to a child's age and maturation; and Emotional Indicators, which reflect his attitudes, concerns, and anxieties. The Developmental Items need not be used as a supplementary means of evaluating Draw-A-Child because they do not add enough new information. If the Goodenough-Harris system is used to score Draw-A-Child, then Koppitz' Developmental Items are certainly unnecessary.

However, the Emotional Indicators are quite valuable, and are recommended as supplements to the McCarthy scoring system. Koppitz' list of 30 indicators includes clinical signs such as gross asymmetry of limbs, shading of body parts, the inclusion of teeth or genitals, and the omission of a major part such as the mouth or legs. To qualify as an emotional indicator, each item had to occur infrequently in the normal population, be unrelated to age or maturation, be considered as an indicator of emotional behavior by Hammer (1958), Machover (1949), or Koppitz herself, and be clinically valid (i.e., differentiate drawings of children with and without emotional problems). Koppitz' (1968) Emotional Indicators thus enhance the examiner's understanding of the child's psychological make-up without duplicating the information provided by the McCarthy and Goodenough-Harris evaluations of Draw-A-Child. Because of the statistical criteria imposed on the Emotional Indicators, some items are differentially valid for boys and girls between the ages of 5 and 10 years. However, most Emotional Indicators are useful for children aged 5 and above. Koppitz' (1968) approach to interpreting the indicators, and her summary of pertinent research, should enable the examiner to apply the Emotional Indicators to the McCarthy drawings produced by kindergarten and primary-grade children.

Two final points deserve comment. First, the examiner should not be troubled that McCarthy instructs the child a draw a *boy* (or *girl*), Goodenough and Harris tell him to draw a *man* (or *woman*), and Koppitz says draw a *person*. Despite the somewhat different instructions, all of the scoring systems reflect a valid assessment of a drawing of a human, young or old. Second, the recommendation to evaluate Draw-A-Child by both the Goodenough-Harris and Koppitz systems is not meant as a criticism of McCarthy's method of scoring the test; a short and straightforward procedure is highly desirable for a multitest battery. However, examiners who have the time, as well as the clinical experience, will benefit greatly by maximizing the information to be derived from an administration of the McCarthy.

### Illinois Test of Psycholinguistic Abilities

Children who are suspected of language disorders and other types of learning disorders are often assessed on both a cognitive and a language-oriented battery to understand fully the nature of their problem. The McCarthy and the ITPA' make a particularly appealing cognitive–language combination for young children; the integration of these two test batteries is discussed below.

The ITPA includes virtually no numerical, gross motor, and fine motor tasks. Consequently, the ITPA profile cannot be used to corroborate the child's performance on McCarthy's Quantitative or Motor Scales. However, the ITPA subtests can be used to enhance the evaluation of the child's verbal, nonverbal, and short-term memory skills. For example, a child with a relatively *high* Verbal Index should perform fairly well on most ITPA auditory–vocal subtests, whereas a child with a *low* Verbal Index might be expected to score poorly on these ITPA tasks.

The child's scaled score on an ITPA subtest, or his average scaled score on two or more subtests, can be compared to his McCarthy Indexes by using Table 8-1. (See p. 183 for a description of how to use the table and how to determine whether two scores reflect consistent or inconsistent functioning.) If the child's Verbal Index is consistent with his average scaled score on the auditory–vocal tasks, then the examiner has twice as much evidence for drawing inferences about a child's level of verbal comprehension and expression than he would have from the McCarthy alone; furthermore, the inferences are based on a much wider sampling of verbal tasks. If, however, the test results are inconsistent, then the causes of the discrepancy should be investigated. The psycholinguistic ages on the separate auditory–vocal tasks should be interpreted in conjunction with the child's verbal test ages to formulate logical hypotheses. One potential source of difference between the child's Verbal Index and auditory–vocal scaled scores is the inclusion of tests of meaningful memory on the McCarthy, versus the inclusion of highly specific linguistic tasks (e.g., Grammatic Closure) on the ITPA.

The child's Perceptual–Performance Index should be compared to his scaled scores on the ITPA visual–motor subtests in the same manner described above for the Verbal Scale. One common cause of differential performance is the substantial fine motor component that characterizes most McCarthy nonverbal tests, but not the ITPA visual–motor tasks. Taken together, the McCarthy and ITPA tasks offer an impressively broad view of the child's nonverbal intelligence.

The child's scores on auditory and visual sequential memory provide additional information about his short-term memory and may be compared to his Memory Index. It is of interest to contrast the child's performance on auditory sequential memory, where the digits are presented at the rate of *2 per second,* with his performance on the McCarthy tasks. Some young children who have difficulty repeating numbers, words, or musical tones presented at the rate of 1 per second can do quite well when the interval between the stimuli is shorter. Visual sequential memory gives the examiner the opportunity to assess the child's short-term memory when the stimuli are presented *only* visually—as opposed to the simultaneous visual and auditory presentation of both Pictorial Memory and Tapping Sequence. Thus, if differences occur between a child's memory scores on the ITPA and the McCarthy, the explanations for the discrepancies may have clinical or educational implications.

The above discussions represent an attempt to incorporate the ITPA into the McCarthy "mold." However, it is also useful to turn the tables and try to fit the McCarthy tasks into the ITPA model. Just as most ITPA tasks can be thought of as measures of verbal or non-verbal intelligence, the McCarthy tests can be analyzed in terms of their psycholinguistic properties. From this perspective, the child's pattern of performance on the McCarthy cognitive tasks may be used to confirm or deny hypotheses derived from the ITPA profile about his psycholinguistic functioning.

A child with a marked discrepancy in the two ITPA channels of communication (auditory–vocal and visual–motor) should also manifest a similar discrepancy on the McCarthy. The Perceptual–Performance tasks all involve visual stimuli and require a motor (rather than vocal) response; consequently, the Perceptual–Performance Index reflects the child's functioning in the visual–motor modality. In contrast, the Verbal and Quantitative Scales are predominantly auditory–vocal. (Exceptions are Pictorial Memory and Counting & Sorting.) The difference between a child's Perceptual–Performance Index and the average of his Verbal and Quantitative Indexes thus provides a good approximation of the discrepancy between his functioning in the visual–motor and the auditory–vocal channels of communication. If this difference is consistent with ITPA findings, then the examiner has more data for drawing inferences about the child's psycholinguistic abilities. If the ITPA and McCarthy yield inconsistent conclusions, then the examiner should reconsider his interpretation of the ITPA profile and integrate the test results from both batteries to generate new hypotheses.

A discrepancy in the child's performance on tasks at the automatic and representational levels of organization can also be checked against his McCarthy profile. Most of the McCarthy Memory tasks are automatic, whereas most of the other cognitive tasks are representational. The lists below indicate the categorization of General Cognitive tests into these two levels of organization.

Automatic

3. Pictorial Memory
6. Tapping Sequence
7. Verbal Memory I
14. Numerical Memory I

Representational

2. Puzzle Solving
4. Word Knowledge
5. Number Questions
8. Right–Left Orientation
13. Draw-A-Child
15. Verbal Fluency
16. Counting & Sorting
17. Opposite Analogies
18. Conceptual Grouping

Four tasks are excluded from the above dichotomy. Verbal Memory II and Numerical Memory II are complex memory tasks (rather than simple rote recall tests) and do not fit nicely into either level of organization. Block Building and Draw-A-Design are also not easily categorized; although both are imitative, neither is very similar to the automatic tasks in the ITPA.

To compare a child's relative ability in the two levels of organization, the examiner should compute his average test age for both the automatic and representational tasks listed above (see Table 6-1 on p. 129). The differences in these average test ages may corroborate or dispute ITPA findings. As with the channels of communication, the examiner should integrate the dual results to formulate sensible hypotheses. When the McCarthy and ITPA are used together, it is not uncommon for an examiner to discover that a child's strength or weakness on the Memory Scale is merely a symptom of a more global integrity or deficit at the automatic level of organization.

The third dimension of the ITPA clinical model is psycholinguistic process, and it relates to reception, association, and expression within both the auditory–vocal and visual–motor modalities. As with the channels of communication and levels of organization, the McCarthy results may be used to "cross validate" ITPA hypotheses pertaining to psycholinguistic processes.

A child who is assessed as having an auditory reception problem based on his ITPA profile should not perform too well on the following McCarthy tasks, all of which place a heavy emphasis on the derivation of meaning from auditory stimuli: Number Questions, Verbal Memory II, Right–Left Orientation, Counting & Sorting, Opposite Analogies, and Conceptual Grouping. Similarly, an auditory association weakness on the ITPA should be accompanied by relatively poor performance on Number Questions, Verbal Fluency, and Opposite Analogies; and a verbal expression deficit should precipitate weak performance in Word Knowledge, Verbal Memory II, and Verbal Fluency.

Within the visual–motor channel, there is an analogous approach for relating McCarthy and ITPA data. A child with an apparent deficit in visual reception should be particularly handicapped on Puzzle Solving and Draw-A-Design, with a severe deficit likely to affect the child's skill on virtually all Perceptual–Performance tasks. Visual association difficulties should lead to poor performance on Puzzle Solving, Right–Left Orientation, and Conceptual Grouping. Finally, a child who is assessed as having poor manual expression would be expected to experience considerable difficulty on the Draw-A-Child test.

Although the above discussion of psycholinguistic processes was oriented toward *deficits* in the various areas, similar integrative procedures would be applied to investigate integrities in one or more processes. For both strengths and weaknesses, consistent performance on the ITPA and McCarthy lends support to the ITPA-generated hypotheses. Discrepant findings should impel the examiner to investigate hypotheses that are more consistent with all of the data collected on the child.

It makes no real difference whether the examiner tries to make the ITPA results conform to McCarthy's scalewise approach to cognition, or if he interprets the McCarthy in accordance with the ITPA clinical model. What is important is that the examiner integrate all of the samples of behavior from both batteries before generating hypotheses laden with educational implications. Interpreting an ability test and a psycholinguistic test in isolation—a common practice—does a disservice to the child.

## FOLLOWING UP HYPOTHESES AND HUNCHES

The administration of supplements to the McCarthy can sometimes be predetermined based on knowledge of the child's age, the reasons for the referral, or the limitations of the McCarthy. However, many supplemental tests, whether administered formally or informally, can only be identified after observing the child in the testing situation and evaluating his performance on the McCarthy. These additional measures may be needed to follow up hypotheses about the child's functioning that are generated by a clinical hunch or by a formal interpretation of his Scale Index and test age profiles.

In general, two types of hypotheses are systematically pursued: (1) those that pertain to the *validity* of the assessment of the child's mental or motor abilities, and (2) those that have implications for diagnosis or educational planning (including remediation), and therefore require verification or clarification. Hypotheses of the first type are generated when the examiner believes that a child's low score on one or more tasks is due to factors other than poor ability. Alternative explanations include sensory loss, speech or language problems, failure to understand the directions, motivation, auditory or visual perceptual difficulties, and interference from extreme emotional states (e.g., anxiety) or disruptive behaviors (e.g., impulsiveness).

The second category of hypotheses may concern a suspected diagnosis such as mental retardation or emotional disturbance; or it may concern an apparent strength or weakness (e.g., nonverbal reasoning) that has educational consequences. Hypotheses of a diagnostic nature should be followed up with instruments designed to measure aspects of the child's functioning that are not tapped by the McCarthy (adaptive behavior, personality, achievement, visual or auditory perception, etc.). The supplementary testing is necessary to round out the picture and permit a competent diagnosis, as discussed earlier in this chapter. Hypotheses that have educational implications should also be pursued if they are to form the basis for making recommendations about the child's educational programming. The latter type of follow-up testing requires the use of instruments that are similar to portions of the McCarthy to verify that the child really does have the hypothesized integrity or deficit, or to determine the extent and breadth of the strength or weakness.

### Testing the Limits on the McCarthy

Supplementary testing is not always necessary for following up hunches or hypotheses. Some questions about the child's functioning can be answered by *testing the limits* on the McCarthy. This clinical technique involves the administration of items under altered conditions to gain greater insight into the child's abilities, and *should always be performed after the entire McCarthy has been administered under standard conditions.* Testing the limits, also known as extension testing, has been described for the various Stanford-Binet tasks and for Wechsler's subtests (Glasser & Zimmerman, 1967; Sattler, 1974; Taylor, 1959; Volle, 1957). Typical modifications are the following: changing the wording of an item to see if failure was due to the child's lack of understanding of the question; giving the child additional cues to see if the correct response can be elicited under special circumstances; administering an item under conditions of reduced pressure, such as without time limits; restructuring the task to allow the child to respond at a more elementary level (e.g., converting a vocabulary test to a multiple choice format); and questioning the child, or using other means, to infer his method of solving a problem.

All of these techniques for testing the limits on the Binet or Wechsler tests may be applied to the separate McCarthy tasks to help the examiner check out hypotheses. However, as with the intelligence tests, *never give a child credit for passing items with modified administration procedures.* His success under the altered conditions offers valuable qualitative information but should not be treated empirically. Even though the computation of "alternate IQs" is sometimes performed based on items administered while testing the limits, we do not advocate this procedure. Sattler (1974, p. 60) has suggested that the alternate score be given cautious interpretation because of the lack of norms. However, we feel it is better *not* to compute alternate scores since they are likely to be misleading and to be misinterpreted. (Indeed, without proper norms, what do standard scores mean?) Examiners who desire quantification of their clinical observations are strongly advised to select supplementary tasks of appropriate content and difficulty level after testing the limits on the McCarthy.

Most McCarthy tasks are readily understood by young children, although a few sometimes present problems. Some youngsters do not understand the concepts "backward" or "opposite," and hence have no idea how to respond to the items of Numerical Memory II and Opposite Analogies, respectively. Others are unaware that they are supposed to repeat the words for items 1–4 of Verbal Memory I in sequence; furthermore, they may have trouble with other aspects of the directions to Verbal Memory I because the examiner's instructions to the child include concepts that are potentially difficult ("some," "many," "after," "finished," "all," "before," "start"). For the same reason, some young children may not understand what they are sup-posed to do for the Verbal Fluency items or for the sorting items in Counting & Sorting.

By testing the limits, the examiner should be able to discern whether a child with a low score on any of the above tasks really was unable to perform the required mental process or whether he failed to understand the directions. For example, the examiner can teach the concept "opposite," using any method that does not involve verbal analogies, and then readminister the Opposite Analogies test, or he can rephrase the instructions to Verbal Memory I, using simpler lan-guage and getting across the notion of repeating the words in order, and then administer the word series again. (The examiner may wish to juggle the order of the words for the second administration or sub-stitute similar words for the actual ones in the items.) As indicated above, even a marked increment in performance does not "count" and cannot change a child's scores. However, when a communication problem becomes the likely explanation for a child's poor perfor-mance on several tasks, the *validity* of his Indexes must certainly be challenged.

The testing-the-limits technique may also be used to determine the degree of a child's deficiency. Some children can solve an item when given a slight clue to the solution, while others may fail even when given many seemingly obvious clues. For Word Knowledge II, the examiner might give clues by saying "A *towel* is in a kitchen or a bathroom—what do we do with it?," or by showing a picture of a *coat* and asking what it is used for. A child who has trouble assembling the puzzles might be told "put the green leaf together" for the Pear item, or the examiner might assemble part of a puzzle and have the child try to complete it. To provide additional clues for Conceptual Grouping, the examiner might continually remind the child of the appropriate category throughout the item ("Remember, only the square ones") or perhaps give feedback for each wrong response to see if the child's behavior can be shaped. Any of the McCarthy cognitive and motor tasks can be modified in similar ways if testing the limits seems desirable, although it is important to remember to wait until the entire battery has been administered with the precise instructions given in the Manual before adapting any task.

Some administrative modifications serve to illuminate the se-verity of a deficiency, whereas others are specifically intended to help pinpoint the cause of the problem. A child can be shown a variety of correct and incorrect reproductions of Draw-A-Design items to see if he can perceive adequately, even if he cannot reproduce the figures. Questions similar to the ones in the Stanford-Binet item "Memory for Stories: The Wet Fall" can be asked about the story in Verbal Memory II if the child cannot retell the story, even after it is read a second time. Success with the modified format suggests an inadequate mechanism for retrieving information that has been stored (good recognition, poor recall). In addition, the questions may be put in multiple choice style to test the limits of a child with an apparent expressive problem.

Adaptations of tasks may also be employed to see if a child's behavioral characteristics hindered his test performance. For example, spontaneously developed Numerical Memory items can be administered to an anxious child during a period of relaxed interchange between child and examiner (perhaps on a comfortable couch) without the anxiety-producing stimuli of a manual, record form, testing table, etc. Similarly, Verbal Fluency items may be readministered without time limits to see if the time pressure inhibited the child's fluency. If the latter approach does not lead to improved performance, then other hypotheses might be explored. The examiner might supply the child with more examples; take turns with the child in naming different animals, pieces of clothing, etc; or give the child a variety of correct and incorrect responses to an item to see if he can distinguish between them.

There is an infinite number of modifications in the McCarthy tasks that can be effected to try to gain insight into a child's performance. The only limitations on the examiner are his own perceptiveness and clinical skill, and his ability to be innovative and flexible during the testing session.

### Selecting Supplementary Tests and Subtests

Testing the limits sometimes suffices as the only means of following up hypotheses, but often it serves as an intermediary between the administration of the McCarthy and supplementary tasks. As indicated above, additional measures may be given to check on the validity of the McCarthy results, or to explore hypotheses that have diagnostic or educational implications. These topics are treated below, in turn.

When the examiner has reason to believe that a child's poor performance on a McCarthy test is *not* due to limited ability, supplementary assessment is often advised. A child who does not seem to comprehend concepts such as "opposite," "backward," "before," or "same" is likely to have difficulty understanding much of what is said to him by his teacher, parents, and peers. The Boehm Test of Basic Concepts (Boehm, 1971) should be given to determine which essential concepts have been learned and which ones have not yet been mastered. Boehm's (1977) suggestions for teaching basic concepts to young children enhance the practical value of her test.

Failure to understand the demands of a task because of a conceptual lack is only one of many ways for a child's test score to be invalid as an estimate of his ability. Children with auditory discrimination problems may also misunderstand the examiner's instructions or questions for various tasks. A child who defines "cow" instead of "towel," who repeats "doll–bark–colt" instead of "doll–dark–coat," or who starts to name things to "write on" instead of "ride on" may have an auditory perceptual problem. An instrument such as Wepman's (1973) Auditory Discrimination Test should be administered to check out this possibility. In addition, language problems may surface during the course of the McCarthy. For example, the child may display poor grammatical structure in his spontaneous speech and his responses to verbal items; or evaluation of his McCarthy profile may suggest a problem with a particular level of organization, channel of communication, or psycholinguistic process (see pp. 191–195). Supplementary testing with some or all of the subtests in the ITPA or Houston Test of Language Development (Crabtree, 1963) should facilitate the diagnosis of a psycholinguistic deficiency if one exists.

Speech or visual perceptual problems, like language problems, can render some of the McCarthy Indexes invalid as indicators of intellectual potential. Suspicions of a speech disorder can be checked out by administering tests such as the Templin-Darley Tests of Articulation (Templin & Darley, 1960) or the Goldman-Fristoe Test of Articulation (Goldman & Fristoe, 1969). The Frostig Developmental Test of Visual Perception (Frostig, Maslow, Lefever, & Whittlesey, 1964) is useful for determining the general level of a child's visual perceptual skills and can identify those with difficulties in this global area. Whenever a speech, visual perception, or other disorder is verified by subsequent testing (by the examiner or by other trained personnel such as speech pathologists and physicians), the child's

McCarthy profile should be reinterpreted to determine which scores provide the best estimates of his intellectual functioning. With preschool children, it is not unusual for the educational or psychological examiner to be the first person to detect a marked sensory loss. If this finding is confirmed, a second testing session should be set up to readminister the McCarthy when the child is wearing corrective lenses or a hearing aid.

Occasionally, the results of the McCarthy cannot be considered as valid estimates of the child's potential because he is unable to answer enough items correctly (e.g., a very young or retarded child who scores 0 on more than half of the tests). In such instances, the child's ability profile should be interpreted tentatively until an infant scale such as the Bayley Scales of Infant Development (Bayley, 1969) can be administered to obtain more reliable measures of his mental and motor functioning.

The preceding discussion has shown how the McCarthy profile may yield invalid estimates of a child's cognitive functioning, and has suggested the type of supplementary testing that can help support such a conclusion. The use of additional measures such as adaptive behavior inventories or projective techniques to confirm diagnoses has been discussed earlier in this chapter, and needs no further elaboration. Hence, the remainder of this section will illustrate (but *not* exhaust) the use of follow-up testing to produce greater understanding of a child's hypothesized strengths or weaknesses on the McCarthy. In most cases, the extra testing is intended to improve the examiner's choice of curricular materials for teaching the child and/or for remediating any known academic difficulties. To make appropriate choices of educational materials and techniques, the examiner must be reasonably sure of the nature of the child's strengths and weaknesses that are uncovered by the investigative approach described in Chapter 6.

Suppose a child has relative strengths on McCarthy tests which require good verbal concept formation (e.g., Word Knowledge, Opposite Analogies). To check out the stability of the finding, longer and more reliable tasks requiring the same abilities might be administered. The examiner could choose one or more of the following: ITPA Auditory Association subtest, WPPSI or WISC-R Similarities and Vocabulary subtests, Stanford-Binet Language and Conceptual Thinking tasks (Sattler, 1974, p. 139), or Detroit Verbal Opposites and Likenesses and Differences tests. Other assessment may also be undertaken to determine if the child's verbal strength extends to reasoning tasks. The measures of social comprehension discussed earlier would serve this purpose well. For school-age children, the Stanford-Binet or Detroit Verbal Absurdities items might also be administered.

Another child might do poorly on Word Knowledge, Verbal Memory II, and Verbal Fluency, leading the examiner to speculate about a verbal expressive problem. By administering additional tasks requiring expressive skills (e.g., ITPA Verbal Expression, WPPSI or WISC-R Comprehension, Detroit Verbal Absurdities), the examiner can judge the accuracy of the hypothesis. If an expression problem does exist, then the child's Verbal Index may not adequately reflect his verbal intelligence. Better estimates of his true ability may be obtained by administering verbal tests which require little or no vocal responding: e.g., Peabody Picture Vocabulary Test (Dunn, 1965), ITPA Auditory Reception and Association subtests, or Wechsler Information subtest.

Numerous supplementary nonverbal tasks can be administered to pursue hypotheses generated by the child's separate scores on the Perceptual–Performance Scale. Consider a child who evidences awkward fine motor coordination and does relatively poorly on the tasks that depend most heavily on this ability (Block Building, Puzzle Solving, Tapping Sequence, Draw-A-Design). In contrast, he does well on Conceptual Grouping, Draw-A-Child (despite a poorly executed figure), and perhaps Right–Left Orientation. The examiner may suspect that the child has well-developed nonverbal concepts and reasoning skills that are masked on tests which place a premium on coordination. Whereas his low level of ability on coordination tasks may be of diagnostic significance, should there be other suggestions of neurological impairment, his potential integrity in nonverbal reasoning has implications for his educational planning. To verify his possible strength, at least one performance test demanding little or no motor coordination should be given. The Columbia Mental Maturity Scale (Burgemeister, Blum, & Lorge, 1972) is an ideal supplement for this purpose and can be given to preschool and school-age children alike.

Other tasks that might be chosen, depending on the child's age, are Raven's (1956) Colored Progressive Matrices, Wechsler's Picture Completion subtest, the ITPA Visual Association subtest, the Detroit Pictorial Absurdities and Pictorial Opposites tests, and the Picture Analogies subtest in the Hiskey-Nebraska Test of Learning Aptitudes (Hiskey, 1966).

Children who do well on the Pictorial Memory and Tapping Sequence tests, when compared with their performance on the tests of auditory memory, may have an exceptional visual memory. This hypothesis may be checked out by administering tests of visual recall ability which do not include an auditory component: the Knox Cube Test (Arthur, 1947), ITPA Visual Sequential Memory subtest, Detroit Visual Attention Span for Objects test, or Hiskey-Nebraska Visual Attention Span subtest. If the hypothesized integrity in visual memory is borne out, its generalizability may be assessed by administering related tasks such as the Detroit Memory for Designs and Visual Attention Span for Letters tests, or the Hiskey-Nebraska Bead Pattern and Memory of Color subtests. Even if supplementary testing does not support the hypothesis of a strong visual memory, it is possible that the child's strength is a good memory when visual and auditory stimuli are presented simultaneously. This hypothesis may be further evaluated by administering the Detroit Oral Directions test or by developing several informal memory tasks which utilize stimuli in both modalities. For example, if the child can read numbers, it would be interesting to see if his digit span increases markedly if each number is exposed visually at the same time that it is spoken by the examiner.

The use of supplementary tests has been illustrated for a few Verbal, Perceptual–Performance, and Memory hypotheses. The same type of approach described for these few examples should be applied to various other hypotheses of deficits or integrities that are generated from a child's McCarthy profile. To pursue hypotheses pertaining to the Quantitative Scale the examiner may select tasks such as the WPPSI or WISC-R Arithmetic subtest, the Detroit Numerical Ability tests, or the arithmetic portions of individual or group achievement tests. Similarly, Motor hypotheses may need verification or clarification, suggesting the use of selected portions of the Southern California Sensory Integration Tests (Ayres, 1972b), the Purdue Perceptual–Motor Survey (Roach & Kephart, 1966), or the Lincoln-Oseretsky Motor Development Scale (Sloan, 1955). The administration of tasks such the WPPSI Animal House subtest, the WISC-R Coding subtest, or the Detroit Motor Speed and Precision test may also contribute to the understanding of the child's motor coordination.

When the necessary supplementary tasks are not included in any tests known to the examiner, then resourcefulness and clinical insight are needed to develop appropriate informal assessment items on the spur of the moment. Another alternative is to use selected portions of the non-normed, but rigorous, assessment technique based on Haeussermann's approach (Jedrysek, Klapper, Pope, & Wortis, 1972) to follow up hypotheses generated from the McCarthy profile. The informed clinician should be able to gain insight into the child's functioning in specific cognitive and motor areas by administering pertinent items from this psychoeducational evaluation of preschool children.

The specific tests the examiner uses for supplementing the McCarthy are not important, and neither is his exact approach. What is important is the examiner's acute awareness of the need for reliable evidence before reaching a diagnosis or setting up a plan for an educational program, in addition to his ability to function as an expert detective within the psychoeducational setting.

## SCREENING FOR POTENTIAL LEARNING PROBLEMS

The early detection of learning disorders is of obvious practical value to the child who is otherwise doomed to academic failure and to all those who must interact with him at home and at school. However, since competent diagnosis requires so much time and effort, it is impractical to evaluate each young child prior to school entrance with the rigor that is appropriate. Consequently, an effective method is needed to detect the high-risk children who would benefit most from a thorough psychoeducational battery.

Many state governments have recognized the need for the mass screening of children who are about to enter school and have passed legislation making such screening mandatory. Unfortunately, the tests used for screening are usually chosen for reasons other than psychometric excellence, with brevity of administration ranking as a high priority selection variable. Although the entire McCarthy may be too long to function as a practical screening tool, a 20–25-minute short form of the McCarthy would make an ideal instrument for large-scale screening of young children. A brief form that correlates substantially with GCI and comprises a sampling of verbal, nonverbal, numerical, and memory tasks would have many advantages.

Besides assessing skills in the typical problem areas of learning disabled children, a McCarthy short form would have norms derived from the representative standardization sample and would be composed of child-oriented tasks geared especially for preschoolers. Furthermore, the GCI has been shown not to discriminate between boys and girls across the age range (Kaufman & Kaufman, 1973b), or between young black and white children (Kaufman & Kaufman, 1973a); and the GCI seems like a better bet than the IQ to "flag" candidates for learning disabilities, based on the results of two studies (DeBoer et al., 1974; Kaufman & Kaufman, 1974) discussed on page 13. Any short form that yields a good estimate of the GCI will also possess these desirable qualities.

### A Six-Test Short Form of the McCarthy

One short form of the McCarthy has been proposed by Kaufman (1977), a six-test abbreviated version of the General Cognitive Scale designed to serve as a screening instrument. The short form was selected to include tests which (1) gradually lead the shy or nonverbal child to verbalization, (2) give proportional representation to the Verbal, Perceptual-Performance, Quantitative, and Memory Scales, (3) correlate substantially with GCI, (4) assess a wide variety of mental functions, (5) do not favor boys or girls, blacks or whites, (6) are especially useful for 3-6-year olds, and (7) are relatively short to administer and score.

The six tests in Kaufman's (1977) short form are Puzzle Solving, Word Knowledge, Numerical Memory, Verbal Fluency, Counting & Sorting, and Conceptual Grouping. Based on the sum of the child's weighted raw score on the six tests (short form score), the examiner computes an estimated GCI. The reliability of the estimated GCI was .90 for the preschool and kindergarten-age children in the standardization sample, and .86 for the school-age youngsters. In addition, the short form and "long form" scores correlated about .92 across the age range. On the average, a child's estimated GCI differed by only 4 points from his actual GCI; the short form, overall, had a standard error of estimate of 6 points (Kaufman, 1977).

Equations are provided by Kaufman (1977) to convert a child's short form score to an estimated GCI-one equation for each quarter year between the ages of 2½ and 8½ years. To facilitate the computation of estimated GCIs, Table 8-3 has been prepared from Kaufman's equations. (Table 8-3 was smoothed to eliminate some slight irregularities in the age-to-age progression of short form scores that result

**Table 8-3**
Short Form Scores Corresponding to Selected GCIs
and Percentile Ranks

| | | | | | | | AGES 2½–5½ YEARS | | | | | | | | |
|---|---|---|---|---|---|---|---|---|---|---|---|---|---|---|---|
| | Esti-mated GCI | 2½ | 2¾ | 3 | 3¼ | 3½ | 3¾ | 4 | 4¼ | 4½ | 4¾ | 5 | 5¼ | 5½ | Percentile Rank |
| | 136 | 31 | 38 | 46 | 51 | 56 | 60 | 64 | 70 | 77 | 84 | 89 | 91 | 92 | 99 |
| +2 SD | 132 | 30 | 36 | 44 | 48 | 53 | 57 | 61 | 67 | 73 | 80 | 85 | 87 | 89 | 98 |
| | 128 | 28 | 34 | 41 | 45 | 50 | 54 | 59 | 64 | 70 | 76 | 82 | 84 | 86 | 96 |
| | 124 | 26 | 32 | 39 | 43 | 47 | 51 | 56 | 61 | 67 | 73 | 78 | 80 | 83 | 93 |
| | 120 | 24 | 29 | 36 | 40 | 44 | 49 | 53 | 58 | 63 | 69 | 75 | 77 | 79 | 89 |
| +1 SD | 116 | 22 | 27 | 34 | 37 | 41 | 46 | 50 | 55 | 60 | 66 | 71 | 74 | 76 | 84 |
| | 112 | 20 | 25 | 31 | 35 | 39 | 43 | 47 | 52 | 57 | 63 | 67 | 70 | 73 | 77 |
| | 108 | 19 | 23 | 29 | 32 | 36 | 40 | 44 | 48 | 53 | 59 | 64 | 66 | 69 | 69 |
| | 104 | 17 | 21 | 26 | 29 | 33 | 37 | 41 | 45 | 50 | 55 | 60 | 63 | 66 | 60 |
| Mean | 100 | 15 | 19 | 24 | 27 | 30 | 34 | 38 | 42 | 47 | 52 | 56 | 59 | 62 | 50 |
| | 96 | 13 | 17 | 21 | 24 | 27 | 31 | 35 | 39 | 43 | 48 | 53 | 55 | 58 | 40 |
| | 92 | 11 | 15 | 19 | 21 | 26 | 30 | 33 | 37 | 41 | 45 | 49 | 52 | 55 | 31 |
| | 88 | 10 | 13 | 16 | 19 | 23 | 27 | 30 | 33 | 37 | 41 | 45 | 48 | 52 | 23 |
| −1 SD | 84 | 8 | 11 | 14 | 16 | 19 | 23 | 27 | 30 | 33 | 37 | 42 | 45 | 48 | 16 |
| | 80 | 6 | 8 | 11 | 13 | 16 | 20 | 24 | 27 | 30 | 34 | 38 | 41 | 45 | 11 |
| | 76 | 4 | 6 | 9 | 11 | 13 | 17 | 21 | 24 | 27 | 30 | 35 | 38 | 42 | 7 |
| | 72 | 2 | 4 | 6 | 8 | 10 | 14 | 18 | 21 | 23 | 26 | 31 | 34 | 38 | 4 |
| −2 SD | 68 | 1 | 2 | 4 | 5 | 7 | 11 | 15 | 18 | 20 | 23 | 27 | 30 | 35 | 2 |
| | 64 | — | — | 1 | 3 | 4 | 9 | 13 | 15 | 17 | 19 | 23 | 27 | 32 | 1 |

*Note.* Compute the child's *short form score* by summing his weighted raw scores on the six tests constituting Kaufman's (1977) short form. Locate the short form score (or the value closest to it) in the column that corresponds to his chronological age. Determine his estimated GCI or percentile rank from the left-most and right-most columns, respectively.

from rigid application of the formulas.) The examiner may enter the appropriate column in Table 8-3 with the child's short form score, and easily determine his estimated GCI and percentile rank. Since only selected short form score values are included in Table 8-3, the examiner may either interpolate or choose the tabled value closest to the child's score to obtain the estimated GCI and percentile rank. Short form scores that are less than the lowest value shown for each age correspond to estimated GCIs "below 64" and percentile ranks of "less than 1;" scores greater than the highest value for each age correspond to estimated GCIs "above 136" and percentile ranks "greater than 99."

**Table 8-3** (continued)

| | | | | | | AGES 5¾–8½ YEARS | | | | | | | |
|---|---|---|---|---|---|---|---|---|---|---|---|---|---|
| | Esti-mated GCI | 5¾ | 6 | 6¼ | 6½ | 6¾ | 7 | 7¼ | 7½ | 7¾ | 8 | 8¼ | 8½ | Percen-tile Rank |
| | 136 | 94 | 96 | 99 | 101 | 104 | 108 | 112 | 115 | 117 | 118 | 119 | 120 | 99 |
| +2 SD | 132 | 91 | 93 | 96 | 99 | 102 | 105 | 108 | 112 | 114 | 115 | 116 | 117 | 98 |
| | 128 | 88 | 90 | 93 | 96 | 99 | 102 | 105 | 109 | 111 | 112 | 113 | 114 | 96 |
| | 124 | 85 | 87 | 90 | 93 | 96 | 99 | 102 | 106 | 107 | 108 | 110 | 111 | 93 |
| | 120 | 82 | 84 | 87 | 90 | 93 | 96 | 99 | 102 | 104 | 105 | 107 | 109 | 89 |
| +1 SD | 116 | 79 | 81 | 84 | 87 | 90 | 93 | 96 | 99 | 101 | 102 | 104 | 106 | 84 |
| | 112 | 76 | 78 | 81 | 84 | 87 | 90 | 93 | 96 | 97 | 99 | 101 | 103 | 77 |
| | 108 | 72 | 75 | 78 | 81 | 84 | 87 | 89 | 92 | 94 | 96 | 98 | 100 | 69 |
| | 104 | 69 | 72 | 76 | 79 | 81 | 84 | 86 | 89 | 91 | 93 | 95 | 97 | 60 |
| Mean | 100 | 65 | 68 | 73 | 76 | 79 | 81 | 83 | 86 | 88 | 90 | 92 | 94 | 50 |
| | 96 | 62 | 65 | 70 | 73 | 76 | 78 | 80 | 82 | 84 | 87 | 89 | 91 | 40 |
| | 92 | 58 | 62 | 67 | 70 | 73 | 75 | 77 | 79 | 81 | 84 | 86 | 89 | 31 |
| | 88 | 55 | 59 | 64 | 67 | 70 | 72 | 74 | 76 | 78 | 81 | 83 | 86 | 23 |
| −1 SD | 84 | 52 | 56 | 61 | 64 | 67 | 69 | 71 | 73 | 75 | 78 | 80 | 83 | 16 |
| | 80 | 49 | 53 | 58 | 61 | 64 | 66 | 68 | 70 | 72 | 75 | 77 | 80 | 11 |
| | 76 | 46 | 50 | 55 | 58 | 61 | 63 | 65 | 66 | 68 | 71 | 74 | 77 | 7 |
| | 72 | 42 | 47 | 52 | 56 | 58 | 60 | 62 | 63 | 65 | 68 | 71 | 74 | 4 |
| −2 SD | 68 | 39 | 44 | 49 | 53 | 55 | 56 | 58 | 59 | 62 | 65 | 68 | 71 | 2 |
| | 64 | 36 | 41 | 46 | 50 | 52 | 54 | 55 | 56 | 59 | 62 | 65 | 68 | 1 |

Table 8-4 provides a means for converting the child's short form score to an estimated General Cognitive Age. The table may be used for children of any age, even those outside of the McCarthy age range, so long as their level of functioning is somewhere within the 2½–8½-year-old band.

*Example:* A 6-year-old girl obtained the following *weighted* raw scores on the six tests in the short form:

| | | | | |
|---|---|---|---|---|
| Puzzle Solving | 8 | Verbal Fluency | 21 |
| Word Knowledge | 18 | Counting & Sorting | 8 |
| Numerical Memory | | Conceptual Grouping | 5 |
| Part I | 4 | | |
| Part II | 0 | | |

Her short form score (sum of the weighted raw scores on the six tests) is 64. Entering the column for 6-year olds in Table 8-3, one finds the value of 65 to be closest to her score of 64. This score corresponds to

**Table 8-4**
Estimated General Cognitive Ages
for Short Form Scores

| Estimated General Cognitive Age | Short Form Score |
|---|---|
| 2½ | 10–18 |
| 3 | 19–26 |
| 3½ | 27–34 |
| 4 | 35–42 |
| 4½ | 43–51 |
| 5 | 52–58 |
| 5½ | 59–65 |
| 6 | 66–72 |
| 6½ | 73–78 |
| 7 | 79–83 |
| 7½ | 84–87 |
| 8 | 88–91 |
| 8½ | 92–95 |

*Note.* Short form score equals the sum of the child's weighted raw scores on the six tests in Kaufman's (1977) short form. Values of less than 10 and greater than 95 correspond to estimated General Cognitive Ages of "below 2½" and "above 8½," respectively.

an estimated GCI of 96, and ranks her at about the 40th percentile for children her age; her estimated General Cognitive Age is 5½ years (see Table 8-4).

When a short form is used to detect children with potential learning problems, the screening process requires two steps. The first step is to administer the short form to a large number of children (e.g., all who are entering kindergarten) to determine which ones should be given the entire McCarthy Scales. Step two involves administering the *remainder* of the McCarthy to the children "flagged" by the short form, and then interpreting the GCI, cognitive and motor profile, and test behaviors to decide whether further psychodiagnostic testing is indicated.

There are several ways of determining whether the entire McCarthy should be administered based on the child's short form score. One way is to set a cutoff score and give the remainder of the battery to all children scoring below the cutoff. The precise cutoff point is arbitrary; it could be all children scoring more than one standard deviation below the mean (estimated GCIs below 84), or any criterion that makes sense in view of the educational goals of a school system and the number of qualified testers on their staff. However, cutoffs should not be used rigidly. Children who "pass" the criterion should be given the complete battery if the examiner detects any behaviors during the administration of the short form that are suggestive of a learning disorder or emotional disturbance. Two of the short form tests, Puzzle Solving and Verbal Fluency, are among the most clinically revealing tasks in the battery (see Chapter 7), increasing the likelihood of observing important behaviors during the abbreviated testing session.

Another reason for administering the entire McCarthy to a child scoring above the cutoff is evidence of *scatter* in the short form profile of test scores. The weighted raw score on each task can be converted to a test age (see Table 6-1 on p. 129), and the range of test ages on the component tasks can be determined. Norms are not available to evaluate significant scatter, so that the examiner will have to rely on clinical judgment. To supplement the examiner's judgment, we suggest that any one of the following general criteria be sufficient for concluding that scatter exists in a child's short form profile: (1) a range of three or four years between the highest and lowest test ages; (2) three or more tests deviating significantly from the child's estimated General Cognitive Age (using the rules provided in Chapter 6); and (3) a substantial discrepancy between tasks on different cognitive scales (e.g., if the average test age on the Verbal tasks is two or three years below the average Perceptual–Performance test age).

When the weighted raw scores for the 6-year-old girl in the above example are converted to test ages, a good deal of variability is evidenced in her profile. Her test ages range from $3\frac{1}{2}$ on Parts I and II of Numerical Memory to $7\frac{1}{2}$ on Verbal Fluency. These three tasks deviate significantly from her General Cognitive Age of $5\frac{1}{2}$, as does her test age of 4 on Conceptual Grouping. Consequently, even though the girl's estimated GCI of 96 indicates average intelligence, the apparent scatter in her profile suggests the need for the administration of the remainder of the McCarthy—and probably other supplementary tests as well—to detect a potential learning disorder.

Thus, the same type of clinical flexibility that should characterize the administration of a psychoeducational battery is desirable even for the interpretation of a short form. Indeed, any screening tool will be maximally successful for detecting large proportions of children with potential learning problems if it is used as a clinical instrument rather than as a means for obtaining a rigid passing or failing score for each child. The fact that the McCarthy short form includes a varied content makes it far more clinically useful than homogeneous instruments, such as picture vocabulary tests, which are often used for screening because they are fairly quick to administer. In addition, the excellent norms that characterize any short form derived from the McCarthy make it better for screening than barely normed or poorly normed tests that have little to recommend them other than a 20- or 25-minute administration time.

### Group Screening with the McCarthy Drawing Tests

The six-test short form described above is but one of many abbreviated versions of the McCarthy that might be used effectively for screening or other purposes. Clinical or educational researchers may wish to select for a short form McCarthy tasks that are geared specifically to a particular educational program or set of curricular materials. For example, in the area of educational evaluation, Rentfrow, Durning, Conrad, and Goldupp (1975) chose to administer only those McCarthy tasks that corresponded to the three main goals of their Head Start program: *intellectual skills* (Pictorial Memory, Verbal Memory, Conceptual Grouping); *societal arts and skills* (Number Questions, Imitative Action, Draw-A-Design, Draw-A-Child, Counting & Sorting); and *language competence* (Word Knowledge, Verbal Fluency, Opposite Analogies).

Another approach is to administer parts of the McCarthy in a group format in order to permit the testing of many children simultaneously. Following the lead of Denis P. McCarthy (1975) and others (Koppitz, 1975, chap. 12) who have found that group administration of the Bender-Gestalt yields reliable and valid results, Reynolds (1977) explored the feasibility of administering Draw-A-Design and Draw-A-Child in a group format. He group administered the two McCarthy drawing tests to 83 youngsters in grades K–2 and found that scores obtained in this fashion correlated significantly with measures of readiness and achievement. Reynolds (1977) also tested 30 of the 83 youngsters on the drawing tests under the standard conditions of individual administration, using a counterbalanced design. He found that scores obtained via group and individual administrations correlated .86 for Draw-A-Design and .82 for Draw-A-Child, even after removing the influence of age. These results suggest that group administration of the McCarthy drawing tests might provide an extremely rapid and practical screening device which could be used in conjunction with other group and individual screening tests. Certainly, tasks similar to Draw-A-Design and Draw-A-Child have been shown in numerous studies to be significantly related to school readiness and academic achievement (e.g., Ilg & Ames, 1972; Kaufman & Kaufman, 1972; Koppitz, 1963, 1968, 1975; Leviton & Kiraly, 1974). Further research is needed, however, to verify that the educationally relevant information provided by drawing tests is indeed obtainable from a group administration of Draw-A-Design and Draw-A-Child.

Pending future research, the administration of the McCarthy drawing tests to children in a group format prior to school entrance would make an ideal screening supplement to Kaufman's (1977) six-test short form. Children who may escape detection by the short form might conceivably be flagged by their scores on the drawing tests or by a clinical evaluation of their designs and human figure drawings. The latter point again underscores the need for the screening process to be conducted or at least supervised closely by qualified individual testers, even if the screening is performed with group-administered tests.

## USE OF THE McCARTHY AS AN ADJUNCT TO OTHER TESTS

The entire preceding portion of this chapter has been based on a single assumption: that the McCarthy is the featured test for assessing the child's cognitive development or intelligence. Even the section on screening presumes that children identified as high risks by the short form will be given the remainder of the McCarthy before any other supplementary tests are considered. However, the WPPSI, WISC-R, or Stanford-Binet is often the featured intelligence test in a battery. For children older than 6½ years, there are logical reasons for choosing the WISC-R or the Binet instead of the McCarthy (see pp. 17–19); but even for preschool and kindergarten-age youngsters, an examiner may simply prefer to include the WPPSI or Binet in a comprehensive battery. In some cases, state laws regarding the classification of exceptional children may demand the use of a conventional IQ test.

By virtue of assessing five major areas of ability and providing scores on 18 separate cognitive and motor tests, the McCarthy looms as a valuable source of supplementary tasks for examiners who use the WPPSI, WISC-R, or Binet. Several of the motor tests, or even the entire Motor Scale, would provide a valuable supplement to the cognitive information yielded by the IQ tests. The combination of Draw-A-Design and Draw-A-Child is a particularly appealing adjunct to the WISC-R because only Coding (and Mazes, which is rarely given) requires the use of paper and pencil. In addition, the Memory Scale provides extremely useful supplementary test data for both the WPPSI and WISC-R, which each include only one optional test of short-term memory.

The various separate McCarthy tasks can be administered to follow up hypotheses based on an intelligence test, just as tasks from the WPPSI, WISC-R, Binet, Detroit, and other batteries may be used to pursue hypotheses generated by the McCarthy profile. The categories devised by Sattler for the Stanford-Binet and applied to the McCarthy (see pp. 147–148) should be particularly useful for selecting tasks to follow up hypotheses about a child's strengths or weaknesses on the Binet. A child who seems to have a weak memory based on a few brief Binet tasks can be given some or all of the Memory Scale. Similarly, apparent strong or weak performance in nonverbal reasoning, visual–motor coordination, numerical reasoning, language development, or conceptual thinking can be verified or disputed by administering the pertinent McCarthy tasks. Other hypotheses can be checked out as well. For example, a child who performs very well on Word Naming, compared to his level on other Binet tasks, might be given Verbal Fluency to see if his apparent facility applies as well when the time limits are shorter and the words to be named fall in a specified category.

Hypotheses generated from the WPPSI and WISC-R profiles may be followed up in the same way. Children who are able to give only one or two oral definitions of the words in Vocabulary might be given both parts of Word Knowledge to establish their level of functioning in this important area of language development. The generalizability of the nonverbal skills of a child earning a very high or very low Performance IQ may be explored by administering tasks quite different from those included on Wechsler's batteries: Tapping Sequence, Right–Left Orientation, Draw-A-Child, and Conceptual Grouping. As another illustration, children who perform poorly on the WPPSI or WISC-R Arithmetic subtest could be given Counting & Sorting and Number Questions. Their scores on the McCarthy number tests may be just as low, suggesting poorly developed numerical ability; or the McCarthy scores may be considerably higher, suggesting that the *timed* nature of Wechsler's Arithmetic items may have been a primary cause of the child's deficient performance.

One frequent component of neuropsychological batteries is the informal assessment of specific cognitive or motor skills. The items or tasks used for informal assessment are usually poorly normed or have no known norms at all, and are sometimes developed on the spur of the moment. Typical informal tasks are standing on one foot, skipping, knowledge of right versus left, bouncing a ball, and visual memory span. When the Binet or a Wechsler scale is used as the measure of academic potential in a comprehensive battery, the well-normed McCarthy tasks may be used for informal assessment. Leg Coordination, Imitative Action, Arm Coordination, Right–Left Orientation, and Tapping Sequence are among the tests that the examiner might find particularly valuable for this purpose. Table 6-1 on p. 129 may be used to obtain a test age for any task administered for informal assessment. Certainly a test age on Leg Coordination, derived from a representative normative sample, is far more meaningful to an examiner than his clinical impressions and subjective norms for isolated items such as walking a straight line or skipping. These suggestions are not intended to curtail the examiner's creativity in developing tasks to meet specific assessment needs. However, when well-normed tasks such as the ones constituting the McCarthy are available and suitable for the immediate demands of the situation, then they should be used in preference to barely normed or novel items.

Finally, some children are tested for a specific reason, such as a speech or language evaluation, or for determining the severity of an emotional disorder. Speech, language, or projective tests are likely to predominate the test battery, with the assessment of cognitive functioning assuming a smaller role. Whereas a general estimate of intellectual functioning represents a desired supplement to a specialized battery of tests, a thorough evaluation of strengths and weaknesses is often unnecessary. In these instances Kaufman's (1977) six-test short form of the McCarthy might be more practical and economical to give than the entire battery.


### EDUCATIONAL PLANNING

Some McCarthy users have expressed a strong desire for educational prescriptions tied directly to a child's profile of scores, not unlike the ITPA-based programs. Such prescriptions would tell teachers or remedial specialists what to do to remediate deficits, in very concrete terms, based on the child's profile of strengths and weaknesses on the McCarthy. Psycholinguistic training programs connected to the ITPA have been used rather widely in the past (e.g., Bush & Giles, 1969; Hartman, 1966; Minskoff, Wiseman, & Minskoff, 1972) and are still quite popular. Unfortunately, research support of these test-related programs has been meager, to say the least, and hard data are simply not available to offer evidence of their success (Newcomer & Hammill, 1976). The lack of research justification does not imply that the current educational programs tied to the ITPA should necessarily be terminated abruptly; indeed, one of the problems with evaluation research is the difficulty in designing studies that are capable of yielding unequivocal results about the effectiveness of an educational program. Nevertheless, Newcomer and Hammill's (1976) documentation of the failure of existing research to support the efficacy of ITPA-related programs, especially the transfer of specific skills to academics, must raise some doubts about psycholinguistic training. Research generated from the positions taken by Newcomer and Hammill (1976), and by their opposition (Bush, Minskoff, & McCleod, in chap. 5 of Newcomer & Hammill, 1976) may ultimately resolve the issues, one way or the other. For now, one pertinent implication is clear: *new educational programs tied directly to tests such as the McCarthy should not be implemented,* except on an experimental basis, until the waters are less muddy.

The research issue is only one reason for opposing educational prescriptions based on McCarthy results. Another stems from the way in which the battery was developed. Tests were included in the McCarthy and assigned to one or more scales based on the test author's clinical experience, the results of factor analysis, and intuitive and functional considerations (Hollenbeck, 1972; Kaufman & Hollenbeck, 1973; McCarthy, 1972, p. 2). McCarthy's goal was to construct a *practical* tool, and she clearly did not operate out of a unified theoretical framework. This approach is in marked contrast to Kirk and his co-workers, who used Osgood's three-dimensional language model as an anchor for developing the ITPA. Thus, whereas the theory underlying the ITPA provides a *logical* rationale for developing test-related educational prescriptions, no such justification exists for the McCarthy.

Like the Wechsler scales and the Stanford-Binet, the McCarthy includes time-tested items that "work" with children; the tasks constituting these batteries, however, were not intended to represent all of the children's important abilities or to come close to exhausting the possibilities. Wechsler, Binet, and McCarthy tasks are *samples of behavior* and should be treated as such. Poor performance on some of the samples does not immediately imply the need to train the child in the weak areas. Rather, the low scores should be treated as symptoms of problems that may be more global or pervasive, and hence likely to transcend the specific task or tasks in the battery. As reiterated throughout this chapter, additional samples of behavior that are not tapped by the McCarthy are needed to complete the picture. Then educational suggestions can be made that are based on a rigorous and, therefore, more reliable set of hypotheses about the child's particular strengths and weaknesses across a broad spectrum of cognitive and motor behaviors.

Some training of specific McCarthy skills is probably warranted. Low scores on Counting & Sorting and Number Questions suggest the need for focusing on basic mathematical concepts, quantitative words, and elementary number operations. Poor performance on Right–Left Orientation, Opposite Analogies, and the early items of Conceptual Grouping suggests an inadequate mastery of the kind of essential concepts that can be taught to young children (e.g., see Boehm, 1977). Finally, if low scores on Conceptual Grouping and Verbal Fluency seem traceable to poor categorical thinking, then it is sensible to teach the basic logical classification skills that are necessary for early school achievement. The other McCarthy tests, probably without exception, should not be trained since poor performance is likely to be symptomatic of a more basic perceptual or cognitive deficit. Even for the several tests mentioned above, low scores should first be explored as possible evidence of more pervasive deficiencies. (See Chapter 6 for a discussion of hypotheses generated from various combinations of the 18 tests.) Only when the more global hypotheses are rejected should specific training be considered.

Granted, future research on the training of specific McCarthy skills may suggest that this educational practice is fruitful for any and all tasks at certain age levels. For now, it is advised that such training be limited to the tests which assess basic foundation concepts such as Counting & Sorting and Conceptual Grouping, and not applied to the majority of the cognitive and motor tests. Instead, the role of the McCarthy profile and the scores on any supplementary measures should be to help choose the most appropriate curricular materials for the child and to suggest the approaches for teaching him that seem the most likely to succeed.

As with Wechsler's scales and the ITPA, a substantial difference between McCarthy's Verbal and Perceptual–Performance Indexes has implications for the modality in which most curricular materials might be geared. In general, a high Verbal Index suggests an emphasis on auditory–vocal materials, whereas a high Perceptual–Performance Index suggests materials having visual stimuli and requiring manipulative responding. However, the perceptive examiner will look beyond global verbal–nonverbal differences and make educational recommendations based on more specific hypotheses as well. For example, a child may have a low Perceptual–Performance Index because of poor motor coordination, but have well-developed visual perceptual and nonverbal reasoning abilities (see the case of Henry M. in Chapter 9). A conscientious clinician will uncover this finding by investigating the test age profile, and perhaps administering a supplementary test such as the Columbia Mental Maturity Scale. An examiner who responds only to the low Perceptual–Performance Index may rule out visual stimuli from the child's curriculum plan and try to remediate the "pervasive" deficit in the visual–motor modality when, in reality, the child's strengths may be in visual perception and nonverbal reasoning.

The entire profile should be considered when selecting educational materials, not just the verbal–nonverbal dichotomy. A child who functions far better in the visual–motor than the auditory–vocal channel should probably be taught to read with visually oriented materials. However, the likelihood of any particular visual material succeeding may be predictable based on other test findings. For example, an examiner may feel that the Peabody Rebus program (Woodcock, 1967) should be tried for a particular child. Since this technique demands good memory skills, the examiner needs to verify that the child has a relatively high Memory Index, or at least evidences a good visual memory on Pictorial Memory, Tapping Sequence, and supplementary tasks such as ITPA Visual Sequential Memory. If the child's memory is not adequate, then a different reading program should be selected—one that is consistent with his entire profile. Similarly, a preschool child who obtains a very high Quantitative Index may be ready to begin an enrichment program in mathematical skills, but the precise curriculum to use should be a function of his verbal ability, short-term memory, and nonverbal skills.

The Memory Scale often provides useful information for determining *how* to teach a child. A youngster with a poor memory, for example, will typically benefit from spaced rather than massed practice, with a brief review preceding each new lesson (e.g., Bryant, 1969). A child who obtains a low Memory Index due to apparent distractibility should be taught in an environment that is as free from distraction as possible, using materials that permit him to focus on one key element at a time (Strauss & Kephart, 1955; Strauss & Lehtinen, 1947). In contrast, a youngster with an exceptional memory may be encouraged to overlearn facts, words, or relationships by rote techniques to help compensate for deficiencies in one or both major modalities.

Fluctuations in the young child's test ages on the Perceptual–Performance and Motor Scales, if interpreted in the context of his complete McCarthy profile, may suggest the need for visual–motor training. Several systems have been developed for this purpose, including the ones designed by Barsch (1967), Frostig and Horne (1964), Getman (1962), and Kephart (1971). The choice of which system, if any, should be attempted will be a function of the specific nature of the child's skills, the severity of his deficiencies, his presenting problems, his age, and the examiner's theoretical orientation. Whenever such training is undertaken, it should be done with the thorough understanding that research is *not* available to document the success of visual–motor programs; although they *may* lead to improved perception, their effects have not been shown to transfer to academic achievement (Hammill, Goodman, & Wiederholt, 1974). Consequently, teachers need to be instructed on the pros and cons of visual–motor training and on realistic goals for their efforts.

Hammill and Bartel (1975) and Myers and Hammill (1976)

present excellent descriptions and critical evaluations of the major visual–motor programs which should be required reading for anyone contemplating, or already involved in, visual–motor training. As Hammill and Bartel (1975, p. 230) state: "In general, perceptual–motor training is viewed as more acceptable for preschool than for kindergarten or school-age children, and is never recommended as a substitute for teaching language, reading, or arithmetic skills."

The research on visual–motor training echoes the results of the psycholinguistic training studies and underscores the advisability of *not* developing an educational program specifically geared to the McCarthy profile. Rather, the goal should be to use an appropriate combination of instruments to convert samples of a child's behavior into hypotheses that have educational significance. The use of multiple instruments for assessment does not deviate from the techniques proposed by many advocates of test-related educational programming. Frostig (1967a, 1967b), for example, suggests using a comprehensive testing program which includes the Wechsler, ITPA, and other perceptual and motor tests, along with her Developmental Test of Visual Perception. Unfortunately, many of the practitioners who adhere to the visual–motor or psycholinguistic training programs do not follow the sound assessment suggestions frequently made by the developers of the programs.

A sensible approach to the translation of McCarthy scores (and scores on supplementary measures) to educational suggestions is to try to match the child's profile of *abilities* to the skills required for various curricular materials. This task requires a thorough knowledge of the methods and materials that are available for preschool and primary-grade children and a careful analysis of the requisite skills for success at different levels of the various programs. Of particular value to the psychological examiner is the regular feature in the *Journal of Learning Disabilities* entitled, "Programs, Materials, and Techniques," as well as books by Frierson and Barbe (1967, Part IV), Hammill and Bartel (1975), Johnson and Myklebust (1967), Lerner (1976, Parts III, IV), Newman (1969, Parts III, IV), Otto, McMenemy, and Smith (1973), Van Riper (1972), and Van Witsen (1967). A handy reference table assembled by Hammill and Bartel (1975, Appendix I) lists educational resources in the areas of gross motor development, perceptual–motor skills, cognitive and language-related activities, social studies, science, mathematics, and social skills; information about each resource, including its purpose, price, and the authors' evaluative comments, are provided in the table.

The books mentioned above generally discuss educational techniques that are geared specifically to the achievement areas of reading, spelling, arithmetic, and writing, or to skills such as perceptual–motor processes and oral expression. The teaching is aimed directly at the problem areas, rather than at skills in a hypothetical hierarchy that will presumably transfer to school achievement. We adhere to this approach to educational planning. The examiner should use the knowledge of a child's profile to facilitate the selection of resources and techniques that can utilize his integrities both to teach the pertinent content areas and to help ameliorate his deficient abilities. Teaching through the child's areas of strength while building up poorly developed skills is an educational strategy that is advocated by most authorities (Lerner, 1976, p. 75).

The above philosophy applies both to remediation, when essential skills or achievement areas are deficient, and to the choice of a preschool or primary-grade curriculum to avoid possible failure. If individualization of instruction is feasible within a preschool or first-grade setting, the examiner can try to match the ability profile of each child tested to a tailor-made set of curricular materials. This degree of flexibility may completely avoid failure for a child destined to have difficulty with conventional curricula and should enhance the achievement of other children as well. When early childhood curricula have clearcut goals and specified methods for achieving them, the examiner should select materials to supplement the required curricular resources. If the examiner's options for individualizing the child's instruction are extremely limited, then suggestions about the best ways of teaching the child within the given context can be beneficial. Knowledge of the theory, goals, and educational materials for various approaches will greatly facilitate the examiner's tasks, as will a thorough understanding of the preschool and primary-grade child. The following references focus on the very young child and on educational programs or techniques geared to his needs: Almy (1975); Evans (1975); Fallon (1973), Frost (1968); Leeper, Dales, Skipper, and Witherspoon (1968); Mott (1974); Reger (1970); Stone, Smith, and Murphy (1973).

Planning remediation for children who are experiencing failure in one or more school subjects is also dependent on the examiner's awareness of the precise methods and materials that have been used to teach the child. Trying to deduce why the existing program is not working can be as important for future decision making as the child's test profile. Knowledge of the unsuccessful program can also prevent the embarrassment of suggesting remedial techniques that are highly similar to the program that is not working. The examiner who is concerned about making meaningful remedial suggestions to teachers should consult some of the sources mentioned above and keep abreast of current research and innovative ideas in the area. For example, Hallenback (1976) has discussed some interesting ideas regarding the use of comic strips for remediation; Harrigan (1976) found research support for teaching beginning readers with syllables instead of phonemes; Schaer and Crump (1976) pointed out the importance of realizing that there has been little evaluation of popular remedial programs; and Schaefer, Heilig, and Rubin (1974) described a Learning Wall which permits young children to interact actively with a life-size projected image. These articles are merely illustrative of the diversity of recent work on remediation; by keeping up with the literature, the examiner can apply pertinent research findings, try new materials, employ innovative uses of ordinary materials, and follow suggested precautions as he tries to solve the problems of each child that is tested.

Although the examiner should always be aware of the available educational resources, he should not be limited by them. It is well within the examiner's role to propose the purchase of a variety of materials and resources to broaden his options for making educational recommendations. In addition, the examiner should take an active part in ensuring the success of a suggested educational program. One way is to informally try out different modes of teaching reading, arithmetic, or spelling during the testing session (after several hypotheses have been generated) to get some subjective impressions of what might work. Whether or not diagnostic teaching is attempted during the evaluation, the examiner should adhere to a systematic policy of following up the effectiveness of his suggestions and making new recommendations based on the feedback he receives from the teachers and on any new pertinent information about the child. Teachers who are experienced at clinical teaching (Lerner, 1976, chap. 6) can assume a large role in the follow-up process. However, the availability of competent teachers is not an excuse for the examiner to terminate his involvement after making an initial set of recommendations. The examiner's orientation is different in many respects from the teacher's, and the dual perspective often facilitates better decision making. In addition, even if the examiner's contribution is minimal during follow-up evaluations, the continuity with the same child should provide him with useful feedback about his ability to translate a test profile into educational suggestions.

It is also important to realize that the child's educational program need not involve an extensive search for dramatic materials or brand new methodology. Just because a child has learning problems does not necessitate that the examiner make intricate or novel recommendations; conventional approaches work quite well for many children, including some who are referred for learning difficulties. Most often effective remediation involves the dynamic application of learning theories and principles of good teaching (Bryant, 1969; Kirk & Kirk, 1971, chap. 8). Teachers who are unfamiliar with the wisdom of various learning theories may be using counter-productive techniques. Although most children may learn despite the teacher's methods, some will be unable to compensate. In these instances, the best educational suggestion may well be to recommend that the teacher adhere to pertinent principles of effective teaching. For example, the examiner may note that the child seems able to learn effectively when he is taught in small steps that increase gradually in difficulty, and that he responds well to praise; these observations can then be translated into operational procedures.

# Chapter 9
## Illustrative Case Reports

The culmination of McCarthy interpretation, including the integration of the test results with additional data, is the comprehensive case report of a child referred for clinical evaluation. The case reports of nine children, ranging in age from 3 years-11 months to 7 years-4 months, are featured in this chapter to illustrate the practical application of the content of Chapters 4–8.

The nine children were either referred to Rutland Center in Athens, Ga., for a suspected behavioral disorder, or they were already in treatment at the Center and were being reevaluated. Rutland Center is a psychoeducational center for evaluating and treating emotionally disturbed children that has served as the prototype for other psychoeducational centers throughout Georgia and around the country; treatment is based on the innovative Developmental Therapy created and designed by Wood (1975).

Each of the children discussed in this chapter was tested on the McCarthy Scales and on other pertinent instruments by Nadeen Kaufman, psychologist at Rutland Center. The illustrative case reports are essentially the reports that she presented at the staff meetings for determining diagnoses and treatments, except for modifications that were made either to preserve the anonymity of the children or to make the reports more consistent with the goals of this book. Although the case reports reflect only the psychological evaluation of

222

the child, it should be noted that each child was examined by a psychiatrist and educational tester as well, and the child's mother was interviewed by a social worker. In addition, all decisions made at the staff meetings were based on the opinions of the professional personnel who participated in the assessment, along with the input of other professionals who were dynamically involved with the child. Only the psychological reports are presented here, rather than the child's complete file, to keep the focus of this chapter on the interpretation of the McCarthy profile, the communication of test results and clinical observations made during the testing, and the integration of the McCarthy with other instruments for decision-making purposes.

The nine cases are presented below, from the youngest to the oldest. As a means of identification, each child is assigned the main diagnostic category agreed upon by the multidisciplinary team at the staff meeting. However, these categorizations are considered *tentative,* pending subsequent feedback from those who interact with the child (teachers, therapists, parents) and the outcome of follow-up evaluations. Furthermore, the use of a single categorical description does not imply a one-dimensional problem and is not intended to detract from the multifaceted pattern of abilities and behaviors that uniquely characterizes each child.

A summary of scores on the McCarthy precedes the case report of each child. The GCI and Scale Indexes are shown, with relative strengths and weaknesses indicated by an "S" and "W," respectively. In addition, the separate tests that are classified as strengths and weaknesses relative to the child's General Cognitive Age are listed, along with their test ages. The age equivalents and the strengths and weaknesses shown in the McCarthy summary are based on tables and computational procedures presented in Chapters 5 and 6. A slight exception to the conventional approach is the method used to determine relative strengths and weaknesses on the scales for Elizabeth T., who obtained a GCI below 50 and scored below 22 on most Scale Indexes. To evaluate her scale profile, Scale Ages were obtained as suggested in Chapter 5, pages 122–124; then strengths and weaknesses relative to her General Cognitive Age were determined by using the same guidelines suggested for the 18 separate tests (see p. 133).

The summaries of McCarthy scores are included for the nine sample children merely to provide an overview of their record form. Ordinarily, information about strengths and weaknesses is marked directly on the front and back of the child's record form; hence, numerical summaries need not appear in most psychological reports.

A final cautionary note merits careful attention. The nine cases presented below are merely illustrative and should *not* foster generalizations about children with learning or behavioral disorders. No attempt was made to choose cases that were representative of children referred for psychological evaluation; indeed, the main criterion for including psychological case reports in this chapter was the degree to which they helped meet the instructional goals of the book. Thus, inferences about the incidence of various disorders or the relationship of background variables (e.g., age, sex, race) to specific disorders are completely unwarranted if based in any way on the sample cases. Similarly, no particular diagnostic significance should be attached to the specific McCarthy profile of any of the nine children. For example, the identical profile of Indexes obtained by a sample child diagnosed as having minimal brain dysfunction might conceivably be earned by a child with a different disorder or by a normal youngster; profiles derive their meaning when interpreted in the context of background information, observed behaviors, and other test data.

Finally, it would be inappropriate to think in terms of "characteristic" McCarthy profiles because of any consistencies that may be evident in a few of the illustrative profiles. Carefully designed research investigations and cross-validation studies with a variety of samples are necessary to uncover the existence of any characteristic profiles for learning or behaviorally disordered children.

### Katie K., Age 3 Years–11 Months: Mental Retardation/Socioeconomic Deprivation

GCI = 61                    General Cognitive Age = 3

| Scale Indexes | | Highlights of the 18 Tests | | | |
|---|---|---|---|---|---|
| | | Strengths | | Weaknesses | |
| Verbal | 29 | Test | Age | Test | Age |
| Perc.–Perf. | 38 | | | | |
| Quant. | 31 | | | | |
| Memory | 38 | Pictorial Mem. | 6 | Word Knowl. | Below 2½ |
| Motor | 28 | Block Build. | 5 | Verbal Flu. | Below 2½ |
| Mean Index | 32.8 | Tapping Seq. | 4½ | | |
| | | Arm Coord. | 4 | | |

## REFERRAL AND BACKGROUND
## INFORMATION

Katie was referred to Rutland Center for evaluation by her day care center teacher who describes her as slow to comprehend, with a short attention span. Katie reportedly doesn't like the day care center, and her mother sees her moodiness and sadness as major problems. At home she doesn't get along with her one stepsister, Jill, aged 7. They fight, but Katie cries in frustration if not allowed to play with Jill (she doesn't have any other friends). Katie's mother describes her as "mean" when she comes home from the day care center, especially to Jill if Jill has stayed home from school that day. Complaining of frequent stomach aches and headaches, Katie runs into things because she doesn't watch where she is going.

At the age of 2 Katie was hit by a car and remained unconscious for about 10 minutes. Her mother said that since then she doesn't participate as much with other children. Very few developmental facts are known about her, since her mother was unable to recount her past milestones, saying that she doesn't know Katie very well. There is a long history of mental problems and family instability, and Katie has lived with her maternal grandmother on and off throughout her life. At present her mother is living with a boyfriend and is not legally divorced. When interviewed, Katie's mother indicated a lack of knowledge of child development and gave the impression that Katie and she do not interact with each other; she also indicated that Katie is given much unsupervised freedom to roam the neighborhood after being dropped off by the day care center bus.

## APPEARANCE AND BEHAVIORAL
## CHARACTERISTICS

Katie, a black girl aged 3 years 11 months, appears to be the size of an average 2½- or 3-year old. Her small figure corresponds to her equally immature speech development. It was difficult to understand her verbal expression, and nonverbal gestures were employed as clues whenever possible by the examiner to facilitate communication. In general she remained silent, and spoke with brief one- or two-word phrases which were extremely poorly articulated. In contrast to this limitation, Katie used her facial expressions to communicate her emotions, and she succeeded in demonstrating her ecstatic pleasure at manipulating the test materials and in "playing" at gross motor activities. On the other hand, Katie grew sad and moody when she was told that she could not keep a toy airplane that was present in the room. She indicated that she had no toys or television at home and managed to convey to the examiner the picture of a truly deprived lonesome little girl.

As she worked on the required tasks, Katie participated cooperatively with open mouth, looking up at the examiner for approval. She labeled things wrongly many times, revealing both visual perceptual problems and lack of basic conceptual knowledge. Katie was impulsive and demonstrated little self-control, opening the test kit and taking materials she was told not to on several occasions. This attempt to control the examiner and the testing situation required repetitious redirection on the examiner's part. On the less structured tasks that demanded more verbal expression she grew overactive and restless. Demanding excessive attention, Katie lacked comprehension of assigned tasks, and therefore had difficulty following directions. There were also indications of fine motor problems as well: e.g., when tapping tunes on a xylophone Katie had trouble releasing the mallet for it to contact the keys. This jerky hesitation appeared as mild neurological dysfunctioning.

TESTS ADMINISTERED

McCarthy Scales of Children's Abilities
Vineland Social Maturity Scale

TEST RESULTS AND INTERPRETATION

On the McCarthy Scales of Children's Abilities, Katie obtained a GCI of 61, which classifies her intelligence as Cognitively Deficient and ranks her at the first percentile for children her age. The chances are good (about 85 percent) that her true GCI is in the 55–67 range. Overall, she performed as well as the average child of 3 years, which is about 1 year below her present chronological age. Katie's test profile was characterized by a high degree of consistency. She scored at a $2\frac{1}{2}$–$3\frac{1}{2}$-year-old level in all of the major areas assessed. Thus, her verbal comprehension, nonverbal intelligence, quantitative skills, short-term memory, and motor coordination were all consistent with her deficient level of functioning.

Only two specific areas of strength were noted. Her visual memory and attention to visual detail were as well developed as the average 5 year old, as she performed well on tasks requiring her to recall visual stimuli (pictured objects, taps on a xylophone) and copy structures made of blocks. She also did relatively well on several tasks that assessed her gross motor coordination in the upper extremities. Her ability to perform such tasks as bouncing a ball and aiming a beanbag at a target were commensurate with her chronological age of almost 4 years, rather than with her mental age of 3. However, on gross motor tasks that are more related to maturation than experience (e.g., standing on one foot, clasping hands), she evidenced 2½–3-year-old performance. Thus, except in areas that are quite susceptible to specific training, Katie's physical development seems to parallel her mental development.

Katie scored below the level of the average 2½-year-old on two tasks—one requiring her to define words, and the other requiring her to name things in various categories (e.g., things to eat). She was thus extremely deficient in her language skills, particularly in her ability to express thoughts verbally. This expressive language problem ties in with her previously referred to speech difficulties.

Subsequent to the psychological evaluation, Katie was assessed on the Vineland Social Maturity Scale to measure her adaptive behavior. The Scale was administered to Katie's mother and to her day care center teacher as well because of the mother's lack of involvement with her daughter. Based on a consensus of their responses, Katie obtained a social age between 2½ and 3 years, corroborating the McCarthy findings and suggesting a diagnosis of mental retardation. On the Vineland, Katie was rated highest in locomotion and lowest in her socialization and communication skills. However, her relatively good locomotion rating seems to be due primarily to her unsupervised freedom (sample item: goes about neighborhood unattended).

## SUMMARY AND RECOMMENDATIONS

Almost 4 years old and small for her age, Katie was referred for evaluation by her day care center, where she was described as slow to comprehend, with a short attention span. At home there is fighting between Katie and her 7-year-old stepsister, and together they live with their mother and her boyfriend under socioeconomically deprived conditions. Medical history includes mention that Katie was hit by a car at age 2 and was unconscious for about 10 minutes.

The present evaluation revealed Katie's very immature level of speech development and verbal expression in general. She was far better able to communicate through animated facial expression, and gave the appearance of a well-motivated child who loves concrete materials to play with. Katie was socially manipulative, demanding of excessive attention, impulsive, and lacking in comprehension of tasks and directions. Both gross and fine motor coordination problems were noted. On the McCarthy Scales Katie obtained a GCI of 61, classifying her as Cognitively Deficient and equivalent to an average 3 year old's performance. Two areas of relative strength—visual memory and gross motor coordination of her upper extremities—were noted, as well as one area of relative weakness: the ability to express herself verbally.

Katie scored at a 2½–3-year-old level on the Vineland Social Maturity Scale, indicating that her social adaptive behavior and her cognitive ability are about equally deficient. She is thus functioning as a mentally retarded child, although there is reason to believe that her mental development has the potential for acceleration. For one thing, Katie has been raised under extremely deprived conditions with few concrete materials available and with limited opportunities for stimulation. She is still young enough to benefit greatly from remedial work involving the use of interesting materials and the development of missing skills and basic concepts. To facilitate a speedier rate of acquiring new learning Katie will require a high degree of stimulation, both with physical objects and with new experiences. A second consideration is the extreme consistency characterizing Katie's behavior. Besides appearing to be the size of a child almost 3, instead of almost 4, she was also about 1 year behind in her emotional, cognitive, language, motor, and social development. Consequently, her 3-year-old mental age may reflect a global maturation lag rather than just an intellectual deficit; if so, then a sudden growth spurt in all areas of functioning would not be unlikely, regardless of any educational intervention that may be tried.

In addition to the cognitive remediation mentioned above, speech therapy is recommended for Katie's poor articulation. She will also require aid in establishing appropriate friendships with other children and to become less dependent upon her 7-year-old stepsister for interaction with others. Reevaluation of Katie after such programs have been initiated for at least 6 months is suggested.

## Matthew B., Age 4 Years-5 Months:
## Delayed Development

GCI = 116          General Cognitive Age = $5\frac{1}{2}$

| Scale Indexes | | Highlights of the 18 Tests | | | |
|---|---|---|---|---|---|
| Verbal | 65(S) | Strengths | | Weaknesses | |
| Perc.–Perf. | 54 | Test | Age | Test | Age |
| Quant. | 59 | | | | |
| Memory | 49 | Opposite Anal. | $8\frac{1}{2}$ | Arm Coord. | 3 |
| Motor | 50 | Word Knowl. | 8 | Pictorial Mem. | $3\frac{1}{2}$ |
| Mean Index | 55.4 | Draw-A-Child | $7\frac{1}{2}$ | Tapping Seq. | $3\frac{1}{2}$ |
| | | | | Leg Coord. | $3\frac{1}{2}$ |
| | | | | Numer. Mem. I | $3\frac{1}{2}$ |
| | | | | Numer. Mem. II | $3\frac{1}{2}$ |
| | | | | Block Build. | 4 |

REFERRAL AND BACKGROUND
INFORMATION

Matthew was referred to Rutland Center for evaluation by his teacher at the private preschool he attends. In the 4-year-old group there he is described as being unable to get along with other children. Whereas his mother doesn't see the problem with other children, she does indicate high priority problems concerning Matthew's short attention span, restlessness, demands for excessive attention, and resistance to discipline. She also is aware of his lack of age-appropriate social skills. At home Matthew lives with his father (a lawyer), mother, and 17-year-old sister. When Matthew was $2\frac{1}{2}$ years old, an older brother, then aged 7, suffered severe brain damage as a result of an accident and was placed in a private institution. Matthew has never had the sudden disappearance of his brother explained to him; it is still a highly emotional topic for his parents who appear unable to discuss it. The lines of communication between family members seem strained in other subjects as well, as seen by the fact that Mr. and Mrs. B. didn't feel it necessary to tell Matthew when his maternal grandfather died recently. Matthew's favorite pastime is reported to be swimming in the family's pool.

## APPEARANCE AND BEHAVIORAL
## CHARACTERISTICS

A cute little 4½-year-old boy with long blond curly hair giving him a more girl-like appearance, Matthew extended his hand and came willingly with the examiner to the testing room. Once there he appeared ready to cooperate and enthusiastic to begin tasks. However, as soon as the first sign of difficulty occurred, this mood subtly changed and Matthew began avoiding frustrating situations by gently—but firmly—attempting to manipulate the examiner and resist direction. He kept changing the tasks' requirements away from the examiner's models and specific structure and redesigning them to simpler tasks of which he was more confident of success. In this manner he continually made statements such as "I want to do it wider, O.K.?" "I'm gonna make this one bigger." "That's enough now, I don't have to do it anymore." He pushed the examiner's hand away to prevent interference with his playing inappropriately with test materials. This refusal to follow directions was accomplished mostly through high level verbal interaction, which demonstrated Matthew's strong skills in communicating his needs to others. It also outlined a rather detailed compensatory system he has devised to help him cope calmly with the frustrations new situations present. The most often used device was stalling for time: when he couldn't perform a given task he would simply state "Wait,——I have to think about that a little bit." He then would disregard the chore as if completed, with no further reflection or attempt to answer. He lacked confidence, and made numerous requests for the examiner's help and approval.

Matthew's voice was phlegmy and he stuttered occasionally during the evaluation. This speech difficulty took the form of both prolongations and repetitions, but was not consistent or severe. Also, Matthew repeated whole long sentences, over and over, unnecessarily. Thus he would tell the examiner something which was immediately responded to, and repeat it again 9 or 10 times in succession directly after hearing the response. Whereas he behaved age appropriately during the most structured tasks, he grew very silly and babyish when given more freedom. For example, he giggled and squealed with delight at the person he drew, and became so deeply involved with immature talk and scribbling that he spent an overly long period of time on this task, refusing to terminate his obvious pleasure.

TESTS ADMINISTERED

McCarthy Scales of Children's Abilities
Supplementary evaluation of Draw-A-Child
WPPSI Information and Comprehension subtests
Informal Sentence Completion test
Family Drawing
Children's Apperception Test

TEST RESULTS AND INTERPRETATION

On the McCarthy Scales of Children's Abilities, Matthew obtained a GCI of 116, which classifies his intellectual ability as Bright Normal and ranks him at the 84th percentile for children his age. Overall, he performed as well as the average 5½-year-old, which is about 1 year above his chronological age. The chances are 85 percent that his true GCI falls somewhere between 110 and 122. He performed relatively well on the Verbal Scale (93rd percentile), while his Indexes on the Perceptual–Performance, Quantitative, Memory, and Motor Scales were quite consistent with his overall level of functioning.

The fact that Matthew's Memory Index was not a statistically significant weakness is deceiving. He actually was very poor (3½-year-old level) in simple rote memory, particularly when the stimuli were not meaningful. However, his strong verbal ability was able to compensate for an otherwise severe memory problem. Thus, whereas he could not repeat random digits spoken by the examiner, or taps on a xylophone, he performed adequately when the stimuli were meaningful to him (e.g., repeating a story).

His strength on the Verbal Scale is worthy of comment. He scored at a remarkably high level (as well as an 8–8½ year old) on highly conceptual tasks requiring the communication of abstract ideas. On other verbal tests, however, his performance ranged from average to very poor. Since Matthew's specific areas of integrity are very "visible" it is likely that Matthew is perceived as being smarter than he really is. Unfortunately, his visual–motor, numerical, and especially short-term memory skills are considerably below this one outstanding strength. Even his good performance in one visual–motor task (Draw-A-Child) was greatly facilitated by his verbal concept formation. He talked throughout the task about the different parts of the body and their functions, and as he spoke he drew crude (but creditable) representations of these parts.

One surprising weakness was evidenced by Matthew in his gross motor coordination. Since he reportedly is described as a good swimmer, one would not have anticipated poor performance on the gross motor tasks on the McCarthy. However, he scored at a 3–3½-year-old level on items such as bouncing a ball, catching a beanbag, and standing on one foot. Therefore, the muscles required for balance and precision of movement are not as well developed as the larger body muscles needed for swimming. In view of Matthew's small stature and overall immaturity, his poor gross motor ability on the McCarthy may reflect a slow rate of maturation.

The WPPSI Information and Comprehension subtests were administered to Matthew to supplement the McCarthy data. Matthew obtained scaled scores of 17 on Information and 12 on Comprehension, corresponding to test ages of 6½ and 4¾, respectively. Thus, on these sociocultural measures Matthew's acquisition of facts was at a significantly higher level than his common sense understanding of social situations. His exceptional Information score is consistent both with the advanced verbal concept formation that he evidenced on the McCarthy and with his advantaged background. The fact that his Comprehension score is not at the level of his other verbal reasoning abilities probably reflects the influence of his poorly developed social and interpersonal skills.

The Sentence Completion form which Matthew partially responded to indicated that he is interested in age- and sex-appropriate toys. It also gave insight into his very concrete preoperational level of thinking, as well as aggressive means of coping with conflict. He appears to enjoy a close relationship with his father, and relates least to his older sister. These findings were found on other measures as well, reinforcing the likelihood of their validity. On the Family Drawing, Matthew drew his older sister towering over the rest of the family members; the person closest in size to himself and to whom he apparently is emotionally close was his father. The figures were all executed with poor motor coordination devoid of details or expression. The composite result was an immature drawing. The human figure Matthew worked on for on overly long time (20 minutes) received a 7½-year-old age level based on the McCarthy's *conceptual* evaluation system. The product was monsterlike and bizarre looking, nevertheless. At his age it is difficult to determine the validity of any emotional indicators; however, both his regressive behavior during the task and the overall picture itself suggest aggressive feelings and immaturity.

The projective story-telling measure, the Children's Apperception Test, evoked the most extreme babyishness from Matthew, and he proceeded to act out his stories with a loud voice interrupted by loud laughing. He expressed special interest in destruction and aggressive behavior. Matthew apparently hears adults say things about him which he doesn't understand, but interprets as positive attributes. For example, he stated "Let's tear down buildings . . . That's rambunctious!" He then giggled and shook with sheer delight. Also filling his stories were the frequent mention of water-related activities (e.g., "they got turned over in the water stream," "went plop down the water stream," "fell in lake," "dripped in lake," etc.). This association occurred with no visual representation of any form of water present. It is difficult to determine whether this resulted from regressive and perhaps enuretic concerns, or whether water represents something more personally meaningful to Matthew (perhaps related to his interest in swimming) that remains uncovered at this evaluation.

## SUMMARY AND RECOMMENDATIONS

Matthew is a small 4½-year-old boy having difficulties in school relating to peers. His mother doesn't feel concerned about this behavior, but reports that he has a short attention span, is restless, and is resistant to discipline at home. Communication between Matthew and his other family members (mother, father, 17-year-old sister) is strained, as his older brother's sudden placement in an institution (which occurred when Matthew was 2½) was never explained to him. During the present evaluation Matthew demonstrated resistance to perform activities on which he feared failure. In a nonaggressive manner he manipulated the situation to better suit his needs and areas of strength. Repeating unnecessarily throughout the session, Matthew grew silly and displayed regressive behavior on the less structured tasks. On the McCarthy Scales of Children's Abilities, Matthew earned a General Cognitive Index of 116, which classifies him at the Bright Normal level of intellectual functioning. Performing relatively well on the Verbal Scale, where he evidenced a remarkably well-developed conceptual level, Matthew demonstrated weakness in simple rote memory and gross motor coordination. On projective measures Matthew indicated a close relationship with his father, inappropriate means for dealing with conflict and expressing emotions, and immaturity. There were also numerous references to water themes, which occurred without any relevant visual stimuli.

Matthew's difficulties with his interpersonal relationships with other children appear to result from his lack of age-appropriate social skills. He needs direction to reduce his regressive and aggressive tendencies and to develop more socially acceptable and productive means for coping with conflict. Mr. and Mrs. B. would benefit from parent counseling to open up lines of communication within the family network. This help could not only improve their own adjustment to their other son's severe injury, but it might also create less tension and greater freedom for the development of more satisfactory behavior on Matthew's part.

At this time there is no evidence of psychopathology or neurological dysfunction; rather, Matthew seems to be behaviorally immature in the Ilg and Ames sense of the term. This apparent developmental delay in nonconceptual areas merits reevaluation when he approaches school age since his behavioral maturity at that time may help determine the most appropriate grade placement for him. It is also suggested that Matthew's rote memory problem be followed up at the future evaluation to check out the possibilities of a specific learning disability.

### Emily S., Age 4 Years–11 Months: Reactive Behavior Disorder/Minimal Brain Dysfunction

GCI = 108          General Cognitive Age = $5\frac{1}{2}$

| Scale Indexes | | Highlights of the 18 Tests | | | |
|---|---|---|---|---|---|
| Verbal | 63 (S) | Strengths | | Weaknesses | |
| Perc.–Perf. | 48 | Test | Age | Test | Age |
| Quant. | 50 | | | | |
| Memory | 49 | R–L Orient. | 8 | Puzzle Solv. | $3\frac{1}{2}$ |
| Motor | 44 | Verbal Flu. | 8 | Numer. Mem. II | $3\frac{1}{2}$ |
| Mean Index | 50.8 | Opposite Anal. | $7\frac{1}{2}$ | Block Build. | 4 |
| | | Concept. Grp. | $7\frac{1}{2}$ | | |

## REFERRAL AND BACKGROUND
## INFORMATION

Emily was referred for evaluation by her mother because of numerous complaints about Emily's behavior at the preschool she has been attending for 8 months. At school, her behavior has been described as immature, manipulative, distractible, resistant to discipline, silly, and aggressive to children and rules. At home with her mother, stepfather, and baby brother, Emily is also difficult to control. She plays roughly and resists routines, as well as showing jealousy of her little brother. Emily enjoys a good relationship with her stepfather (her natural father died when she was 1 year old; remarriage occurred when she was 3½ years old). Mrs. S. has been described as providing inconsistent discipline and structure in the home, alternating between shows of frustration and indecision.

Results of a testing session 3 months ago showed Emily to have a Stanford-Binet IQ of 107, with strengths in the areas of memory and language, and visual–motor weaknesses. Testing behavior was consistently overactive with attempts made to verbally control the situation. Tentative diagnosis of a reactive behavior disorder was made at that time, with concern about a potential learning disorder.

The present evaluation was requested to provide a clearer picture of Emily's separate abilities. Mrs. S. mentioned that she had administered 5 mg of ritalin (according to a recent decision made by her doctor) on the day of the present testing.


## APPEARANCE AND BEHAVIORAL
## CHARACTERISTICS

Emily, a pretty 5-year-old girl with long blond hair, brought her cap gun to the testing session and proceeded to shoot it off several times before placing it down on the table as requested. Laughing and talking excessively, she demonstrated hyperactive restlessness as she demanded excessive attention from the examiner. Emily proved highly distractible and also frequently hummed and sang during test activities. Great immaturity and regressive, silly behavior was noted. For example, Emily acted out many of the examiner's words, licked her pencil point, mouthed the examiner's instructions in mimicry, blew out her breath on the test materials, etc.

Most extreme of all the many annoying behaviors Emily presented was her resistance to discipline, direction, and structure. She managed to hold on tight to the manipulator role she quickly established for herself. Whether demonstrating her boredom with loud, fake yawning, or responding to the examiner's casual comments with rhymes (even when she couldn't make "sensible" content), Emily set herself in opposition to the demands of the evaluation. Yet, despite Emily's contrariness, which seemed to reflect her "joy of misbehaving" more than anything else, she enjoyed being the center of attention and accepted redirection often enough to permit valid assessment of her abilities. Indeed, she exerted considerable effort when responding to the actual test items. For example, while naming as many things as possible in a brief time (e.g., things to wear), she was visibly "straining" to come up with a variety of acceptable responses for each item.

## TESTS ADMINISTERED

McCarthy Scales of Children's Abilities
ITPA: Visual Closure and Visual Association subtests
Family Drawing
Children's Apperception Test

## TEST RESULTS AND INTERPRETATION

On the McCarthy Scales of Children's Abilities Emily obtained a GCI of 108, which classifies her intelligence as Average and ranks her at the 69th percentile for children her age. Overall she scored as well as a typical 5½-year-old. There is an 85 percent likelihood that her true GCI is between 102 and 114.

Emily demonstrated an exceptional strength in verbal comprehension and expression (90th percentile), while revealing consistently Average performance in other areas of functioning: nonverbal intelligence, numerical facility, short-term memory, and motor coordination.

Her Average level of functioning on nonverbal tasks is misleading. She displayed considerable scatter on the Perceptual–Performance Scale, ranging from 3½-year-old behavior when solving picture puzzles to 8-year-old behavior when demonstrating knowledge of right versus left. Actually, her scores on the Perceptual–Performance tests may be dichotomized. She did well not only on the right–left task, but also scored at a 7½-year-old level on a test of logical classification skills. Both of these tasks require well-developed nonverbal reasoning and verbal concept formation (even though they are on the Perceptual-Performance Scale). Conversely, she scored at about a 4-year-old level (within the $3\frac{1}{2}$-$4\frac{1}{2}$-year-old range) on five tasks measuring visual-motor coordination, including design copying.

When this dichotomy is coordinated with her excellent verbal skills, a clear pattern emerges. Emily is very strong in her verbal conceptual development, functioning as well as the average 7-year-old child on tasks measuring this ability. There is thus a striking 3-year difference between her knowledge of verbal concepts and her visual-motor skills. Whereas she evidences rich acquisition of language skills, performing at a superior level on a creative task (in which she revealed great originality and flexibility of thought) and on analogies, Emily is seriously depressed in her visual-motor functioning. Emily's pattern of successes and failures on the Stanford-Binet (noted above) is consistent with this conclusion, and therefore reinforces its validity.

After the entire McCarthy was completed, the picture puzzles were reintroduced to test the limits. Emily was given structured verbal clues to help her solve the puzzles she had previously failed, and she was encouraged to talk out loud while assembling the pieces. With these extra cues she was able to solve even the hardest McCarthy puzzle, indicating adequate visual perception and also demonstrating that she can use her good verbal ability to facilitate her nonverbal performance.

The ITPA Visual Closure and Visual Association subtests were then administered to continue to explore her functioning in the visual-motor modality. Her scaled score of 41 on Visual Closure (psycholinguistic age of 5 years-3 months) gave additional evidence of adequate visual perception. On Visual Association, a measure of nonverbal reasoning that does not depend on motor coordination, Emily obtained a scaled score of 29 (age 3 years-10 months). This score is significantly below her McCarthy GCI and suggests deficient reasoning when Emily cannot (or does not) rely on her well-developed verbal concept formation.

The sizable discrepancy in Emily's verbal and nonverbal functioning is suggestive of minimal brain dysfunction. Her testing behaviors, such as extreme restlessness and distractibility, help substantiate this conclusion. When she is placed in an academic setting it is likely that her problem will translate into learning difficulties in school.

During the Family Drawing, Emily was quite silly, laughing at her drawing of her mother. The initial product of her mother consisted of a head with circle eyes and nose and a straight line mouth; long pencil strokes extended upward, representing hair. Seconds after her laughing stopped, however, she grew more serious, stating "I drew her with a mad face—I want to make her happy. I need to erase the yucky head." She then proceeded to erase the "figure," and instead drew a head with only eyes, and two straight lines on either side which she called a chair. Emily interpreted this as a satisfactory change, commenting "Now she has a happy face . . . she's sitting on a chair." The only other person she drew in her family was herself. The picture was poorly constructed, repeating the low level of visual–motor development displayed previously on the Perceptual–Performance tests. It also suggests the possibility of concern over approval from her mother with potential conflict involving the father figure.

The projective story-telling Children's Apperception Test reiterated the theme of male figure conflict. The father figure appears benign via defenses used to render him harmless. Emily equates strangers with intruders who take others' possessions away. There were also several indications of sibling rivalry; e.g., in one picture a baby boy is seen as gloating over his closeness with the mother, while the child-hero is left behind.

Emily demonstrated regressive behavior, both verbally in her stories, and nonverbally with her test behaviors. Her overall immaturity is in direct contrast to a major theme in her story responses: that of reaching for greater independence. She openly states this need to be treated in a more grown-up manner with the accompanying frustration at still being ascribed a little girl's status and role. Also revealed was Emily's lack of understanding of cause and effect relationships on human emotion. For example, a calm character "found out he was so mad" rather than arrive at that state as a logical consequence of provocation. Emily seeks and receives support from her family, and especially sees her mother as nurturative.

## SUMMARY AND RECOMMENDATIONS

A 5-year-old girl who is difficult to control both at home and in nursery school, Emily was described as immature, manipulative, overactive, and aggressive to children and rules. Reported to have a Stanford-Binet IQ of 107, tentative diagnosis of reactive behavior disorder has been considered, with concern about the possibility of a learning disorder. During the present evaluation Emily repeated her unruly behavior, and even though she had taken 5 mg of ritalin before coming, she was extremely hyperactive both verbally and motorically.

On the McCarthy Scales of Children's Abilities, Emily achieved a General Cognitive Index of 108, classifying her intelligence as Average, but also revealing a profile of significant strengths and weaknesses. Functioning with exceptional strength in her verbal comprehension and expression, she displayed relatively poor visual–motor coordination. Her nonverbal reasoning ability was facilitated by her good verbal concept formation. Combined with her distractible and overactive behavior, Emily's test performance suggests the presence of minimal brain dysfunction, likely to result in school learning problems in an academic setting. All other drawing tests underscored the same conclusion.

Projective measures indicated great immaturity with regressive behavioral tendencies accompanied by the desire for independence. Emily is apparently struggling over a dependence–independence dichotomy with the inability to delay the gratification of having "grown-up" possessions and freedom. She also demonstrates confusion over emotional states and their causation. Emily's relationship with her family produces anxieties which leave her jealous of her baby sibling, fearful of her mother's disapproval, and ambivalently drawn to and yet fearful of her stepfather.

An overview of Emily's behavioral symptoms and emotional problems suggests a reactive behavior disorder in addition to apparent minimal brain dysfunction. Both types of disturbance seem to be affecting Emily's behavior, and each is a high priority concern for treatment.

Several recommendations can be made at this time. First, a check on Emily's ritalin dosage is strongly indicated, with an increase probably needed. In addition, Emily is young enough to benefit from a program of visual–motor training and gross motor exercises. Starting with activities within her capability (such as clay or finger painting) and progressing to playing ball, her motor skills should begin gradual improvement. Visual perceptual materials such as picture puzzles, formboards, marbles, and mazes will also be suitable to begin with. Since she apparently knows various perceptual facts (such as those pertaining to logical classification), she needs broad experience applying these rules to new visual situations. Her strength in verbal concept formation suggests that verbal *labeling* might be effective in solving perceptual problems. By having Emily describe alternative solutions out loud, her excellent verbal expression can facilitate her nonverbal reasoning and planning ability just as it did in the puzzle-solving activity noted earlier. Emily herself used both singing and rhyming to supplement her verbal responses, and careful incorporation of music and poetry will probably prove beneficial as a teaching vehicle and motivational device. Considering Emily's high level of verbal concept formation, limmericks might easily become a medium through which factual content can be presented.

Emily needs parental relationships clarified, with her role in the family clearly identified. This clarity is essential not only for Emily herself, but also to help her parents' individual functioning toward their daughter. Management will be facilitated by tight structure and well-defined limits. Emily possesses good enough verbal reasoning and comprehension to benefit from logical discussion aimed at explaining rules and regulations within the family system. Consistency and communication are mandatory elements in any successful program in dealing with Emily.

### Ralph Y., Age 5 Years–3 Months:
### Childhood Schizophrenia

GCI = 98                    General Cognitive Age = 5

| Scale Indexes | | Highlights of the 18 Tests | | | |
|---|---|---|---|---|---|
| Verbal | 40 | Strengths | | Weaknesses | |
| Perc.–Perf. | 53 (S) | Test | Age | Test | Age |
| Quant. | 57 (S) | | | | |
| Memory | 31 (W) | Concept. Grp. | 7½ | Tapping Seq. | Below 2½ |
| Motor | 42 | R–L Orient. | 7 | Leg Coord. | Below 2½ |
| Mean Index | 44.6 | Draw-A-Child | 7 | Verbal Mem. I | 2½ |
| | | Numer. Mem. II | 7 | Verbal Mem. II | 2½ |
| | | Word Knowl. | 6½ | | |
| | | Numer. Mem. I | 6½ | | |
| | | Opposite Anal. | 6½ | | |

## REFERRAL AND BACKGROUND INFORMATION

Ralph is presently enrolled at Rutland Center, where he has received Developmental Therapy for 5 months. He is described as a boy with very poor gross motor coordination, immature speech, and several neurological "soft" signs of impairment. Behaviorally, he lacks appropriate social skills for a child his age. He acts out, resists discipline, and is fearful of new situations. Also noted is his whirling, aggressive tendencies, and bizarre behavior such as talking to the palm of his hand. On one previous attempt to evaluate him, Ralph refused to cooperate with the examiner and caused the termination of the testing session with no new information obtained. The present evaluation was planned to gain better insight into his behavioral problems and to facilitate better rapport with Ralph. His therapist, to whom he is able to relate without fear, sat silently in the testing room throughout the evaluation.

## APPEARANCE AND BEHAVIORAL CHARACTERISTICS

Ralph is a very tall 5-year-old boy who appears as well developed physically as an average 7-8-year old. He hid his face by turning his body into his chair when the examiner and his therapist approached him. He appeared upset and on the verge of tears, but with his therapist's help he was able to separate from his mother and enter the examiner's testing room. Whereas his articulation was poor, Ralph spoke freely and offered a continual flow of conversation and comment. His language content frequently drifted away from the demands of the tasks at hand and took on a bizarre quality. For example, on a task requiring him to repeat digits, Ralph responded to the stimulus 2-5-8 with "Old MacDonald Had a Farm." This response was stated matter-of-factly by him, sandwiched in between correct responses and sincere attempts. On the same task, he responded to one item with "that's not my phone number" in an air of concern and puzzlement.

On a task requiring him to recall a set of common objects he had just seen on a picture card, Ralph incorporated these objects into a series of unrelated sentences rather than just supply the necessary words. On a verbal memory task in which Ralph was requested to repeat a short series of unrelated words, he was unable or unwilling to respond appropriately, and instead gave his free association as word responses. He apparently knew this was not what he was supposed to do, because he belligerently added the statement "I copied that" after each associative answer. This type of losing touch with the specific goal-oriented behavior demanded by the testing situation implies an inability to control his impulses, as well as a need to make all of his words meaningful to *himself* in some esoteric way.

Ralph worked in a reflective manner on visual perceptual tasks that absorbed his interest, such as putting together cut-up puzzles. He used a trial-and-error approach, but he was slow to perceive relationships. Whereas he "saw" his mistakes, his insight didn't occur quickly enough for him to correct them within time limits. He perseverated on this task, refusing to give up working on one item for an unduly long time.

There was much aggression in Ralph's behavior toward the examiner and the test materials. On the less structured gross motor tasks he threw the beanbag in a deliberate aim at the examiner as fast and hard as he could manage. This behavior also occurred with the ball. Ralph appeared excited and happy on these occasions, and took delight in the chaos he created within the room. He proceeded to aim at the ceiling light fixture, etc., and was finally brought back to task by his previously dormant therapist, who again withdrew after Ralph resumed a more cooperative manner.

Ralph's activity level during most of the testing was high. Whereas he proved capable of sitting still when he was task absorbed, on most occasions he sat in his chair, tipping it all the way back on its two back legs until both he and it fell over backward. He kept falling over backward (without hurting himself apparently) throughout the evaluation. This falling especially occurred during verbal tasks which did not require him to manipulate concrete objects. For a spell in the middle of the session, he ran back and forth in the center of the room, in each direction, ending his run with a slide and fall.

In all, Ralph was relating primarily to *himself,* not to the examiner or his therapist, or (in some cases) to the tasks at hand.

TESTS ADMINISTERED

McCarthy Scales of Children's Abilities
Projective Drawings

TEST RESULTS AND INTERPRETATION

Ralph's GCI of 98 ± 6 places him in the 45th percentile for children his own age, which represents an Average level of performance. His scores on the specific scales exhibited much scatter, ranging from an Index of 31 on Memory (3rd percentile) to 57 on the Quantitative Scale (75th percentile). His Indexes on the Verbal and Motor Scales were midway between these extremes, and were consistent with his Average GCI. Relative to Ralph's overall score, his Quantitative

Index reflects a strength, indicating his facility in dealing with numbers and his good understanding of quantitative concepts. His Perceptual–Performance Index of 53 (60th percentile) also suggests a relative strength in visual–motor coordination and nonverbal reasoning when manipulating concrete materials.

Despite Ralph's poor performance on the Memory Scale, one cannot conclude that he is deficient in short-term memory. An analysis of the separate short-term memory tasks constituting the scale is revealing. His ability on both parts of the numerical memory task (repeating digits both forward and backward) was a relative *strength* for him. Performing at the $6\frac{1}{2}$–7-year-old age level, Ralph gave evidence of his previously mentioned facility with numbers. However, on the Verbal Memory test (repeating words, sentences, and a story), and on a task requiring Ralph to copy a sequence of notes tapped by the examiner on a xylophone, his failure to cooperate was probably the main reason that he registered at only a $2\frac{1}{2}$-year-old level of ability. On the Verbal Memory test he free associated, apparently choosing not to comply with the "rules of the game." Similarly, on the task with the xylophone, Ralph preferred to bang violently in random, aggressive strokes, rather than trying to copy the appropriate model. Whereas it is conceivable that Ralph actually possesses $2\frac{1}{2}$-year-old level skills, it is not likely, considering his good memory for digits. Hence, the low Memory Index is probably a reflection of his behavior disorder rather than a poor short-term memory. Some evidence for this hypothesis came later in the session during a relaxed moment when the examiner attempted to test the limits on Verbal Memory by informally assessing Ralph's span for semantic stimuli. He was able to repeat several series of three words spoken by the examiner, a feat he could not perform during the regular test; however, be became silly when longer word series and sentences were tried, so the informal testing was discontinued.

A careful analysis of Ralph's relative strengths and weaknesses on the numerous specific tests which make up the scales reveals an interesting and consistent pattern. He was highly successful on the high level tasks requiring abstract, conceptual thought. This degree of excellence was evidenced by a $6\frac{1}{2}$–7-year-old level of performance on a variety of tasks cutting across the Verbal and Perceptual–Performance Scales. He excelled in the following conceptual tasks: defining concrete and abstract words, drawing a picture of a boy, demonstrating knowledge of the spatial concept right versus left, utilizing logical classification skills, and providing opposites to verbal analogies. His Average GCI of 98 was limited in part by his failure to cooperate on two memory tasks and in part by his average or below average ability in the more convergent tasks such as copying designs. However, his good conceptual ability gives us insight into Ralph's greater ability in abstract reasoning and hence potential success in school-related achievement.

The only relative weakness that could not be attributed to Ralph's behavioral problems was seen in a gross motor coordination task, Leg Coordination. Here he exhibited extremely poor gross motor functioning, as he was unable to stand on one foot, walk backward, or walk on tiptoes. Whereas he successfully walked a straight line, his overall ability ranked him below the average 2½-year-old. Interestingly, he was at an average level for his age in gross and fine motor tasks involving his arms and hands (except for awkward pencil manipulation). Ralph seems to have established cerebral dominance (right handed) based on observation of his preferred hand on motor tasks. Despite the apparent neurological integrity in this area, his extremely poor performance on Leg Coordination suggests the definite possibility of some degree of neurological impairment.

Although the Bender-Gestalt Test could not be administered because Ralph's tolerance for structured tests dwindled rapidly after the completion of the McCarthy, an examination of his design-copying skills was made during one McCarthy test, Draw-A-Design. On this test, Ralph performed at a 5-year-old level, which matches his chronological age. Therefore, his visual perceptual skills are probably intact. From a qualitative point of view, Ralph's errors fell into two primary categories: perseveration and rotation.

Ralph's free art expressions were primarily on the representational level, although some kinesthetic scribbling occurred right alongside his more meaningful efforts. On all four drawings that he completed spontaneously, and in his Draw-A-Child production for the McCarthy, Ralph displayed a great many emotional indicators. These deviations are frequently associated as manifestations of emotional disorder. His drawings all had certain characteristic qualities of execution: they were out of bounds, constructed impulsively with rapid movements, and were basically uninhibited. Out of the turmoil of his long, aggressive strokes evolved a narrow range of repetitive themes. Young children draw what's important to them. People predominate, then animals follow a normal hierarchy of subject matter. Ralph's thoughts, as revealed through his drawings, turn outward; they are less intimate personal statements. First, with the exception of one fireman who was drawn swathed in hoses, there are no human relationships or people represented. Ralph drew (1) a fire station scene; (2) a fire in progress with several ongoing attempts at controlling it being carried out; (3) a big cloud with great rain; and (4) grass being hosed down with water in a darkened sky containing both moon and shaded sun. The last picture had a series of "8's" written over it. The subject and style of the drawings conjure an air of foreboding. The pictures portray ominous signs and destruction, along with indications of anxiety and difficulties in interpersonal relationships. Ralph appears predominantly involved with *things*. In response to the examiner's probing about his possible fear of fire, or concern over its destructive nature, or even mention about how hot a fire is, Ralph came up with cold, emotionless observations. In one of his drawings, there were striking inconsistencies of thought. Here again, the picture was devoid of people.

In the Draw-A-Child task, Ralph began by drawing a long vertical line in the center of the page, dividing it in two. The picture of the boy was filled in on the right half, and on the left he drew a spiraling set of circles which he carried over across the line onto the boy. When questioned, he called this "wind," and later referred to it as a "tornado." Here we see a mechanism for maintaining structure within the task: the vertical dividing line—which may also help him compartmentalize fearful stimuli.

It is interesting to note traditional symbolic interpretations of fire as a theme in drawings: the combination of anger and need for warmth (love).

## SUMMARY AND RECOMMENDATIONS

Ralph is a 5-year-old boy, physically resembling an average 7-8-year-old, who currently attends Rutland Center. During the evaluation, Ralph's language content often drifted away from the demands of the tasks and took on a bizarre quality. He related to neither the examiner nor to his therapist, who was present; his behavior indicated an inability to control his impulses, as well as the need to make all of his words meaningful to *himself* in some esoteric way. Ralph exhibited spells of hyperactivity, as well as aggressive behavior toward the examiner and the test materials.

On the McCarthy Scales Ralph's General Cognitive Index of 98 places him in the Average level of intellectual functioning, although this is probably an underestimate of his potential. Relative to this level of ability, strengths were exhibited on the Quantitative and the Perceptual–Performance Scales, while his poor performance on the Memory Scale indicated a relative weakness. However, this finding does not imply a poor memory, necessarily, because his score on the Memory Scale was depressed by his apparent lack of cooperation on two tests. Overall, he performed best on high level tasks requiring abstract, conceptual thought, and worst on gross motor activities involving his lower extremities.                         ·

Ralph's free art expressions displayed a great number of emotional indicators. Most significant is the relative absence of people and human relationships from all of the spontaneous pictures he drew, and his predominant involvement with things and destructive forces.

Based on the results of this evaluation, it is recommended that Ralph be thoroughly examined by a neurologist for suspected neurological impairment. It is essential that Ralph continue the Developmental Therapy he has been receiving, since he is deficient in maintaining appropriate interpersonal relationships and gives evidence of schizophrenic behavior.

### Dennis C., Age 5 Years–7 Months:
### Minimal Brain Dysfunction

GCI = 75                    General Cognitive Age = $4\frac{1}{2}$

| Scale Indexes | | Highlights of the 18 Tests | | | |
|---|---|---|---|---|---|
| | | Strengths | | Weaknesses | |
| Verbal | 41 | Test | Age | Test | Age |
| Perc.–Perf. | 31 (W) | | | | |
| Quant. | 39 | | | | |
| Memory | 30 (W) | Leg Coord. | $7\frac{1}{2}$ | R–L Orient. | 3 |
| Motor | 50 (S) | Arm Coord. | $6\frac{1}{2}$ | Numer. Mem. I | 3 |
| Mean Index | 38.2 | Block Build. | 6 | Verbal Mem. I | 3 |
| | | Pictorial Mem. | 6 | Tapping Seq. | $3\frac{1}{2}$ |
| | | Number Quest. | 6 | Draw-A-Des. | $3\frac{1}{2}$ |
| | | Verbal Flu. | 6 | Numer. Mem. II | $3\frac{1}{2}$ |
| | | Verbal Mem. II | $5\frac{1}{2}$ | Concept. Grp. | $3\frac{1}{2}$ |
| | | Opposite Anal. | $5\frac{1}{2}$ | | |

## REFERRAL AND BACKGROUND
INFORMATION

Dennis was referred to Rutland Center for evaluation by his teacher at the day care center where he attends preschool classes. In school he is reported to demand excessive attention, not to follow or comprehend directions, and to be unable to express his feelings appropriately. Lacking age-appropriate skills, forgetful, and restless, Dennis' behavior at home with his mother and three younger siblings is described similarly. There is no father present in this economically deprived family situation.

## APPEARANCE AND BEHAVIORAL
CHARACTERISTICS

A well-dressed and good-looking black boy of about 5½, Dennis smilingly entered the testing room and continued this easy-going and friendly style of interaction for the duration of the session. He was eager to please the examiner, and this desire was clearly evident as he directed his attention to required tasks. Dennis' frustration tolerance was high, and he used a slow trial-and-error method of attack on perceptual activities. There were indicators of perseveration as Dennis recreated items that he had responded to earlier and repeated the examiner's verbal instructions; left–right confusion was apparent when he frequently switched his choice of preferred hand on gross motor events. Other neurologically associated signs included poor fine motor coordination (e.g., he held a pencil awkwardly). Dennis experienced difficulty in keeping his attention from focusing on irrelevant perceptual details when responding to test items, and this figure–ground problem turned up on several different measures.

Dennis' most characteristic behavioral pattern was his lack of impulse control coupled with an extremely poor short-term memory. He simply forgot even simple statements that were said to him just seconds before. This difficulty was especially evident for less meaningful or more lengthy stimuli; if the input dealt with subjects that Dennis could easily associate with concepts already understood by him, he was far better able to maintain the memory trace. Although he genuinely was giving full cooperative efforts, Dennis went off on tangents during which he responded to his own needs rather than to the demands of the testing situation. For example, he began banging on a toy xylophone harder and harder rather than concentrate on the structured tune-copying task; he spontaneously drew a second figure on the Draw-A-Child subtest, and subsequently continued scribbling in "hair" while laughing at his creation; and he grouped a set of blocks by his set of rules instead of conforming to the requirements of this logical classification task. An immature child, Dennis' test responses were interspersed with silly giggling as he reacted to his own internal sense of humor.

## TESTS ADMINISTERED

McCarthy Scales of Children's Abilities
Bender-Gestalt
Supplementary evaluation of Draw-A-Child
ITPA: five subtests at the "automatic" level of organization
Stanford-Binet: one memory task
Children's Apperception Test
Vineland Social Maturity Scale

## TEST RESULTS AND INTERPRETATION

On the McCarthy Scales of Children's Abilities, Dennis obtained a GCI of 75, which classifies him in the Borderline range of intelligence and ranks him at the 6th percentile for children his age. His cognitive functioning was at the level of the typical 4½-year-old, which is 1 year below his chronological age. In addition, the chances are good (about 85 percent) that his true GCI falls somewhere within the 69–81 range. Hence, his true level of functioning may conceivably be Dull Normal, Borderline, or Cognitively Deficient.

On the five separate scales of the McCarthy, Dennis exhibited scatter in his specific areas of functioning. He was relatively strong (50th percentile) in his motor coordination, but displayed weaknesses (3rd percentile) in both his short-term memory and his nonverbal expression of intelligence. His verbal comprehension and numerical reasoning skills, on the other hand, were consistent with his Borderline ability.

Further analysis of his profile proved interesting. Dennis' *gross* motor coordination was outstanding (about the 7-year-old level); but in *fine* motor coordination tasks he performed more poorly (3½–4½-year-old level), and he appeared uncomfortable when handling both a pencil and a xylophone mallet.

·

The most striking finding concerned Dennis' short-term memory. He was truly deficient (3–3½-year-old behavior) in tasks demanding recall of *nonmeaningful* stimuli—e.g., numbers, isolated words and phrases, and notes on a xylophone. In great contrast, he performed at a 5½–6-year-old level on *meaningful* memory tasks; that is, he was able to recall pictures of common concrete objects and he was able to retell most of a short story. Thus, he has a hard time remembering even a short stimulus, but is able to recall much longer stimuli as long as they relate to his existing conceptual framework. Without adequate context clues, Dennis' memory problem hinders his understanding of many things people may say to him. When this difficulty occurs he appears to lack comprehension, when in fact he does not remember exactly what he was told. However, other portions of the test battery revealed that when Dennis *is* reached he has a good store of basic facts and concepts, a creative skill reflecting original and flexible thought patterns, and the ability to express these thoughts appropriately. Despite Dennis' ability to handle the concepts he has learned, his short-term memory still limits the rate at which he incorporates new concepts.

It is also important to note that in a design-copying task on the McCarthy, Dennis revealed visual perceptual problems, as he had figure–ground confusions and had a difficult time analyzing designs into their component parts. This difficulty was also found on the Bender-Gestalt test, on which Dennis obtained a Koppitz error score of 16. Whereas this performance, being about one standard deviation below the mean for children his age, is still within the normal range, it is more equivalent to that of a child less than 5 years old. Dennis demonstrated his impulsivity here too, as he spontaneously wrote his attempts at an "i" and a "z," in between designs.

Dennis' product on the Draw-A-Child subtest of the McCarthy was evaluated by the Goodenough-Harris scoring system and assigned a standard score of 86, which is consistent with his Borderline GCI. The person drawn was missing many parts (i.e., arms, hands, feet, ears, neck, hair) and included teeth—figural aspects which are very common for young children of Dennis' age and of no particular significance for emotional interpretation.

Supplementary evaluation was undertaken to follow up some of the hypotheses indicated above. First, a testing-the-limits procedure was used for Draw-A-Design to investigate Dennis' visual perception.

For each McCarthy design, the examiner drew five figures and asked Dennis to pick out the one that matched the model. Whereas he was able to do this successfully for most of the designs, he revealed considerable visual perceptual difficulties with the three designs containing diagonals and intersecting lines. The ITPA Visual Closure subtest was given to check on Dennis' apparent figure–ground problem (mentioned above); his scaled score of 21 (psycholinguistic age of 2 years-11 months) verifies the severity of his perceptual difficulty in this area.

Other selected ITPA subtests were administered as well. Dennis performed poorly on Visual Sequential Memory (scaled score, 24; age, 3 years-10 months) and Auditory Sequential Memory (scaled score, 26; age, 3 years-2 months), offering additional support for his poor memory for nonmeaningful stimuli. Whereas his poorly developed abilities on the two ITPA memory tests and on Visual Closure might reflect a more global deficiency at the automatic level of responding, this does not seem to be the case; i.e., he was able to score at about an age-appropriate level on two other automatic tasks— Auditory Closure and Sound Blending (scaled scores of 33 and 37, respectively).

One Stanford-Binet task was given to provide an additional piece of evidence about Dennis' meaningful memory—the listening comprehension subtest "Memory for Stories: The Wet Fall" at Year VIII. Although Dennis failed this task, passing four of the six questions instead of the necessary five, he demonstrated again that he can remember stimuli that are laden with meaning.

Dennis' responses to the Children's Apperception Test picture stimulus cards produced stories which were replete with perceptual confusions and strong yearnings for a male parent figure. Several picture cards were misinterpreted due to extreme figure–ground difficulties; also evident were two- versus three-dimensionality confusions. The total results were that some stories' contents were distorted. Those pictures which were appropriately seen elicited fantasy tales of dominant male figures who were seen as leaders, protectors, and supervisors. Mothers, although well intentioned, were primarily ineffective in meeting the child's nurturance needs. Instead, the child-hero is portrayed as capable and autonomous in an environment which is potentially threatening and dangerous. There was an air of desperation about Dennis' described competition between mother and father over possession of the son; both father and son express mutual affection, but the child's place is with the mother. Isolation and projection/ introjection were the available defense mechanisms used by Dennis to cope with the depicted conflicts.

After the evaluation, Dennis' mother was given the Vineland Social Maturity Scale to evaluate his adaptive behavior. Overall, his Social Age was slightly above 5 years, which is close to his chronological age and indicates normal adaptive behavior. He was rated highest on locomotion, resulting from his good gross motor skills and the limited supervision he receives at home. Because of his problems in following simple instructions and in impulse control, he was rated lowest in the areas of communication and self-direction, respectively.

Dennis' true GCI (75 ± 6) ranks him somewhere between the Cognitively Deficient and Dull Normal levels of intelligence. However, his normal social maturity indicates that he is not functioning as a mentally retarded child. In view of his weak memory, visual perceptual problems, and lack of impulse control, a diagnosis of minimal brain dysfunction is suggested.

## SUMMARY AND RECOMMENDATIONS

Referred by his day care center, where he is reported to demand excessive attention and not to follow or comprehend directions, 5½-year-old Dennis was cooperative, evidenced high frustration tolerance, and had a good attention span during the present evaluation. Revealing an extraordinarily weak short-term memory and lack of impulse control, Dennis' GCI of 75 classifies him in the Borderline level of intellectual functioning. A relative strength was demonstrated in gross motor abilities, and relative weaknesses in short-term memory of non-meaningful stimuli, nonverbal intelligence, and visual perception. These perceptual difficulties reappeared in all subsequent measures, with special deficiencies in figure–ground distinctions. Projective devices indicate that Dennis misses the male relationship of a nonpresent father. Minimal brain dysfunction is suspected based on the test results and behavioral observations.

Dennis is highly motivated to please and perform well academically; this desire portends well for his management. He needs help to establish a mediational process in between his impulses and actual behavior. Dennis will fare better if verbal interaction with him is associated with concepts that he has already acquired; in this manner he will have a better chance to set up an internal organization of retrieval. His memory problem is quite severe and must be treated as a primary consideration, since it delays Dennis' general learning.

New learning stimuli need to be short, with highly meaningful content. New facts must always be taught in close association with already incorporated knowledge. Extra context clues can be liberally sprinkled throughout every lesson. Lessons need to be extremely short, and they will necessitate frequent review sessions. It is far better to administer new learnings in ten 3-minute batches, and to distribute review to a likewise number of brief drill periods that will reinforce the newly acquired material, than to expect Dennis to ingest information in one class-oriented teaching session. He simply will not respond desirably unless his special needs are catered to. Also essential for him is continual overlearning of new material until he has reached an automatic level of response. In this manner the degree of mediation between stimulus and response will be lessened, making for less dependence on an already inadequate retrieval system.

Visual perceptual exercises also need to be incorporated for Dennis' remedial program. A daily supplementary training session should be initiated at once, and Dennis should never be required to answer questions based on visual input without accompanying verbal explanations.

Perhaps a male model could be provided for him (e.g., a Big Brother, etc.) to help satisfy his strong desire for a father–son relationship.

### Henry M., Age 6 Years–1 Month:
### Minimal Brain Dysfunction

GCI = 104                    General Cognitive Age = 6

| Scale Indexes | | Highlights of the 18 Tests | | | |
|---|---|---|---|---|---|
| Verbal | 64 (S) | Strengths | | Weaknesses | |
| Perc.–Perf. | 36 (W) | Test | Age | Test | Age |
| Quant. | 54 | | | | |
| Memory | 63 (S) | Verb. Mem. I | Above 8½ | R–L Orient. | Below 2½ |
| Motor | 39 (W) | Verb. Mem. II | Above 8½ | Block Build. | 4 |
| Mean Index | 51.2 | Concept. Grp. | 8½ | Draw-A-Des. | 4 |
| | | Pictorial Mem. | 8 | | |
| | | Word Knowl. | 8 | | |
| | | Numer. Mem. II | 8 | | |
| | | Counting & Sort. | 7½ | | |
| | | Opposite Anal. | 7½ | | |

## REFERRAL AND BACKGROUND
## INFORMATION

Henry was referred for evaluation by his parents, who received complaints from his teacher, describing him as "loud, nervous, unwilling to follow commands or adhere to limits." He is aggressive to other children and throws temper tantrums. This behavior is most likely to surface during unstructured time, and he has also been observed to be inconsistently hyperactive.

Mrs. M., who divorced Henry's natural father when Henry was 1½ years old, feels that her present husband (who adopted Henry) has a better relationship with her son than she does. When Henry was 5 years old his grandfather, with whom the family had been living, died. Mr. and Mrs. M. feel that this affected the child. Henry has been in day care centers since he was 9 months old, and it is in group situations that he demonstrates his needs for excessive attention.

Presently Henry is in a nursery class for 4 year olds, a play-oriented, less structured environment, where he was placed after 2 weeks of inappropriately aggressive behavior in a kindergarten class. At home with his baby brother and parents, he is highly manipulative, has low frustration tolerance, short attention span, and is in constant motion. Nine months ago, he obtained a Stanford-Binet IQ of 125.

## APPEARANCE AND BEHAVIORAL
## CHARACTERISTICS

A very handsome boy of average physical development, Henry exploded into the testing room and proceeded to explore every inch of this new surrounding. Once he was calmed down and directed to the tasks presented by the examiner, he was moderately cooperative, maintained good eye contact, and sought approval and reassurance for his performances. Initially he demonstrated some anxiety when he realized that some of his responses were being timed; this factor might also account for his wishing to repeat each completed item (regardless of his degree of success) as if it were a new stimulus once again. Despite the fact that this repetition was not permitted, the behavior did not drop out of his repertoire for most of the standardized testing procedures.

Besides holding a pencil clumsily, Henry exhibited an awkward gait and other mild suggestions of neurological dysfunctioning. His total lack of left versus right directionality, as well as the compensatory behaviors he demonstrated during a design-copying test (i.e., numerous rotations of the paper; only one glance at the stimulus models) give heightened credence for this possible impairment. Most significant of all, however, was his progressively deteriorating hyperactive–distractible behavior. Each minute that elapsed brought with it less and less control of his impulses and far greater immature, manipulative, and out-of-bounds behavior. During the final segment of the evaluation, a projective story-telling test, Henry proceeded to physically act out each of his very brief responses. The room was filled with his loud noises and wild grabbing at everything he came into contact with. His predominant disposition to redirection was resistance and he made continual attempts to physically and verbally control the examiner.

TESTS ADMINISTERED

McCarthy Scales of Children's Abilities
Bender-Gestalt
Supplementary evaluation of Draw-A-Child
Columbia Mental Maturity Scale
Children's Apperception Test

TEST RESULTS AND INTERPRETATION

On the McCarthy Scales of Children's Abilities, Henry obtained a GCI of 104 ± 6, which classifies him in the Average range of intelligence and ranks him at the 60th percentile for children his age. However, this overall Index does not adequately reflect Henry's true functioning. On the Verbal and Memory Scales he performed at a Superior level (91st percentile), which was strikingly higher than his Borderline to Low Average level (about 10th percentile) on the Perceptual–Performance and Motor Scales. Thus, he excelled in verbal comprehension and expression and short-term memory but was relatively deficient in visual perceptual ability, manipulation of concrete materials, and motor coordination. Only his quantitative ability was consistent with his overall Average level of performance.

Henry is a child with superior potential coupled with a severe deficit in the visual perceptual modality. Despite his intellectual ability, his deficiency makes him a prime candidate for a learning disability when he starts the primary grades of school. He performed at a 4–5-year-old level on two drawing tasks: copying designs and drawing a child. This poor performance, along with a qualitative evaluation of his productions, underscores his visual-motor difficulties. Henry also demonstrated no knowledge of right versus left and he displayed mixed hand dominance during the administration of the Motor Scale. Altogether, the behavioral and test-related evidence is highly suggestive of minimal neurological impairment. In contrast to his fine motor problems, Henry demonstrated age appropriate functioning on noncognitive gross motor tasks (e.g., catching a beanbag, standing on one foot). Henry's most outstanding abilities (equivalent to the average 8½-year-old child) were on several memory tasks involving verbal labeling and a visual task of logical classification where the emphasis was on *conception* rather than on perception.

Based on Henry's good performance on the latter task, the Columbia Mental Maturity Scale was administered to check on his nonverbal abstract reasoning when the influence of coordination is controlled. Henry scored at a Superior level on the Columbia, obtaining an Age Deviation Score of 122, which is consistent with his McCarthy Verbal Index and his Stanford-Binet IQ. Therefore, despite Henry's visual–motor coordination difficulties, his nonverbal intelligence is as well developed as his verbal comprehension and expression. The fact that Henry's GCI of 104 is considerably lower than his Binet IQ is also of interest, since research has suggested that discrepancies of that sort may be associated with minimal brain dysfunction.

The Koppitz scoring system of the Bender-Gestalt earned Henry an error score of 18. This finding indicates that his level of visual–motor development is almost three standard deviations below the mean for children his age; it is equivalent to children below the age of 5. His errors were significantly associated with brain injury in children his age, and three emotional indicators were revealed as well: progressively increasing size of figures, large size of figures, and expansion. Interpretation of these signs create an amazingly consistent picture of Henry's emotional nature, for they are all associated with low frustration tolerance, explosiveness, acting out behavior, and impulsivity in children. Whereas this performance is more acceptable on the protocols of younger, preschool children, for Henry it is supportive evidence of neurological impairment. Clinical evaluation of the boy Henry drew in the Draw-A-Child test added to the consistency of his behavioral and test findings. Several aspects of his figure (e.g., gross asymmetry of limbs) have been found to be associated with aggressiveness, impulsiveness, poor coordination, and neurological dysfunction.

After the Bender-Gestalt was administered, the examiner briefly investigated Henry's visual perception. For several of the Draw-A-Design and Bender items he was asked to select the correct design from among four or five figures drawn by the examiner. He was able to select the correct response quickly and easily each time, even though some of the wrong responses were very similar to the model, suggesting adequate visual receptive skills.

By the time the projective story-telling test was attempted, it was apparent that Henry's ability to remain task oriented was quickly diminishing. He went through the picture cards giving brief responses and exhibiting much resistance. However, even during these verbalizations he demonstrated inappropriate expression of feelings and inappropriate affect. His degree of regression was overwhelming as a defense mechanism; the picture cards simply became too "real" as he proceeded to physically act out every scene. In addition to this immaturity and lack of inner control, there was some display of confusion over sex identification, as the main child characters were seen as girls and the mother figure was assigned the role of punisher.

## SUMMARY AND RECOMMENDATIONS

Henry, a 6-year-old boy who is currently displaying inappropriately aggressive behavior in his preschool situation, is described by his mother as highly manipulative with low frustration tolerance, short attention span, and constant physical activity. His behavior worsens in unstructured group situations, where he demonstrates excessive need for attention. During the present evaluation Henry was hyperactive, distractible, and demonstrated many soft signs suggestive of neurological malfunctioning. On the McCarthy Scales of Children's Abilities, Henry's GCI of 104 (Average) does not adequately describe his intellectual functioning. He displayed significant strengths on the Verbal and Memory Scales and significant weaknesses on the Perceptual–Performance and Motor Scales. Henry has a severe deficit in his visual–motor coordination, although there is evidence that his receptive skills are adequate and that his nonverbal reasoning is superior. His verbal comprehension and expressive abilities are excellent, all together setting the stage for a child destined to experience difficulties functioning in the academic setting.

Since Henry appears to exhibit minimal brain dysfunction, it is imperative that his parents receive counseling as to how to best meet

Henry's needs and help him to control his own impulsive and acting out behavior, as well as education about the nature of neurological impairment. He will probably improve his functioning in situations where limits are clearly defined and the environment well structured. Henry's school setting is probably adding to his lack of self-control, allowing regression to surface as an available coping style. Perhaps a change in his school group structure might also aid in eliciting better behavior from him.

Henry's excellent verbal comprehension and expression and abstract reasoning ability can be used to facilitate his visual perceptual and fine motor performance. By pairing his strengths with these areas of deficiency, his overall level of functioning will be greatly improved. Gradually, the "crutch" that his fine verbal ability, memory, and reasoning provided him with can be withdrawn. Once the intended associations have been successfully made, his weak areas in the visual-motor modality will have a chance to develop. To help this process, paper-and-pencil activities, such as Frostig-style daily exercise work sheets, should provide additional preacademic experience. At some time in the near future it is recommended that the Purdue Perceptual Motor Survey be administered to help provide further data for analyzing Henry's greatest remedial needs.

It is strongly recommended that a complete neurological evaluation be made; most likely he will be placed on medication for hyperactivity.

### Jonathan P., Age 6 Years–5 Months: Psychoneurotic Anxiety Reaction

GCI = 85          General Cognitive Age = $5\frac{1}{2}$

| Scale Indexes | | Highlights of the 18 Tests | | | |
|---|---|---|---|---|---|
| | | Strengths | | Weaknesses | |
| Verbal | 47 | Test | Age | Test | Age |
| Perc.–Perf. | 42 | | | | |
| Quant. | 36 (W) | Verb. Mem. II | Above $8\frac{1}{2}$ | Numer. | |
| Memory | 50 | Tapping Seq. | $8\frac{1}{2}$ | Mem. I | $3\frac{1}{2}$ |
| Motor | 43 | Pictorial Mem. | 8 | | |
| Mean Index | 43.6 | Leg Coord. | $7\frac{1}{2}$ | | |
| | | Verb. Mem. I | 7 | | |

## REFERRAL AND BACKGROUND INFORMATION

Jonathan was referred to Rutland Center for evaluation by his school, where he is described as demanding excessive attention and engaging in constant activity. His first-grade teacher states that he has difficulties listening and following directions. He has previously received treatment at a speech and hearing clinic for poor articulation and now receives speech therapy at his school. At home Jonathan lives with his three older sisters and two younger stepsisters, as well as his mother and stepfather. Bedwetting has been a continual problem for him, and his mother reports his hyperactivity and stuttering as major areas of difficulty. She also describes the household as highly structured by her husband, who feels that Jonathan isn't masculine enough because he plays with his sisters. A nonaffectionate but well-meaning man, Jonathan's stepfather of 1 year hasn't observed Jonathan's lack of available boys to play with in the neighborhood. Jonathan apparently is experiencing insecurities at home and difficulties both academically and behaviorally at school.

## APPEARANCE AND BEHAVIORAL CHARACTERISTICS

His big blue eyes almost hidden under long blond bangs, Jonathan is a handsome 6½-year-old boy of average physical development. He offered much spontaneous conversation which was both relevant and communicative; but his severe and pervasive articulation errors made his speech extremely difficult to fully comprehend. This problem did not deter him from talking, nor did he appear frustrated or embarrassed at the examiner's need for repetitions. Interestingly, at no time during the evaluation did any sign of stuttering appear, even though this was listed as one of his presenting problems. He smiled frequently, cooperated willingly, and maintained good eye contact throughout the bulk of the session. Toward the latter part, however, he grew more restless and asked "Am I through?" and "Can I go now?" frequently. This anxiety to leave appeared during a projective story-telling test, and very well may have resulted from his being required to deal with topics uncomfortable to him. Of course, his ability to attend for a whole morning's session may be limited and therefore instrumental in creating his desire to terminate rather abruptly. However, it is important to realize that Jonathan sat with full attention directed at the examiner and the tasks presented to him without wavering his concentration up to this final chore. This behavior is in direct contradiction to the other major presenting problems ascribed to Jonathan: his short attention span, distractibility, and hyperactivity. As a matter of fact, he was physically controlled, sitting still in his seat and dealing appropriately both with the manipulatible objects present as well as with purely verbal stimuli.

Besides the examiner needing repetition to decipher Jonathan's poorly articulated speech (e.g., he made frequent letter substitutions and dropped the final sounds off most words), Jonathan himself required constant repetition of the examiner's instructions, etc. This listening difficulty occurred even when he was fully attending to the tasks at hand.

The most characteristic behavior displayed by Jonathan was his inhibited self-control. Despite the fact that he talked freely, he was afraid to make direct statements of desired confrontation, and he "softened" any such occurrences. For example, when he couldn't figure out how to solve a cut-up picture puzzle, he started singing quietly while working at unsuccessful trial-and-error combinations "Something's wrong with this puzzle—a part is missing—something's wrong with this puzzle," etc. However, he was unable to ask the examiner directly whether or not the puzzle was indeed missing a piece. He also found it necessary to express himself indirectly when he obviously wished to misbehave during a gross motor task, and instead used his hand and arm as the "disobedient one." When the examiner redirected him back to task, he slapped his hand hard to punish it for its "transgressions." Apparently Jonathan's tendency toward repressed emotional expression goes along with his internalized knowledge of right versus wrong.

TESTS ADMINISTERED

McCarthy Scales of Children's Abilities
WISC-R Information and Comprehension subtests
Bender-Gestalt
Supplementary evaluation of Draw-A-Child
Informal Piagetian tasks: number and prenumber skills
Wepman Auditory Discrimination Test, Form IIA
Children's Apperception Test

TEST RESULTS AND INTERPRETATION

On the McCarthy Scales of Children's Abilities, Jonathan obtained a GCI of 85, which places him in the Dull Normal category and ranks him at the 17th percentile for children his age. His functioning is equivalent to that of the average 5½-year-old child. The chances are 85 percent that Jonathan's true GCI is somewhere between 79 and 91. Therefore, although his true level of functioning is probably Dull Normal, it may well be either Borderline or Average.

On the five separate scales of cognitive and motor abilities, Jonathan's Scale Indexes ranged from 36 on Quantitative to 50 on Memory. (The mean and standard deviation of each specific scale is 50 and 10, respectively.) This 14-point spread represents an average amount of scatter and thus is not unusual. Relative to his overall level of performance, Jonathan's low Quantitative Index represents a significant weakness. However, his Memory Index of 50, as well as his Verbal Index of 47, Motor Index of 43, and Perceptual–Performance Index of 42, all do not vary significantly from his own mean performance. Thus Jonathan's verbal comprehension and expression, nonverbal reasoning, visual–motor coordination, short-term memory, and gross motor coordination are all about equally well developed and are consistent with his overall GCI of 85. His Quantitative Index was superior to only 9 percent of children his own age, revealing a clear weakness in his knowledge of number concepts and facts and his ability to manipulate numerical symbols.

An examination of the separate McCarthy tests is rather revealing, as his individual abilities reached as low as 3½-year-old performance on one task, and extended above the 8½-year-old level on another task. His significant strengths were primarily in short-term memory tasks. He scored at or above the 8½-year-old level on tests requiring him to recall the names of pictures of common objects, to repeat a short story read to him, and to tap sequences of notes on a xylophone. Note that these areas of strength do not only reflect above average performance for his mental age, they are 2 years or more above his chronological age. His exceptional performance in these memory tasks leads one to wonder why his overall Memory Index was not a strength for him. The answer lies in his inadequate ability to recall digits. The 3½-year-old behavior mentioned above was in a task requiring him to repeat digits in the same order spoken by the examiner. Thus we see that Jonathan's inability to manipulate numerical symbols is so pervasive that he cannot even rely on his superb short-term memory to "bail him out" on this numerical task.

Relative to Jonathan's mental age of 5½, he demonstrated only one other significant strength or weakness on the individual tests: a relative strength in a noncognitive gross motor task involving the lower extremities. Jonathan obtained a perfect score in this task, as he was able to perform such acts as skipping, standing on one foot, and walking backward. His 7½-year-old level of performance in this task reflects adequate physical development and suggests intact neurological organization. Further support for this observation came from the fact that Jonathan displayed consistent right-handed behavior (i.e., he established hand dominance) when bouncing a ball, catching and throwing a beanbag, and drawing. Interestingly, even though Jonathan demonstrated internal awareness of his own laterality, he gave evidence that he did not know right from left in a cognitive test of this spatial skill.

Because the McCarthy is relatively free of culturally saturated items, the WISC-R Information and Comprehension subtests were administered as supplementary measures. On Information, Jonathan obtained a scaled score of 5, which ranks him at the 5th percentile for children his age. This score indicates a poverty in his store of acquired basic facts, but more than that it reinforces his poor quantitative skills. Examination of his pattern of responses revealed that he performed poorest on the number-related information items (e.g., "How many legs does a dog have?" "How many days make a week?"). Therefore, Jonathan's numerical deficiency not only involved solving oral problems and recalling digits; it even extended to his inability to master age-appropriate quantitative facts. On the socially relevant Comprehension subtest, Jonathan obtained a scaled score of 9 (37th percentile), which is significantly higher than his Information score but is consistent with both his GCI and Verbal Index.

Several informal Piagetian tasks were administered to Jonathan to better understand his numerical ability. He was given tasks measuring one-to-one correspondence and conservation of number, as well as prenumber tasks such as ordination, cardination, and logical classification. He performed at about a 5½-year-old level on these tasks; although he could not conserve number, he did fairly well on the tasks considered by Piaget to be prerequisites for mastering number operations. As on the standardized ability tests, Jonathan did most poorly on the Piagetian tasks specifically requiring number manipulation or a numerical response (as opposed to tasks which assess quantitative concepts nonverbally).

Because of Jonathan's constant need for repetition and clarification of the examiner's words, the Wepman Auditory Discrimination Test was administered. He obtained a score of −1 (below average discrimination ability), indicating that his speech articulation problem is receptive as well as expressive.

Jonathan's Bender-Gestalt productions earned him a Koppitz error score of 12, which indicates that his level of visual–motor development is within the average range for children his age. Specifically, 12 errors is the mean score achieved by the average 5½-year-old, so Jonathan's performance was commensurate both with his overall mental age on the McCarthy and with his drawing competencies demonstrated on the McCarthy drawing tests. Most of his errors were rotations or distortions of shape, and there were no significant emotional indicators present.

Using the Goodenough-Harris scoring system to evaluate Draw-A-Child, Jonathan received a standard score of 91, which is entirely consistent with his Dull Normal level of mental maturity. His drawing of a boy on the McCarthy included extremely large petal-like fingers and toes with the corresponding omission of both hands and feet. He also omitted the mouth, body, and neck. Omissions are generally viewed as signs of immaturity, with omission of the mouth in particular reflecting feelings of anxiety, insecurity, and withdrawal (including passive resistance). These conclusions were reinforced by the inclusion of a tiny head. In all, the figure appeared almost grotesque, reflecting Jonathan's intense feelings of inadequacy and very poor self concept.

Jonathan's responses on the Children's Apperception Test, a projective story-telling test, were largely stereotypical and nonproductive. It was here that he first appeared visibly anxious and voiced his desire to leave. His brief stories tended to deny the conflict content in the stimulus pictures, with defenses of repression and denial, undoing and ambivalence providing story resolutions. Whereas his stories were innocuous and nonthreatening, his defenses apparently were not good enough to disclaim the anxiety that surfaced in his physical behavior.

## SUMMARY AND RECOMMENDATIONS

Jonathan is a 6½-year-old boy who is described both at school and home as hyperactive, distractible, and possessing a short attention span. He is additionally troubled by poorly articulated speech and stuttering. Jonathan's mother reports a rather rigidly structured homelife engineered by his stepfather of 1 year, with whom he and his five sisters live. There has been indication of his stepfather's disapproval of Jonathan's "feminine interests" in playing house with his sisters, despite the absence of available boy peers. During the present evaluation there were no evidences of either stuttering, hyperactivity, distractibility, or a short attention span. Jonathan worked with full concentration and cooperation for most of the session, the only exception occurring during a projective story-telling test which appeared to make him uncomfortable. In general Jonathan appeared to be a very self-controlled child who is experiencing difficulties communicating his feelings despite the fact that he is able to offer much spontaneous conversation. His performance on the McCarthy Scales of Children's Abilities indicates his intelligence to be in the Dull Normal category (GCI, 85) with a mental age equivalent to an average 5½-year-old child. Jonathan revealed a significant weakness on the Quantitative Scale relative to his own level of performance. He appears deficient in number concepts and facts, with limited ability to manipulate numerical symbols. On the specific tests he demonstrated strength in short-term memory tasks—as long as numbers were not involved. Other measures revealed Jonathan's average visual–motor development and reaffirmation of his Dull Normal mental ability. Projective devices established his anxieties, insecurities, poor self-concept and feelings of inadequacy. Also evident were his use of various defenses: regression and denial, undoing and ambivalence. They did not appear able to control his anxiety, however, and he coped with his conflict by wishing to escape.

In view of Jonathan's specific personality attributes, his reported bedwetting seems to be one of his few available emotional releases outside the reach of an otherwise alert ego. Whether he is expressing passively aggressive resentment against his parents—or regressive desires to return to the days before his natural father (who he reportedly likes) separated from him at age 2—is unknown. However, maintaining a repressed unconscious wish is certainly consistent with the kinds of coping behaviors Jonathan has already displayed. His on-and-off stuttering may also be part of such a general behavioral pattern.

Whereas schedules and routines typically provide stability and a sense of security for young children, at times it becomes advisable to relax family demands and allow more flexibility in a child's life. This seems to be the best course for dealing with Jonathan's problems at present. He appears unable to handle the pressures at home. Perhaps his emotional vulnerability is a stage that he will be better able to cope with given more personal freedom within which to explore his own feelings. Hopefully, in a less threatening, more nurturative environment he will begin to communicate his feelings and therefore have a better chance of meeting his needs. Jonathan has had much indirect pressure placed upon him in recent years: from ages 2 to 5 he had no male model in a household of many females, all older. When a new father appeared, there was the contrast of a strongly dominant male to attend to. He has had much stress in establishing his own identity. It is also recommended that Jonathan's mother and stepfather both receive counseling to help them better understand their son and appropriate means of interacting with him in the family setting.

Since Jonathan fared much better when performing Piaget's numerical and prenumerical tasks than on the more traditional arithmetic assessment, remedial techniques in this area will probably be more successful if they use a Piaget-based hierarchical teaching approach. It is not known at this time whether his quantitative weakness stems from a kind of "number phobia," if he has simply not been able to acquire appropriate numerical information, or if he has a brain-related number disorder. Jonathan's basic concepts appear more developed than his skill with digits, and at this time the stress should be on nonthreatening and more success-producing work time.

It is suggested that Jonathan's speech therapist be contacted to confirm that he is receiving adequate treatment for both a receptive and an expressive articulation problem. His school teacher might require counseling in this matter. If it is possible, institute a program of after school tutoring by a male.

### Elizabeth T., Age 7 Years-0 Months: Mental Retardation

GCI = Below 50                    General Cognitive Age = $3\frac{1}{2}$

| Scale Indexes | | Age | Highlights of the 18 Tests | | | |
|---|---|---|---|---|---|---|
| | | | Strengths | | Weaknesses | |
| Verbal | 26 | $4\frac{1}{2}$ (S) | Test | Age | Test | Age |
| Perc.–Perf. | Below 22 | $3\frac{1}{2}$ | | | | |
| Quant. | Below 22 | $2\frac{1}{2}$ (W) | | | | |
| Memory | 22 | 4 | Pictorial Mem. | 6 | R–L Orient. | Below $2\frac{1}{2}$ |
| Motor | Below 22 | $3\frac{1}{2}$ | Verbal Mem. II | $5\frac{1}{2}$ | Count. & Sort. | Below $2\frac{1}{2}$ |
| | | | Draw-A-Child | 5 | Block Build. | $2\frac{1}{2}$ |
| | | | Verbal Flu. | 5 | Number | |
| | | | | | Quest. | $2\frac{1}{2}$ |
| | | | | | Tapping Seq. | $2\frac{1}{2}$ |
| | | | | | Leg Coord. | $2\frac{1}{2}$ |

## REFERRAL AND BACKGROUND
## INFORMATION

Elizabeth was referred to Rutland Center for evaluation by her teacher at an institution for the mentally retarded where she currently resides Mondays through Fridays and attends a TMR primary class. Concern over increased jargon speech, self-talk, and sexual acting out are among the reported presenting problems encountered at the institution; at home her mother describes Elizabeth as demanding excessive attention, distractible, restless, and resistant to discipline. She does not get along with her father, and an incident was related in which he physically "grabbed her around the waist" and frightened her during a drunken episode. Both parents, once alcoholics, are currently controlling this problem successfully. Of her five siblings at home (three sisters, aged 1, 6, and 10; two brothers aged 5 and 11), she fights most with her younger brother.

Her maternal grandfather had a history of seizures, and at 10 months of age Elizabeth suffered from spinal meningitis. One year ago there was an epileptic seizure, and Elizabeth is currently taking phenobarbital twice daily. Weighing 99 pounds, she has been on an unsuccessful diet; on weekends her craving for food is very difficult for her mother to control. Along with the various sexual acting out reports from the institution for the retarded (e.g., excessive masturbation) is a noted resistance to male figures. Difficult to test, a Leiter IQ of "about 74" was obtained for Elizabeth 1½ years ago.

## APPEARANCE AND BEHAVIORAL
## CHARACTERISTICS

A 7-year-old girl who is not only greatly overweight but is also tall and large boned, Elizabeth gives the physical appearance of a child at least 2 years older. Her eyes have weak muscle balance, and her right eye is especially prone to "wander" without the accompaniment of its mate. She exhibited restless and distractible behavior, proceeding to investigate and touch everything in sight. Elizabeth was unaware of the social situation she was in and evidenced a lack of impulse control and little anxiety. She frequently made comments like "can't do it," but with extremely tight control and structure she was able to accept redirection and attend to each task. Elizabeth made many aggressive attempts to manipulate both the examiner and the testing situation (e.g., telling the examiner to be quiet when she wanted to listen to a siren outside; humming in a loud monotone, then whistling, to drown out the examiner's instructions for a nonverbal task). Elizabeth maintained very little eye contact and varied her restlessness with lying her head down on the table. Her language development was at about a 3- or 3½-year-old level. There were grammar and articulation difficulties, and basically telegraphic speech—but neither jargon nor self-talk occurred during the evaluation.

Elizabeth's desperate desire to ingest anything edible was clearly demonstrated during the testing session. When giving creative verbal responses on a McCarthy subtest, she managed to perform relatively well when telling all the animals she could think of, or things to wear, etc. However, when asked to tell all the things to eat that she could, Elizabeth acted out an eating orgy, smacking her lips and using her whole body to express this apparently greatly gratifying experience. When the session was over, Elizabeth was given a large piece of bubble gum by the examiner, which she promptly swallowed, and then grabbed the paper bag it had come from to help herself to anything else should could find.

## TESTS ADMINISTERED

McCarthy Scales of Children's Abilities
Bender-Gestalt
Vineland Social Maturity Scale
Children's Apperception Test

## TEST RESULTS AND INTERPRETATION

On the McCarthy Scales of Children's Abilities, Elizabeth scored below the norms for 7 year olds, achieving a GCI of less than 50. This score classifies her as Cognitively Deficient with an overall level of functioning equivalent to the average 3½-year-old child. Her best ability was in the area of verbal comprehension (age 4½), and her most deficient area was in quantitative skills (2½-year-old level). Her short-term memory, nonverbal reasoning, and motor coordination were consistent with her overall level of 3½ years.

Elizabeth performs best when she is able to associate new stimuli to things that she already knows. This tendency was evidenced in a number of ways. She was able to achieve a 5-year-old level of behavior when drawing a picture of a girl (a meaningful task), but performed at only a 3-year-old level when copying abstract (i.e., meaningless) designs. Furthermore, she evidenced good short-term memory (5½-6-year-old behavior) when the content to be recalled was either pictures of common objects or a brief story. This ability surpassed by far her 2½-3½-year-old performance on memory tasks which were devoid of meaning (e.g., taps on a xylophone, digits). She also evidenced a relative strength in a verbal task measuring creativity. Here she was able to name many different things in specified categories, again showing her ability to succeed on tasks that are meaningful and call upon her past experiences.

It is important to note that Elizabeth's retardation is not confined to the cognitive sphere. She performed at the level of the average $2\frac{1}{2}$–3-year-old on tasks designed to assess gross motor skills. On these tests she revealed her inadequacy in such activities as bouncing a ball and catching a beanbag, and she was particularly uncoordinated when required to use her legs. For example, she was not able to stand on one foot even for 1 second, and she could not maintain her balance while walking on a 9-foot tape. In addition, she achieved a Social Age between 3 and $3\frac{1}{2}$ on the Vineland Social Maturity Scale, which was administered to Elizabeth's mother directly after the evaluation. In her social adaptive behavior, Elizabeth's retardation was most profound in the areas of eating, occupation (she has virtually no skill at self-occupation), and self-direction.

The Bender-Gestalt test was impossible to evaluate for traditional errors—virtually no part of any of the attempted reproductions were correct. This extraordinarily low level of visual–motor development involved both the receptive perceptual process as well as all mediation and motor expression of the design-copying task. A qualitative evaluation of her figures indicates approximately a $3$–$3\frac{1}{2}$-year-old level of development, which is consistent with her design-drawing competence on the McCarthy and with other measures of her cognitive, motor, and adaptive development. The human figure drawing Elizabeth made on the Draw-A-Child subtest of the McCarthy was greatly deficient from a perceptual–motor point of view, but when scored conceptually it revealed that her knowledge of body parts was functioning at a much higher level.

On the Children's Apperception Test, a projective story-telling measure which requires the child to respond to picture stimulus cards, Elizabeth made genuine attempts to communicate her thoughts and emotions verbally. She expressed a great need for nurturance, and was overly concerned with the child-hero being disciplined and controlled. The environment is perceived as threatening, and she apparently has deep fears of male figures. A repetitive theme throughout her stories was such statements as "the man's gonna get us," or mention of "Bad Daddy." The anxieties relate to physical harm from father figures. Women are viewed as nurturant and also as the primary discipliner.

Yet, however potent the mother is depicted, she too is powerless to protect the child from "the man," etc., and she herself is in danger as well. Elizabeth fears desertion by the mother figure. Many defense mechanisms were inconsistently employed, the main ones being regression, repression and denial, and reaction formation. There was evidence of some loose association and tangential thinking, but this finding was probably due to her weak controls rather than to pathological causation.

## SUMMARY AND RECOMMENDATIONS

Elizabeth is a very large, overweight 7-year-old girl who is currently a resident at an institution for the retarded. Her teacher reports jargon speech, self-talk, and sexual acting out, and her mother (who sees her on weekends) describes her distractibility, restlessness, and resistance to discipline. Elizabeth does not get along with her father or younger brother, and has been called resistant to male figures at the institution. As an infant she suffered spinal meningitis and 1 year ago she was put on a daily dosage of phenobarbital after an epileptic seizure. During the present evaluation Elizabeth was distractible and manipulative, but redirectable once strong limits were set. Demonstrating a delayed language disorder with some dysphasic characteristics, but neither of the presenting speech problems, Elizabeth appeared quite obsessed with food and eating. Her GCI on the McCarthy was below the norms for children her age and can only be described as "below 50." With an overall level of functioning equivalent to a 3½ year old, Elizabeth's best ability was in verbal comprehension and her greatest weakness was in numerical skills. Both her Bender-Gestalt productions and her human figure drawing were equally deficient, revealing her retarded level of visual–motor development. On the Vineland Social Maturity Scale, her mother rated Elizabeth at a 3–3½-year-old level in her social functioning, completing the picture of her overall retarded development. On projective measures, Elizabeth expressed her need for nurturance, fear of losing her mother's support, and feelings of restriction by having many demands for "good" behavior placed on her. Also weighing on her mind is her apparent fear of males, as this was a repetitive theme in her stories.

Certain recommendations can be made for Elizabeth based on this evaluation. She has revealed enough cognitive integrities to be considered teachable; however, she will learn best when she can associate new stimuli to things she already knows. Any successful teaching situation will therefore need to call upon her past experience and be sure to focus on meaningful variables if she is expected to remember. Reading to her about the things she knows might prove fruitful. Elizabeth needs gross motor work as well as fine motor and cognitive remediation.

Elizabeth is a girl who is retarded and brain damaged, and thus she has a variety of behaviors which are typically associated with *both* of these conditions. Her relationship with males needs exploring and improvement, despite the great difficulties in communicating with her. Her excess weight is not a simple matter to deal with either. Considering that her figure has the indication of either some breast development or fat deposits located in this part of her anatomy, it is seriously suggested that a medical examination be made to determine if there is any endocrine gland disorder. There is always the possibility that she may be acting out sexually and masturbating excessively due to the precocious sex hormone secretions.

## George A., Age 7 Years–4 Months: Brain Damage

GCI = 72      General Cognitive Age = $5\frac{1}{2}$

| Scale Indexes | | Highlights of the 18 Tests | | | |
|---|---|---|---|---|---|
| Verbal | 44 (S) | Strengths | | Weaknesses | |
| Perc.–Perf. | 25 (W) | Test | Age | Test | Age |
| Quant. | 33 | | | | |
| Memory | 38 | Verb. Mem. I | Above $8\frac{1}{2}$ | Puzz. Solv. | $3\frac{1}{2}$ |
| Motor | Below 22 (W) | R–L Orient. | 8 | Tapping Seq. | $3\frac{1}{2}$ |
| Median Index | 33 | | | Leg Coord. | $3\frac{1}{2}$ |
| | | | | Arm Coord. | 4 |
| | | | | Draw-A-Des. | 4 |
| | | | | Concept. Grp. | 4 |

## REFERRAL AND BACKGROUND INFORMATION

George, who is presently in a Rutland Center treatment class, was originally referred for evaluation by his teacher, who described him as aggressive toward children and rules, manipulative, and possessing low frustration tolerance and severe visual perceptual problems. He has also been observed to be self-destructive and immature.

Previous testing found him to be brain damaged and to display evidence of an "inadequate personality."

At home in an economically and culturally deprived rural, isolated environment, George is continually exposed to aggressive family models. He has infrequent and negative contact with his stepfather, a 23-year-old half-brother recently released from a mental institution who beats him, and a pathological mother who treats him as a severely retarded child (her other child, a 10-year-old girl, resides in an institution for the mentally retarded). This is George's second year in kindergarten, where he is frequently absent. His medical history reports mother medicated during pregnancy, a difficult labor, very late developmental milestones, and other problems all suggestive of organicity. The present evaluation was made to obtain updated information on George's cognitive, motor, and emotional functioning.

## APPEARANCE AND BEHAVIORAL CHARACTERISTICS

George, a small 7-year-old black boy, appeared quite unkempt as he entered the testing room. His face was dirty and sported a bad cut, and his shirt was torn. He was tired and yawned frequently throughout the session. George cooperated with the examiner more out of acquiescence than due to well-motivated spirit. Little show of anxiety surfaced as he proceeded to talk to himself and sing while performing various tasks. When fine motor activities were required of him, George displayed very poor motor control, as his hands shook while working slowly and his fingers tended to curl up. His visual receptive abilities proved more developed than his motoric expression. For example, he was able to acknowledge errors in the picture puzzles he put together, but was helpless to correct them.

Much immature and regressive behavior persisted during the evaluation, as George acted out many of his sentences and brief stories in response to a projective story-telling test. He lacked impulse control, laughed inappropriately, and on one occasion he withdrew from an uncomfortable situation by covering his eyes with his hands.

The most disturbing aspects of George's behavior were his recounting of bizarre stories of sadism, hostility, and aggression, and his sudden violent attacks on whatever materials were available during the evaluation. His description of werewolves was filled with admiration rather than fear, and his detailed discussion of his beating a rat to death and then handling it gave one the impression of unhealthy emotional development with little superego functioning. This aggression translated to physical expression when during quiet and calm interaction with the examiner George brutally slammed his first down on whatever materials were being worked with, while verbalizing some relevant hostile phrase indicating his motivation and awareness.

TESTS ADMINISTERED

McCarthy Scales of Children's Abilities
Bender-Gestalt
Supplementary evaluation of Draw-A-Child
Informal Sentence Completion Test
Children's Apperception Test

TEST RESULTS AND INTERPRETATION

On the McCarthy Scales of Children's Abilities, George obtained a GCI of 72, which classifies him in the Borderline level of intelligence and ranks him at the 4th percentile for children his own age. Overall he functioned as well as the average 5½-year-old, which is almost 2 years below his chronological age. His true GCI is likely (85 percent chance) to fall somewhere between 66 and 78, indicating that his actual level of functioning is conceivably Cognitively Deficient rather than Borderline.

On the separate scales George exhibited much scatter in his cognitive and motor abilities. A relative strength was noted on the Verbal Scale (28th percentile), which was in marked contrast to his deficiencies on both the Perceptual–Performance and Motor Scales (below the first percentile). Therefore he has adequate (but still below average) skills in verbal comprehension, concept formation, and expression, but is strikingly weak in his nonverbal and motoric functioning. This profile of scores is highly suggestive of brain dysfunction, with the greatest deficit occurring in the right hemisphere.

As mentioned earlier, his fine motor coordination is obviously impaired; this deficiency was reflected in his 3½-4-year-old performance on tasks requiring him to tap keys on a xylophone and to copy designs. Of extreme relevance is the finding that his *gross* motor behavior is equally impaired, as he performed at the same 3½-4-year-old level on noncognitive tasks such as standing on one foot, walking backward, bouncing a ball, and catching a beanbag.

Further examination of his test scores indicates a deficiency not only in his coordination but also in his nonverbal reasoning. Again, he performed at only the 3½–4-year-old level on two visual perceptual tasks stressing organization of perceived materials (classifying blocks, solving puzzles). Even his visual receptive abilities are not entirely intact, as he displayed some figure–ground confusions in the design-copying task. This diffuse display of neurological malfunctioning probably goes beyond minimal brain syndrome and points to a more pervasive organicity.

George's functioning within the auditory–vocal channel was extremely consistent across a wide variety of tasks; he functioned at about a 6½-year-old level. His only performance that "marred" the consistency was his excellent memory for words and sentences (better than that of the average 8½-year-old child). Also, despite his probable brain involvement, he scored at an 8-year-old level on a task requiring discrimination of right versus left.

George's GCI of 72 on the McCarthy is 20 points lower than his WISC-R Full Scale IQ of 92 (obtained almost 1 year ago). Research has shown that children with brain dysfuntion tend to obtain GCIs that are about 15 points below their IQs, so the present findings are not incongruous with the past test results. In addition, the striking difference between George's Verbal and Perceptual–Performance scores on the McCarthy corresponds well to his very large Verbal–Performance IQ discrepancy on the WISC-R. The main difference between the two testings concerns the *level* of his verbal ability. He scored at the High Average level on the WISC-R, but was in the Average range on the McCarthy.

On the Bender-Gestalt, George made 17 errors using Koppitz' scoring system, which is more than three standard deviations below the mean for children his age, and is below the level of the average 5-year-old. Most of his errors were either distortions of shape or problems with integration of the different parts of a figure. A qualitative evaluation of his errors on the McCarthy Draw-A-Design test also revealed a preponderance of distortion (especially disproportion) errors and problems of integration. Of the 17 errors on the Bender, 10 were significantly associated with brain injury; although George committed only two rotation errors, both were highly significant indicators of brain injury. In addition, George traced several Bender and McCarthy designs with his finger before drawing them and required an unusually long time to complete each drawing test—behaviors which are associated with brain injured children.

George's responses to the projective Sentence Completion test were quite interesting, not in their ability to shed light on his sources of anxieties and defense mechanisms, but in revealing his internalization of socially appropriate—even stereotypical—response patterns. It is difficult to ascertain whether he answered primarily by stimulus–response "phrase associations" or by thought-out expressions (e.g., "I wish *at stars*;" "I cry when *I'm sad*"). In some way George has at least partially assimilated verbalizations of "correct" and "expected" behavior despite his obvious lack of having truly experienced this degree of social awareness.

The Draw-A-Child subtest on the McCarthy Scales was evaluated by the Goodenough-Harris scoring system and was assigned a standard score of 86. It is evident here that George's body concept and nonverbal concept formation, while certainly below average for his age, is a functional aspect of his overall cognitive development, which he was able to express even with his severe fine motor limitations. The fact that the subject he chose to draw (even with the instruction to "draw a boy . . . etc.") was a monster ("Harry the Werewolf") is viewed as the child's perceiving himself as being different from others, as not being quite human. Other emotional indicators (i.e., slanting figure, poor integration of parts of figure, omission of nose and hands) are primarily associated with poor coordination, impulsivity, and poorly integrated and labile personality.

On the Children's Apperception Test, George aligned himself with the male identity figure. The stories he made up in response to the stimulus picture cards displayed his sense of comfort with the male aggressive role and little superego. However, when he cast a female (mother) in this role, he was unable to cope with the dynamics of the story he created. Thus he revealed ineffective defenses other than denial of the actual story element, leading to ultimate rejection of the card. In general the environment was pictured as hostile and dangerous, and George demonstrated inappropriate expression and lack of understanding of emotional feelings.

## SUMMARY AND RECOMMENDATIONS

George is a small 7-year-old black boy who has been previously diagnosed as brain damaged and severely emotionally disturbed. His home environment is inadequate both economically and emotionally, meeting few of his needs and exposing him instead to aggression and pathological behaviors by family members. During the present evaluation he displayed little anxiety and consistently immature and aggressive behavior. On the McCarthy Scales his GCI of 72 classified him in the Borderline level of intelligence and indicated his overall functioning to be equivalent to that of a 5½-year-old. Wide scatter appeared, as a significant strength was noted on the Verbal Scale, in marked contrast to significant weakness on both the Perceptual–Performance and Motor Scales. The test response pattern on the McCarthy and Bender-Gestalt was highly suggestive of pervasive neurological dysfunctioning. Various projective measures yielded a composite picture of an impulsive child with little superego and inadequate coping styles for dealing with stress. There was also evidence of conflict over females in punitive roles.

It is imperative that George continue his present therapeutic classes. Teaching techniques should minimize the use of visual clues and instead stress his good verbal memory. Since his auditory–vocal channel of communication appears adequately developed, both a phonics approach and a linguistic orientation to the teaching of reading might prove most successful. To help him compensate for his behavioral and personality limitations, a programmed series or one incorporating the use of machines could reduce some of the inevitable difficulties that will be encountered. George would benefit by spending as little time at home as possible. If his after school leisure time could be carefully structured with whatever available activities or meetings could be found for him, then perhaps the debilitating effect of his family might be reduced. One such activity might help his academic deficiency in the visual–motor modality: a daily supplementary program of perceptual–motor training that can easily fit into his after school time. Limiting these exercises, taken from a Kephart- or Ayres-designed teaching method, to a mere 15 or 20 minutes a day may very well lead to some improvement in this area.

# References

Almy, M. *The early childhood educator at work.* New York: McGraw-Hill, 1975.

Anastasi, A. *Differential psychology.* (3rd ed.) New York: Macmillan, 1958.

Arthur, G. *A point scale of performance, revised form II: Manual for administering and scoring the tests.* New York: The Psychological Corporation, 1947.

Ayres, A. J. *Sensory integration and learning disorders.* Los Angeles: Western Psychological Services, 1972. (a)

Ayres, A. J. *Southern California Sensory Integration Tests.* Los Angeles: Western Psychological Services, 1972. (b)

Bakan, P. The eyes have it. *Psychology Today,* 1971, *4,* 64–69.

Baker, H. J., & Leland, B. *Examiner's handbook: Detroit Tests of Learning Aptitude* (Rev. ed.). Indianapolis: Bobbs-Merrill, 1967.

Bakwin, H., & Bakwin, R. M. *Clinical management of behavior disorders in children.* Philadelphia: W. B. Saunders, 1966.

Bannatyne, A. *Language, reading, and learning disabilities.* Springfield, Ill.: Charles C Thomas, 1971.

Bannatyne, A. (Ed.) Programs, materials, and techniques. *Journal of Learning Disabilities,* 1973, *6,* 102–108.

Bannatyne, A. Diagnosis: A note on recategorization of the WISC scaled scores. *Journal of Learning Disabilities,* 1974, *7,* 272–274.

Barsch, R. *Achieving perceptual-motor efficiency.* Seattle: Special Child, 1967.

Bayley, N. *Manual for the Bayley Scales of Infant Development.* New York: The Psychological Corporation, 1969.

Beery, K., & Buktenica, N. A. *Developmental Test of Visual–Motor Integration.* Chicago: Follett, 1967.

Bellak, L., & Bellak, S. S. *Children's Apperception Test manual* (5th ed.). Larchmont, N.Y.: C.P.S. Co., 1971.

Belmont, L., & Birch, H. G. Lateral dominance and right–left awareness in normal children. *Child Development,* 1963, *34,* 257–270.

Bender, L. *Bender Motor Gestalt Test: Cards and manual of instruction.* New York: American Orthopsychiatric Association, 1946.

Bereiter, C. Review of race and intelligence: The fallacy behind the race–IQ controversy. *Contemporary Psychology,* 1973, *18,* 455–456.

Berry, M. F. *Language disorders of children: The bases and diagnoses.* New York: Appleton-Century-Crofts, 1969.

Birch, H. G., & Belmont, L. Auditory–visual integration, intelligence and reading ability in school children. *Perceptual and Motor Skills,* 1965, *20,* 295–305.

Birch, H. G. & Lefford, A. Intersensory development in children. *Monographs of the Society for Research in Child Development,* 1963, *28, #5.*

Boehm, A. E. *Manual for the Boehm Test of Basic Concepts.* New York: The Psychological Corporation, 1971.

Boehm, A. E. *Boehm resource guide for basic concept teaching.* New York: The Psychological Corporation, 1977.

Bryant, N. D. Some principles of remedial instruction for dyslexia. In H. Newman (Ed.), *Reading disabilities.* Indianapolis: Bobbs-Merrill, 1969.

Burgemeister, B. B., Blum, L. H., & Lorge, I. *Columbia Mental Maturity Scale* (3rd ed). New York: Harcourt Brace Jovanovich, 1972.

Burns, R. C., & Kaufman, S. H. *Actions, styles, and symbols in Kinetic Family Drawings (K-F-D).* New York: Brunner/Mazel, 1972.

Buros, O. K. (Ed.). *The seventh mental measurements yearbook.* Highland Park, N.J.: Gryphon Press, 1972.

Bush, W. J., & Giles, M. T. *Aids to psycholinguistic teaching.* Columbus, Ohio: Charles E. Merrill, 1969.

Bush, W. J., & Waugh, K. W. *Diagnosing learning disabilities* (2nd ed.). Columbus, Ohio: Charles E. Merrill, 1976.

Carrow, E. Assessment of speech and language in children. In J. E. McLean, D. E. Yoder, & R. L. Schiefelbusch (Eds.), *Language intervention with the retarded.* Baltimore: University Park Press, 1972.

Carrow, E. *Test for Auditory Comprehension of Language* (5th ed.). Austin, Tex.: Learning Concepts, 1973.

Chalfant, J. C., & King, F. S. An approach to operationalizing the definition of learning disabilities. *Journal of Learning Disabilities,* 1976, *9,* 228–243.

Chalfant, J. C., & Scheffelin, M. A. *Central processing dysfunctions in children: A review of research.* Washington, D.C.: Government Printing Office, 1969.

Clawson, A. *The Bender Visual Motor Gestalt Test for children.* Los Angeles: Western Psychological Services, 1962.

Clements, S. D. *Minimal brain dysfunction in children: Terminology and identification—phase one* (NINDB Monograph No. 3, U.S. Public Health Service Publication No. 1415). Washington, D.C.: Department of Health, Education, and Welfare, 1966.

Cohen, J. A. The factorial structure of the WISC at ages 7-6, 10-6, and 13-6. *Journal of Consulting Psychology,* 1959, *23,* 285–299.

Copel, S. L. *Psychodiagnostic study of children and adolescents.* Springfield, Ill.: Charles C Thomas, 1967.

Crabtree, M. *Houston Test of Language Development.* Houston: Houston Press, 1963.

Crawford, J. E. *Children with subtle perceptual–motor difficulties.* Pittsburgh: Stanwix House, 1966.

Cruickshank, W. M. (Ed.). *Cerebral palsy: Its individual and community problems* (2nd ed.). Syracuse, N.Y.: Syracuse University Press, 1966.

Davis, E. E. Review of the McCarthy Scales of Children's Abilities. *Measurement and Evaluation in Guidance,* 1974, *6,* 250–251. (a)

Davis, E. E. Review of the McCarthy Scales of Children's Abilities. *TPGA Journal,* 1974, *3,* 57–59. (b)

Davis, E. E. Concurrent validity of the McCarthy Scales of Children's Abilities. *Measurement and Evaluation in Guidance,* 1975, *8,* 101–104.

Davis, E. E., & Rowland, T. A replacement for the venerable Stanford-Binet? *Journal of Clinical Psychology,* 1974, *30,* 517–521.

Davis, E. E., & Slettedahl, R. W. Stability of the McCarthy Scales over a 1-year period. *Journal of Clinical Psychology,* 1976, *32,* 798–800.

Davis, E. E., & Walker, C. Validity of the McCarthy Scales for Southwestern rural children. *Perceptual and Motor Skills,* 1976, *42,* 563–567.

Davis, F. B. Interpretation of differences among averages and individual test scores. *Journal of Educational Psychology,* 1959, *50,* 162–170.

DeBoer, D. L., Kaufman, A. S., & McCarthy, D. The use of the McCarthy Scales in identification, assessment, and deficit remediation of preschool and primary age children. Symposium presented at the meeting of the Council for Exceptional Children, New York, April 1974.

DiLeo, J. H. *Children's drawings as diagnostic aids.* New York: Brunner/Mazel, 1973.

Doll, E. A. *Vineland Social Maturity Scale: Condensed manual of directions* (Rev. ed.). Circle Pines, Minn.: American Guidance Service, 1965.

Dunn, L. M. *Expanded manual for the Peabody Picture Vocabulary Test.* Circle Pines, Minn.: American Guidance Service, 1965.

Evans, E. D. *Contemporary influences in early childhood education* (2nd ed.). New York: Holt, Rinehart & Winston, 1975.

Fallon, B. J. (Ed.). *40 innovative programs in early childhood education.* Belmont, Calif.: Lear Siegler/Fearon, 1973.

Frierson, E. C., & Barbe, W. B. (Eds.). *Educating children with learning disabilities: Selected readings.* New York: Appleton-Century-Crofts, 1967.

Frost, J. L. (Ed.). *Early childhood education rediscovered.* New York: Holt, Rinehart, & Winston, 1968.

Frostig, M. Education of children with learning disabilities. In E. C. Frierson & W. B. Barbe (Eds.), *Educating children with learning disabilities.* New York: Appleton-Century-Crofts, 1967, pp. 387–398. (a)

Frostig, M. Testing as a basis for educational therapy. *Journal of Special Education,* 1967, *2,* 15–34. (b)

Frostig, M., & Horne, D. *The Frostig program for the development of visual perception.* Chicago: Follett, 1964.

Frostig, M., Maslow, P., Lefever, D. W., & Whittlesey, J. R. B. *The Marianne Frostig Developmental Test of Visual Perception.* Palo Alto, Calif.: Consulting Psychologists Press, 1964.

Garrett, J. F. Cerebral palsy. In J. F. Garrett (Ed.), *Psychological aspects of physical disability.* Washington, D.C.: U.S. Government Printing Office, 1952, pp. 60–67.

Gesell, A., & Amatruda, C. S. *Developmental diagnosis* (2nd ed.) New York: Paul B. Hoeber, 1947.

Getman, G. N. *How to develop your child's intelligence.* Leverne, Minn.: G. N. Getman, 1962.

Glasser, A. J., & Zimmerman, I. L. *Clinical interpretation of the WISC.* New York: Grune & Stratton, 1967.

Goldman, R., & Fristoe, M. *Goldman-Fristoe Test of Articulation.* Circle Pines, Minn.: American Guidance Service, 1969.

Goodenough, F. L. *Mental testing.* New York: Rinehart & Co., 1949.

Guilford, J. P. A system of the psychomotor abilities. *American Journal of Psychology,* 1958, *71,* 164–174.

Guilford, J. P. *The nature of human intelligence.* New York: McGraw-Hill, 1967.

Hallenback, P. N. Remediating with comic strips. *Journal of Learning Disabilities,* 1976, *9,* 11–15.

Hammer, E. F. *The clinical application of projective drawings.* Springfield, Ill.: Charles C Thomas, 1958.

Hammer, E. F. The House-Tree-Person (H-T-P) drawings as a projective technique with children. In A. I. Rabin & M. R. Haworth (Eds.), *Projective techniques with children.* New York: Grune & Stratton, 1960, pp. 258–272.

Hammill, D. D., & Bartel, N. R. *Teaching children with learning and behavior problems.* Boston: Allyn & Bacon, 1975.

Hammill, D. D., Goodman, L., & Wiederholt, J. L. Visual–motor processes: What success have we had in training them? *The Reading Teacher,* 1974, *27,* 469–478.

Harrigan, J. E. Initial reading instruction: Phonemes, syllables or ideographs. *Journal of Learning Disabilities,* 1976, *9,* 74–80.

Harris, D. B. *Children's drawings as measures of intellectual maturity.* New York: Harcourt, Brace, & World, 1963.

Hartman, A. S. *Preschool diagnostic language program.* Harrisburg, Pa.: Department of Public Instruction, 1966.

Haworth, M. R. *The CAT: Facts about fantasy.* New York: Grune & Stratton, 1966.

Hellmuth, J. (Ed.). *Learning disorders.* (Vol. 3). Seattle: Special Child, 1968.

Hiskey, M. S. *Hiskey-Nebraska Test of Learning Aptitude.* Lincoln, Nebr.: University of Nebraska, 1966.

Hollenbeck, G. P. A comparison of analyses using the first and second generation little jiffy's. *Educational and Psychological Measurement,* 1972, *32,* 45–51.

Hufano, L., & Hoepfner, R. Review of the McCarthy Scales of Children's Abilities. *Measurement and Evaluation in Guidance,* 1974, *6,* 251–254.

Ilg, F. L., & Ames, L. B. *School readiness* (New ed.) New York: Harper & Row, 1972.

Inhelder, B., & Piaget, J. *The early growth of logic in the child.* New York: Norton, 1969.

Jedrysek, E., Klapper, Z., Pope, L., & Wortis, J. *Psychoeducational evaluation of the preschool child.* New York: Grune & Stratton, 1972.

Jensen, A. R. How much can we boost IQ and scholastic achievement? *Harvard Educational Review,* 1969, *39,* 1–123.

Jensen, A. R. Test bias and construct validity. *Phi Delta Kappan,* 1976, *58,* 340–346.

Johnson, D. J., & Myklebust, H. R. *Learning disabilities: Educational principles and practices.* New York: Grune & Stratton, 1967.

Kagan, J. Impulsive and reflective children: Significance of conceptual tempo. In J. Krumboltz (Ed.), *Learning and the educational process.* Chicago: Rand-McNally, 1965.

Kaslow, F. A therapeutic creative arts unit for children with learning disabilities. *Academic Therapy,* 1972, *7,* 297–306.

Katz, E. A "Survey of Degree of Physical Handicap." *Cerebral Palsy Review,* 1954, *15,* 10–11.

Kaufman, A. S. Analysis of the McCarthy Scales in terms of Guilford's structure of intellect model. *Perceptual and Motor Skills,* 1973, *36,* 967–976. (a)

Kaufman, A. S. Comparison of the performance of matched groups of black children and white children on the Wechsler Preschool and Primary

Scale of Intelligence. *Journal of Consulting and Clinical Psychology,* 1973, *41,* 186–191. (b)

Kaufman, A. S. Comparison of the WPPSI, Stanford-Binet, and McCarthy Scales as predictors of first grade achievement. *Perceptual and Motor Skills,* 1973, *36,* 67–73. (c)

Kaufman, A. S. Factor analysis of the WISC-R at eleven age levels between 6½ and 16½ years. *Journal of Consulting and Clinical Psychology,* 1975, *43,* 135–147. (a)

Kaufman, A. S. Factor structure of the McCarthy Scales at five age levels between 2½ and 8½. *Educational and Psychological Measurement,* 1975, *35,* 641–656. (b)

Kaufman, A. S. Note on interpreting profiles of McCarthy scale indexes. *Perceptual and Motor Skills,* 1975, *41,* 262. (c)

Kaufman, A. S. Do normal children have "flat" ability profiles? *Psychology in the Schools,* 1976, *13,* 284–285. (a)

Kaufman, A. S. A new approach to the interpretation of test scatter on the WISC-R. *Journal of Learning Disabilities,* 1976, *9,* 160–168. (b)

Kaufman, A. S. A McCarthy short form for rapid screening of preschool, kindergarten, and first grade children. *Contemporary Educational Psychology,* 1977, *2,* 149–157.

Kaufman, A. S., & DiCuio, R. F. Separate factor analyses of the McCarthy Scales for groups of black and white children. *Journal of School Psychology,* 1975, *13,* 10–18.

Kaufman, A. S., & Hollenbeck, G. P. Factor analysis of the standardization edition of the McCarthy Scales. *Journal of Clinical Psychology,* 1973, *29,* 358–362.

Kaufman, A. S., & Kaufman, N. L. Tests built from Piaget's and Gesell's tasks as predictors of first grade achievement. *Child Development,* 1972, *43,* 521–535.

Kaufman, A. S., & Kaufman, N. L. Black–white differences at ages 2½ to 8½ on the McCarthy Scales of Children's Abilities. *Journal of School Psychology,* 1973, *11,* 194–204. (a)

Kaufman, A. S., & Kaufman, N. L. Sex differences on the McCarthy Scales of Children's Abilities. *Journal of Clinical Psychology,* 1973, *29,* 362–365. (b)

Kaufman, A. S., & Kaufman, N. L. Social-class differences on the McCarthy Scales for black and white children. *Perceptual and Motor Skills,* 1975, *41,* 205–206.

Kaufman, A. S., & Kaufman, N. L. Research on the McCarthy Scales and its implications for assessment. *Journal of Learning Disabilities,* 1977, in press.

Kaufman, A. S., Zalma, R., & Kaufman, N. L. The relationship of hand dominance to the motor coordination, mental ability, and right–left awareness of young normal children. In preparation.

Kaufman, N. L. A study of the creative verbal abilities of children having minimal brain dysfunction. Unpublished manuscript, 1973.

Kaufman, N. L., & Kaufman, A. S. Comparison of normal and minimally brain dysfunctioned children on the McCarthy Scales of Children's Abilities. *Journal of Clinical Psychology,* 1974, *30,* 69–72.

Kephart, N. C. *The slow learner in the classroom* (2nd ed.). Columbus, Ohio: Charles E. Merrill, 1971.

Kessler, J. W. *Psychopathology of childhood.* Englewood Cliffs, N.J.: Prentice-Hall, 1966.

Khanna, J. L. (Ed.). *Brain damage and mental retardation* (2nd ed.). Springfield, Ill.: Charles C Thomas, 1973.

Kinsbourne, M., & Smith, W. L. (Eds.). *Hemispheric disconnection and cerebral function.* Springfield, Ill.: Charles C Thomas, 1974.

Kirk, S. A., & Kirk, W. D. *Psycholinguistic learning disabilities.* Urbana, Ill.: University of Illinois Press, 1971.

Kirk, S. A., McCarthy, J. J., & Kirk, W. D. *Examiner's manual: Illinois Test of Psycholinguistic Abilities* (Rev. ed.). Urbana, Ill.: University of Illinois Press, 1968.

Koppitz, E. M. *The Bender-Gestalt test for young children.* New York: Grune & Stratton, 1963.

Koppitz, E. M. *Psychological evaluation of children's human figure drawings.* New York: Grune & Stratton, 1968.

Koppitz, E. M. *The Bender-Gestalt test for young children.* Vol. 2: *Research and application, 1963-1973.* New York: Grune & Stratton, 1975.

Lambert, N., Windmiller, M., Cole, L., & Figueroa, R. *Manual for the AAMD Adaptive Behavior Scale, public school version (1974 Rev. ed.)* Washington, D.C.: American Association on Mental Deficiency, 1975.

Leeper, S. H., Dales, R. J., Skipper, D. S., & Witherspoon, R. L. *Good schools for young children.* New York: MacMillan, 1968.

Lerner, J. W. *Children with learning disabilities* (2nd ed.). Boston: Houghton-Mifflin, 1976.

Leviton, H., & Kiraly, J. The effects of a short training program on the Draw-A-Man test scores of pre-school children. *Educational and Psychological Measurement,* 1974, *34,* 435–438.

Machover, K. *Personality projection in the drawing of the human figure.* Springfield, Ill.: Charles C Thomas, 1949.

Machover, K. Human figure drawings of children. *Journal of Projective Techniques,* 1953, *17,* 85–91.

Machover, K. Sex differences in the developmental pattern of children as seen in human figure drawings. In A. I. Rabin & M. R. Haworth (Eds.), *Projective techniques with children.* New York: Grune & Stratton, 1960, pp. 238–257.

McCarthy, D. Factors that influence language growth: Home influences. *Elementary English,* 1952, *29,* 421–428, 440.

McCarthy, D. Identifying and helping children with language disabilities. In V. J. Glennon (Ed.), *Frontiers in elementary education.* Syracuse: Syracuse University Press, 1954, pp. 25–36.

McCarthy, D. Affective aspects of language learning. In A. H. Kidd & J. L. Rivoire (Eds.), *Perceptual development in children.* New York: International Universities Press, 1966, pp. 305–343.

McCarthy, D. Language disorders and parent–child relationships. In R. L. Noland (Ed.), *Counseling parents of the ill and the handicapped.* Springfield, Ill.: Charles C Thomas, 1971, pp. 269–284.

McCarthy, D. *Manual for the McCarthy Scales of Children's Abilities.* New York: The Psychological Corporation, 1972.

McCarthy, D. P. The feasibility of a group Bender-Gestalt test for preschool and primary school-aged children. *Journal of School Psychology,* 1975, *13,* 134–141.

Meeker, M. N. *The structure of intellect.* Columbus, Ohio: Charles E. Merrill, 1969.

Meeker, M. N. Glossary for SOI factor definitions: WISC-R analysis. Available from SOI Institute, 214 Main St., El Segundo, Calif., 1975.

Meeker, M., & Shadduck, R. D. *Evaluation: SOI abilities workbook.* Manhattan Beach, Calif.: Institute for Applied SOI Studies, 1973.

Mercer, J. R. *Labeling the mentally retarded.* Berkeley, Calif.: University of California Press, 1973.

Mercer, J. R., & Lewis, J. F. *SOMPA—System of Multi-cultural Pluralistic Assessment: Parent interview manual.* New York: The Psychological Corporation, in press.

Minskoff, E., Wiseman, D. E., & Minskoff, J. G. *The MWM program for developing language abilities.* Ridgefield, N.J.: Educational Performance Associates, 1972.

Mott, M. *Teaching the pre-academic child.* Springfield, Ill.: Charles C Thomas, 1974.

Mussen, P. H., Conger, J. J. & Kagan, J. *Child development and personality* (3rd ed.). New York: Harper & Row, 1969.

Myers, P. I., & Hammill, D. D. *Methods for learning disorders* (2nd ed.). New York: John Wiley & Sons, 1976.

Natchez, G. (Ed.). *Children with reading problems.* New York: Basic Books, 1968.

Newcomer, P. L., & Hammill, D. D. *Psycholinguistics in the schools.* Columbus, Ohio: Charles E. Merrill, 1976.

Newman, H. (Ed.). *Reading disabilities.* Indianapolis: Bobbs-Merrill, 1969.

Ornstein, R. E. *The psychology of consciousness.* San Francisco: W. H. Freeman, 1972.

Ornstein, R. E. (Ed.). *The nature of human consciousness.* San Francisco: W. H. Freeman, 1973.

Otto, W., McMenemy, R. A., & Smith, R. J. *Corrective and remedial teaching* (2nd ed.). Boston: Houghton-Mifflin, 1973.

Palmer, J. *The psychological assessment of children.* New York: John Wiley & Sons, 1970.

Rabin, A. I., & Haworth, M. R. (Eds.). *Projective techniques with children.* New York: Grune & Stratton, 1960.

Raven, J. C. *Guide to using the Coloured Progressive Matrices* (Rev. order). London: H. K. Lewis, 1956.

Read, K. H. *The nursery school* (3rd ed.) Philadelphia: W. B. Saunders, 1960.

Reger, R. (Ed.). *Preschool programming of children with disabilities.* Springfield, Ill.: Charles C Thomas, 1970.

Rentfrow, R. K., Durning, K., Conrad, E., & Goldupp, O. Use of three new instruments in a Head Start program evaluation. *Psychology in the Schools,* 1975, *12,* 34–39.

Reynolds, C. R. Use of the McCarthy drawing tests as a group screening instrument. Paper presented at the meeting of the National Association of School Psychologists, Cincinnati, March 1977.

Roach, E. G., & Kephart, N. C. *The Purdue Perceptual–Motor Survey.* Columbus, Ohio: Charles E. Merrill, 1966.

Sapir, S. G., & Nitzburg, A. C. (Eds.). *Children with learning problems.* New York: Brunner/Mazel, 1973.

Sattler, J. M. Analysis of functions of the 1960 Stanford-Binet Intelligence Scale, Form L-M. *Journal of Clinical Psychology,* 1965, *21,* 173–179.

Sattler, J. M. *Assessment of children's intelligence* (Rev. reprint). Philadelphia: W. B. Saunders, 1974.

Schaefer, F., Heilig, M., & Rubin, S. Project "me:" A new approach to media in the education of learning disabled children. *Journal of Learning Disabilities,* 1974, *7,* 76–86.

Schaer, H. F., & Crump, W. D. Teacher involvement and early identification of children with learning disabilities. *Journal of Learning Disabilities,* 1976, *9,* 91–95.

Shellenberger, S., & Lachterman, T. Usability of the McCarthy Scales of Children's Abilities in the intellectual assessment of the Puerto Rican child. Paper presented at the meeting of the National Association of School Psychologists, Kansas City, March 1976.

Shirley, H. F. *Pediatric psychiatry.* Cambridge, Mass.: Harvard University Press, 1963.

Shuey, A. M. *The testing of Negro intelligence* (2nd ed.). New York: Social Science Press, 1966.

Sloan, W. The Lincoln-Oseretsky Motor Development Scale. *Genetic Psychology Monographs,* 1955, *51,* 183.

Stone, L. J., Smith, H. T., & Murphy, L. B. (Eds.). *The competent infant: Research and commentary.* New York: Basic Books, 1973.

Strauss, A. A., & Kephart, N. C. *Psychopathology and education of the brain-injured child* (Vol. 2). New York: Grune & Stratton, 1955.

Strauss, A. A., & Lehtinen, L. *Psychopathology and education in the brain-injured child* (Vol. 1). New York: Grune & Stratton, 1947.

Taylor, E. M. *Psychological appraisal of children with cerebral defects.* Cambridge, Mass.: Harvard University Press, 1959.

Templin, M. C. & Darley, F. L. *The Templin-Darley Tests of Articulation.* Iowa City: Bureau of Educational Research and Service, State University of Iowa, 1960.

Terman, L. M., & Merrill, M. A. *Stanford-Binet Intelligence Scale: Manual for the third revision, form L-M.* Boston: Houghton-Mifflin, 1973.

Thorndike, R. L., & Hagen, E. *Measurement and evaluation in psychology and education* (4th ed.). New York: John Wiley & Sons, 1977.

Thurstone, L. L., & Thurstone, T. G. Factorial studies of intelligence. *Psychometric Monographs,* 1941, No. 2.

Thurstone, L. L., & Thurstone, T. G. *Examiner manual for the SRA Primary Mental Abilities: Primary.* Chicago: Science Research Associates, 1948.

Thurstone, L. L., & Thurstone, T. G. *Examiner manual for the SRA Primary Mental Abilities for ages 5 to 7* (3rd ed.). Chicago: Science Research Associates, 1953.

Torrance, E. P. Retooling education for creative talent: How goes it? *Gifted Child Quarterly,* 1974, *18,* 233–239. (a)

Torrance, E. P. *Torrance Tests of Creative Thinking: Directions manual and scoring guide.* Lexington, Mass.: Ginn & Co., 1974. (b)

Torrance, E. P. *Administration, scoring, and norms manual: Thinking Creatively in Action and Movement* (Research ed.). Athens, Ga.: Georgia Studies of Creative Behavior, Dept. of Educational Psychology, University of Georgia, 1976.

Van Riper, C. *Speech correction: Principles and methods* (5th ed.). Englewood Cliffs, N.J.: Prentice-Hall, 1972.

Van Witsen, B. *Perceptual training activities handbook.* New York: Teachers College Press, 1967.

Volle, F. O. A proposal for "testing the limits" with mental defectives for purposes of subtest analysis of the WISC Verbal Scale. *Journal of Clinical Psychology,* 1957, *13,* 64–67.

Wechsler, D. *Manual for the Wechsler Preschool and Primary Scale of Intelligence.* New York: The Psychological Corporation, 1967.

Wechsler, D. *Manual for the Wechsler Intelligence Scale for Children—Revised.* New York: The Psychological Corporation, 1974.

Wender, P. H. *Minimal brain dysfunction in children.* New York: Wiley-Interscience, 1971.

Wepman, J. M. *Auditory Discrimination Test* (Rev. ed.). Chicago: Language Research Associates, 1973.

Wisland, M. V. *Psychoeducational diagnosis of exceptional children.* Springfield, Ill.: Charles C Thomas, 1974.

Wolman, B. B. (Ed.). *Manual of child psychopathology.* New York: McGraw-Hill, 1972.

Wood, M. M. (Ed.). *Developmental therapy.* Baltimore: University Park Press, 1975.

Woodcock, R. W. *Peabody rebus reading program.* Circle Pines, Minn.: American Guidance Service, 1967.

Ysseldyke, J. E., & Samuel, S. Identification of diagnostic strengths and weaknesses on the McCarthy Scales of Children's Abilities. *Psychology in the Schools,* 1973, *10,* 304–307.

Zamm, M. Reading disabilities: A theory of cognitive integration. *Journal of Learning Disabilities,* 1973, *6,* 95–101.

Zimmerman, I. L., & Woo-Sam, J. The utility of the Wechsler Preschool and Primary Scale of Intelligence in the public school. *Journal of Clinical Psychology,* 1970, *26,* 472.

Zimmerman, I. L., & Woo-Sam, J. Research with the Wechsler Intelligence Scale for Children: 1960–1970. *Psychology in the Schools,* 1972, *9,* 232–271.

# Author Index

# Subject Index